AN UNCONVENTIONAL WIFE

An Unconventional Wife

the life of Julia Sorell Arnold

Mary Hoban

SCRIBE

Melbourne • London

Scribe Publications
18–20 Edward St, Brunswick, Victoria 3056, Australia
2 John St, Clerkenwell, London, WC1N 2ES, United Kingdom
3754 Pleasant Ave, Suite 100, Minneapolis, Minnesota 55409 USA

Published by Scribe 2019

The author acknowledges with gratitude the assistance provided by the
Hazel Rowley Literary Fellowship.

Printed and bound in Australia by Griffin Press

Scribe Publications is committed to the sustainable use of natural resources
and the use of paper products made responsibly from those resources.

9781925713442 (Australian edition)
9781912854387 (UK edition)
9781947534827 (US edition)
9781925693539 (e-book)

CiP records for this title are available from the National Library of Australia
and the British Library.

scribepublications.com.au
scribepublications.co.uk
scribepublications.com

To my mother

Contents

Mama, before she got married, according to Aunt Emilia, was a firecracker, a tempestuous redhead, with thoughts of her own about liberty and equality for women. But then along came Papa, very serious and tall, with thoughts of his own too, about ... liberty and equality for women. The trouble was in the coinciding subject matter.

Introduction

I discovered Julia Sorell Arnold in the pages of her grandson's memoirs. He was the renowned English scientist and first director-general of UNESCO, Sir Julian Sorell Huxley. She is a fleeting presence in his book, but nonetheless a startling one. On a January day in Hobart in 1856, as her husband was being received into the Catholic Church, Julia, a staunch Protestant, collected a basket of stones, walked to the church, and *smashed the windows with this protesting ammunition ...*

These words immediately evoked a long-forgotten memory from my childhood when I too threw stones. I had joined a motley group of young Catholic kids making their feelings of rejection palpable as they tossed 'yonnies', or little stones, onto the roof of the building where the local Brownies were meeting. It was claimed the Brownies wouldn't accept Catholics as members. I don't remember testing the allegation, nor even being particularly interested in being a Brownie, but I did like the idea of testing my arm. No windows were in our sights, though, just the roof, and most of the yonnies didn't even carry that far, but we exorcised our demons and believed the Brownies felt our presence at their meeting.

Strangely, though, it was not the stone throwing that stood out in my memory of that day, nor even the satisfaction it engendered. Instead, it was my mother's unambiguous reprimand, rendered with utter conviction, that 'young ladies do not throw stones'. How then, I thought, could Julia Sorell, a woman at the forefront of her society, a mother of three, have done exactly that? What drove her to behave in such a dramatic, 'unladylike' way? What emotion was inscribed into each of her tossed stones? Was it bigotry, anger, ignorance, or something else — despair perhaps? How could such a public and violent demonstration in the middle of the Victorian era be understood?

Her behaviour was too compelling to put aside, but in a world where biography has traditionally focused on quest, on achievement, on destination, how would I ever uncover the life of an ordinary woman whose oblique and private life was determined by whose daughter she was and whose wife or mother or even grandmother she became? Such lives may be the stuff of novels, but they have rarely been deemed worthy of biography. It's all very well for Virginia Woolf to call for the true history of the girl behind the counter rather than the hundred-and-fiftieth life of Napoleon or the seventieth study of Keats, but who apart from Virginia Woolf might be interested in reading it and what publisher would be brave enough to take it on? Only recently, a reviewer of a biography about Betsy Balcombe — as a young girl she had shared a house with Napoleon — reflected that she *was, after all, a fairly insignificant character, one who had no perceptible impact or influence on the great man*. Why then, he asked, was there interest in this girl? Why indeed! Seldom are the letters or papers of such people gathered in archives or recorded in newspapers or books. Almost never are their names and deeds etched onto monuments or their portraits hung on gallery walls. This absence is emblematic of a deeper reality about the lives of women, governed as they have been by the routines and rhythms of domestic life and the expectation that they be quiet, never shrill, never loud, certainly never scream or do anything that might shatter glass or disturb the peace.

I was fortunate with my stone-thrower. Julia Sorell was born in Hobart Town in 1826, the granddaughter of Lieutenant-Governor William Sorell of Van Diemen's Land and Anthony Fenn Kemp, the so-called 'father of Tasmania'. Whether he gained that name because he had eighteen children or because he was one of the wealthiest and most influential of the early white settlers is unclear. Julia's marriage propelled her into one of the most eminent intellectual families of Victorian England. Her father-in-law was the renowned educationalist Thomas Arnold of Rugby School, and her brother-in-law the poet and essayist Matthew Arnold. One of her daughters became a bestselling novelist at the end of the nineteenth century, another became a suffragette and journalist, while another established a school for girls that still exists today. A granddaughter was the author Janet Penrose, who married and worked alongside one of the great historians of their generation, George Macaulay Trevelyan, while two of Julia's grandsons, Julian Huxley and his brother, the novelist Aldous Huxley — most famous for his dystopian novel *Brave New World* — distinguished themselves in twentieth-century science and literature. Precisely because of these connections, many of Julia's letters have been saved, and through these and other documents and biographies relating to the wider Arnold and Sorell families, it is possible to extract her from the covers of married life and to paint a portrait of a woman living through an extraordinary period, when the fields of education, science, politics, industry, feminism, and religion clashed and converged, creating a new landscape and forging profound change.

You might wonder at that word 'religion', but Julia lived in an era when church bells charted the passage of time and when the brand of one's religion mattered deeply. From the time Henry VIII proclaimed himself the head of the Anglican Church — the new Church of England — and declared Catholics, and any others who did not conform to Anglicanism, traitorous to the English nation, anti-Catholicism had evolved as a core element of Englishness. It was the norm in the circles Julia was reared in; it took root in Australia from the very beginning of white settlement; and it was still in play when I threw my yonnies. But as people became more literate and a more democratic and industrialised state began to take shape, intense cultural and intellectual debate erupted about the place of religion. Among the key leaders, on opposing sides of this 'culture war', were Thomas Arnold of Rugby and John Henry Newman, two men of significant influence on Julia as she lived the effects of these changes in the colonial societies of Hobart and Dublin, in the great manufacturing town of Birmingham, and in the intellectual centre of Oxford.

For all the wonder and luck of discovering Julia's own letters, there was also great disappointment that so many had been destroyed. If only she had kept a diary, one of those 'wretched friends', into whose pages she poured out her heart. But she did not or, if she did, it too has been destroyed. Yet such gaps only made me more determined to delve deeper and wider, and the further I went, the more I felt I had been thrust into a novel by George Eliot or Charlotte Brontë, written in an era when a woman's desires and quests were always secondary to the man at the centre; when, according to the law, her condition as a married woman was coverture — under the cover, influence, power, and protection of her husband. But what happened in this world when the contractual exchange of feminine docility and obedience for masculine power and provision failed?

Slowly, as the arc of Julia's life unfolded, her 'ordinary life' revealed a powerful tale of sexual politics where two deeply committed lovers differed fundamentally in their understanding of the marriage contract. It is a story of one woman and all women in its depiction of the complexity of marriage, the drama of betrayal and abandonment, the humiliation of failure. It is a story of how women lived with and apart from men, of how they endured loss, and of the boundaries that existed in their lives. It is the story of the forces that have shaped our lives and the lives of those who have come before us.

The Family of
Julia Sorell Arnold

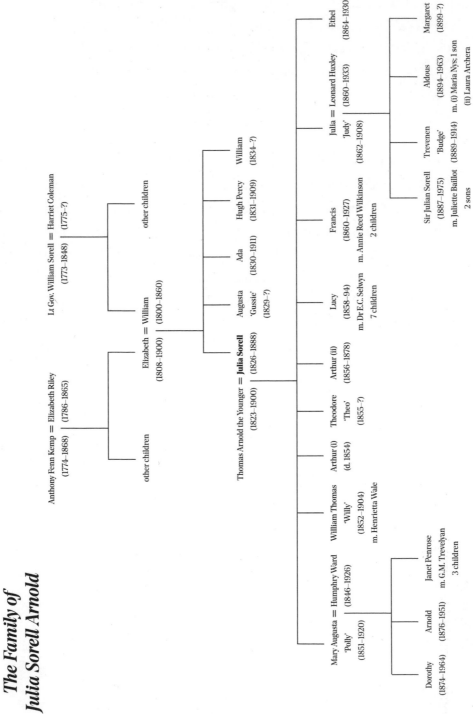

Anthony Fenn Kemp = Elizabeth Riley
(1774–1868)   (1786–1865)

Lt Gov. William Sorell = Harriet Coleman
(1773–1848)   (1775–?)

other children

Elizabeth = William
(1808–1900)   (1800–1860)

other children

Thomas Arnold the Younger = **Julia Sorell**
(1823–1900)   (1826–1888)

Augusta   Ada   Hugh Percy   William
'Gussie'   (1830–1911) (1831–1909)   (1834–?)
(1829–?)

Mary Augusta = Humphry Ward
'Polly'   (1846–1926)
(1851–1920)

William Thomas   Arthur (i)   Theodore   Arthur (ii)   Lucy   Francis   Julia = Leonard Huxley   Ethel
'Willy'   (d. 1854)   'Theo'   (1856–1878)   (1858–94)   (1860–1927)   'Judy'   (1860–1933)   (1864–1930)
(1852–1904)   (1855–?)   m. Dr E.C. Selwyn   m. Annie Reed Wilkinson   (1862–1908)
m. Henrietta Wale   7 children   2 children

Dorothy   Arnold   Janet Penrose
(1874–1964)   (1876–1951)   m. G.M. Trevelyan
                            3 children

Sir Julian Sorell   Trevenen   Aldous   Margaret
(1887–1975)   'Budge'   (1894–1963)   (1899–?)
m. Juliette Baillot (1889–1914)   m. (i) Maria Nys; 1 son
2 sons   (ii) Laura Archera

The Family of
Thomas Arnold the Younger

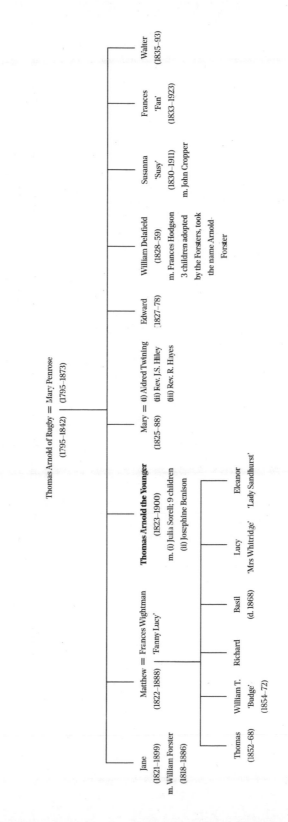

Thomas Arnold of Rugby = Mary Penrose
(1795–1842) (1795–1873)

Jane
(1821–1899)
m. William Forster
(1818–1886)

Matthew = Frances Wightman
(1822–1888) 'Fanny Lucy'

Thomas Arnold the Younger
(1823–1900)
m. (i) Julia Sorell; 9 children
(ii) Josephine Benison

Mary = (i) Aldred Twining
(1825–88) (ii) Rev. J.S. Hiley
(iii) Rev. R. Hayes

Edward
(1827–78)

William Delafield
(1828–59)
m. Frances Hodgson
3 children adopted
by the Forsters, took
the name Arnold-
Forster

Susanna
'Susy'
(1830–1911)
m. John Cropper

Frances
'Fan'
(1833–1923)

Walter
(1835–93)

Thomas
(1852–68)

William T.
'Budge'
(1854–72)

Richard

Basil
(d. 1868)

Lucy
'Mrs Whitridge'

Eleanor
'Lady Sandhurst'

1

A Tumultuous Inheritance

The dreadful shuddering finally ceased, and Julia knew instinctively that the *Calcutta* had reached the channel. Abandoning any pretence at packing her portmanteau, she gathered her brothers and sisters and gleefully sought the deck. Just a little further north was Hobart, and waiting there on the wharf would be her beloved father. It had been nearly three years since she had seen him, and if at times during that period Julia had believed she would never see him again, she felt she could still smell the jacket he had worn when he had given her a last hug and she could still hear the sound of the oars as his form vanished into the mist. These had remained with her, but now, as she reached the deck, it felt as if these sensations were surging out of her body, no longer needing to dwell inside her.

Even the air around her bristled. The wide expanse of blue sky held no warmth, and the wind, unchallenged on its route from the Antarctic, whistled by her, unsettling a flock of screeching birds from their nesting roosts. Julia watched them rise above the trees on the bank, and, as she did, her eye caught the swinging gibbet in the tree. It was holding two blackened bodies. She remembered such sights, but her little brother, standing close to her, was puzzled. She did not explain it to him. Instead she took his face in her hands and turned it away. He would grow oblivious soon enough to the gruesome colliding with the exquisite. Van Diemen's Land was like that, its shimmering surface had always belied a grim, silent underside.

When she turned her head back to look at those receding bodies, she was struck by how much they resembled the hanging Christs that had lined the cloistered hallways of her school in Brussels, and she was back there again in the midst of those whispering, condescending girls who had belittled her for being 'la fille anglaise', the girl who could not recite her rosary and whose mother was said to be very bad. She had grown to hate them and their morbid, gothic Catholicism. It was one thing to hear her grandfather talk about his ancestors who had been expelled from Catholic France, but it was quite another thing to be with those girls, who believed that ghoulish nonsense about the Saviour's blood shielding them while they lied and bullied. Those hanging bodies might recede behind the ship, but the pain of that spite would not.

As Hobart came into view and the babble from her fellow passengers rose, Julia remained strangely quiet, uneasy and unknowing. She had left Hobart as a child and now she was returning as a young woman, ready to enter society. But without her mother, and with her wider family divided, how would she be treated? Would she be accepted, or would she always have to bear the mark of scandal? She had spent the voyage home determined to loosen the hardness that had formed in her during these last few years. She wanted only love and laughter to fill her days and, until those swinging bodies swayed before her, she had believed she had thrown overboard all the sadness and the bitterness and the hatred. But the past was not so easily cast aside.

Three years before, in February 1839, when Julia Sorell had sailed from Hobart, she'd had no inkling that her life was about to change dramatically. She had turned twelve just six months earlier. In the lead-up to the voyage, there had been bitter disputes between her parents. Her mother, Elizabeth, had insisted that her children should see Europe just as she had done as a child, and had pressured her father relentlessly until he submitted to her plan. He would come to bitterly regret his decision, but it was inevitable. Julia's father was a gentle man, while her fiery mother was used to having her own way. It ran in her family. So did betrayal.

Both Julia's grandfathers, Anthony Fenn Kemp and William Sorell, were men of power in the colony. Anthony Fenn Kemp was one of its richest and most rambunctious characters, a man who let nothing stand in his way — a man it was not safe to contradict. He had a long history of opposing authority in the colonies, having been prominent among the group of officers who had instigated the famous Rum Rebellion in 1808, and had been court-martialled for his behaviour. When he settled in Van Diemen's Land, he continued to build not only his fortune, but also his reputation for trouble, and his tendency to governor-baiting, on one occasion being thrown out of Government House for *extreme rudeness*. William Sorell, appointed Lieutenant-Governor in 1817, was a professional military man, administratively adroit and well-regarded, but with a less-than-spotless personal life. It was inevitable that these two men would clash, and when they did, their very public political battles became the stuff of colonial history, making Kemp's previous skirmishes with governors appear minor. But it would be Sorell's tempestuous private life that brought their children together.

Unbeknown to the colonists, 'Mrs Sorell' was not the Governor's wife but his mistress, Louisa Kent. Sorell had abandoned his wife years before in England, leaving her with their six children. Anthony Fenn Kemp had discovered this when Louisa Kent's husband, Lieutenant William Kent, brought an action in London against Sorell 'for criminal conversation'. This coyly named suit could be brought by an injured husband for damages against an alleged seducer of his wife. Kemp kept it to himself until Sorell suspended him from the magistracy for being *the most seditious, mischievous and the man least meriting favour or indulgence from the Government in the whole settlement*. Kemp retaliated immediately by exposing the Governor's private life and complaining bitterly that his mistress accompanied him to church and that they and their children were seen parading about in the government carriage. It mattered little to Kemp that he himself had abandoned a mistress and two children in Sydney. He was now spearheading a campaign to have Sorell recalled from his position as Governor.

It took nearly six years and a far-reaching Commission of Inquiry before this objective was achieved, by which time Kemp, now used to the ways of Sorell and uneasy at the prospect of a new governor, chaired a committee of fifteen influential citizens petitioning the King to allow Sorell to remain. It was too late.

But in early 1825 in the months leading up to Sorell's departure from the colony, his eldest legitimate son, also named William, arrived in Hobart to confront his father over the destitution and pain he had caused his family when he had abandoned them. Whether young William managed to gain any help for his family is unknown, but his own fate was determined the moment he saw a beautiful and lively young woman sitting across the aisle in church. In her, he believed he had found everything he could wish for — that the seventeen-year-old Elizabeth Kemp was the daughter of his father's old rival was immaterial. Their courtship was swift and on 24 September 1825, at St David's Church in Hobart, William and Elizabeth married. The young couple settled in New Town, and within months Elizabeth was pregnant. Their first child, Julia Sorell, was born on 17 August 1826.

Julia's first years were lived in the family home in New Town. She was an energetic, engaging child, full of abundant love for everything around her: dogs, horses, flowers — it mattered not. And she loved the clatter and chatter when the large family — her mother was one of eighteen children — would gather at her grandfather Kemp's big mansion, Mount Vernon, outside Hobart. When the nursery in New Town witnessed the addition of Augusta in 1829 and Ada in 1830, Julia spent more time with her gentle, loving father who continued to marvel at his good fortune in meeting and marrying the beautiful, vivacious Elizabeth. The nursery expanded further when Julia's younger brothers were born, Percy, in 1831, and then William in 1834, but by that time this stable, joyful world was beginning to dissolve.

Julia's mother was young, beautiful, and a force. She had inherited her father's energy and his temper, and, soon after little William's birth, she fell into a fretful humour. Elizabeth was bored with her children and bored with her quiet, sensible husband who was content with his work, his family, and his life in the colony. She was bored too with the small world of Hobart. She wanted to escape. Young, beautiful, fierce, and now restless. It was a dangerous combination.

Elizabeth's ennui began to evaporate when she met Major George Deare of the 21st Fusiliers, who arrived in Hobart in 1833. In his scarlet coat and with his adventurous tales, he was a vivid contrast to the staid and reserved William. The fiery Elizabeth fell in love with him while the spirited, impressionable Julia, a keen observer of her world, watched. She saw the glances they exchanged, their heads close together, their lingering touches. And she listened, too. Children have an instinct for emotional truth, even if they cannot understand its import. It was no coincidence that Elizabeth decided it was time to send Julia to boarding school.

Ellinthorp Hall was the most fashionable school in the colony, and there Julia began learning French, writing, arithmetic, and geography, useful and ornamental needlework, drawing, dancing, and, for an additional charge of six pounds and six shillings, music. This extra fee was not wasted on her, for music would become an abiding passion of Julia's. She made friends very easily at Ellinthorp — her engaging, animated nature ensured this — but she missed her younger brothers and sisters, and she missed her father. She wished she could return home, and take all her friends with her.

When she realised that would not happen, she adapted herself to the pulse of her new life until that day in 1838 when the school was attacked by a small band of bushrangers. There was just enough time for the teachers and girls to pile heavy furniture against the doors and to block up the windows with mattresses, pillows, and cushions, leaving only apertures for the gun barrels, before they sat waiting, silently and fearfully, trying to interpret the sounds of the attack — the scrambling, the running, the gunshots, and finally the silence as their attackers turned and disappeared into the bush. If Julia had hoped a bushrangers' attack might cause her mother to bring her home, she was to be disappointed.

Back in Hobart, Elizabeth Sorell was not thinking about her daughter at all, and she certainly did not want her nearby. Her affair with George Deare had intensified, and when he received notice that his regiment was being posted to India, together they began plotting Elizabeth's escape. It was no easy matter. As a married woman, she would need a satisfactory motive for leaving, she would need her husband's approval, and she would need his money. Adroitly, she worked on William. It was time, she said to him, that their children, particularly their daughters, saw something of the world, as she had when young. Of course, she understood that William would not be able to leave his work, but surely she could take the children? Framed in such a way, William could not refuse her. Elizabeth booked her passage, and that of their children, to England.

Julia was summoned home and, while she watched her mother dress for the ball to farewell George's regiment, she was told of the planned journey to Europe. Excitement fought with unhappiness. She was deeply unsettled. The next day, in between hearing her mother's description of the ball — Lieutenant-Governor and Lady Franklin in attendance, rooms wonderfully illuminated, tables spread with a sumptuous supper, a profusion of wines and toasts — Julia sought answers to all the questions bubbling inside her. Why wasn't her darling father coming with them? How long would she be away for? Would she ever go back to Ellinthorp Hall? Couldn't she return there before they sailed to say a proper goodbye to all her friends? There were no answers, only more talk of the ball.

Julia's unease rose further when, amidst the packing and the farewells, she came to understand that not everyone supported her mother's scheme. The thick Georgian walls of her grandfather Kemp's mansion could not shroud his anger for there was no moderation in his condemnation of his daughter for going, or of William for allowing her to go.

On 3 February 1839, as the *Auriga*, a 232-ton barque under Captain Chalmers, sailed down the Derwent River, Julia watched her father's figure disappear from sight. She was too young to understand that lives are swept along by those very ordinary moments when one decision is made rather than another, when a moment's action renders consequences that reverberate down through the years. All she knew was that she had been ripped from her father, her friends, and her school.

The voyage was a long one, but Julia found life on board absorbing. After the excitement and the confusion of departure, when cargo was stowed here and there, cabins allocated, hatches closed, sails raised, and ropes unfurled, her days assumed a rhythmic pattern. On that small vessel, a dot on a great expanse of water, only the present mattered. As an upper-deck passenger Julia was spared the grim fare served to the steerage passengers — the hard brown biscuits, tasting like sawdust and alive with weevils, and the repulsive-smelling pea soup, so thick a spoon could stand in it — but the rotten food and the cramped conditions did nothing to dent her envy of them. Song and laughter abounded below deck and when she could escape her mother, she sought to join them, to watch, as they did, the flights of the Cape pigeons and albatrosses, or to observe the men and boys fishing for dolphin or shark. And when they sang at night, she would creep onto the deck to listen, staring wide-eyed at the black cloth sprinkled with clusters of small diamonds that sparkled in the void above her.

When the weather prevented her from going on deck, Julia would amuse her younger sisters and brothers with stories from her boarding school. They never tired of hearing about the day the bushrangers attacked, and the boys, keen for their own adventure, would pester her with questions. Would pirates soon appear on the horizon? And if they did, would the Captain give orders for all the muskets and cutlasses to be brought up and put in readiness for an attack? And when the pirates were captured, would the Captain make them walk the plank? Would they be able to watch? Julia tried to share their enthusiasm, but she remembered her fear during that attack on the school. It was like a hard grip on the throat. She never wished to struggle for breath again.

On a glorious day in May 1839, the *Auriga* finally docked in England. Julia thought it *one of the loveliest days that it was possible to conceive* and would remember that, and her feet first touching English soil, for years to come. She watched with excitement as the movement and noise around her took shape, storing it up to tell her father in her next letter, but there was no time for writing. London was not her mother's destination, and, within a day, Julia and her brothers and sisters were shepherded onto a steamboat going to Antwerp. From there, a train took them to Brussels, where their grandfather, the former Governor Sorell, and Mrs Kent were now living. Julia did not know it, but her mother's ruthless campaign was nearly done. Elizabeth Sorell settled her children with their grandfather and disappeared. She had a rendezvous to keep with Major Deare. Once reunited, the couple fled Brussels immediately to join Deare's regiment stationed in India.

Julia did not understand at first what had happened. Her grandfather kept asking her questions about her mother's plans. Had she spoken of where else they might be going? Had her mother met any friends in London or on the boat? Days later, he summoned her to his study, where he told her that her mother would not be returning to Brussels and that she and her brothers and sisters would be staying with him until he could return them to their father. Julia did not know the words to speak. Nor did she understand how that moment would change her, how she would come to loathe those who lied to her or who broke her trust in them. And she had no inkling then that she would never see her mother again. How could she ever find the words to explain any of this to Percy and little William? Gussie and Ada might understand some of what she had to tell them, but not the little boys. She could only hold them close.

Brussels in the late 1830s was one of Europe's most intriguing cities. It was no accident that Thackeray's heroine Becky Sharp found a home in Brussels, a haven for radicals and bohemians full of *second-rate dandies and roués, widow-ladies who always have a lawsuit and very simple English folks who fancy they see 'Continental society'*. More than two thousand British residents lived there, many among them fleeing from creditors or seeking to escape the rigidities of the moral and class systems that prevailed in England. It was no accident, either, that the former Governor Sorell and Mrs Kent lived there. It was one city where the unmarried couple were accepted.

In their grandfather's house, surrounded by strangers in a strange city, this small band of children — twelve-year-old Julia, ten-year-old Gussie, Ada at nine, Percy eight, and the baby William, just five years old — drew closer together. In the face of their mother's abandonment, the younger ones turned to Julia, and, disguising her own bewilderment and anger, she sought to comfort them. There was no explanation, simply its effects.

They heard the raised voices behind closed doors, the broken-off sentences, but the silence seemed even louder. While Julia waited and dreamed of being rescued, of returning to her father and to her old life in Van Diemen's Land, she felt a hard, dark thing settle inside her.

She began to grow up quickly in this raffish city, with its never-ending cavalry parades, its bustling alleyways, its parks full of chestnut trees, and always the sound of church bells. She excelled at French, picked up a little German and some Dutch, mothered her younger brothers and sisters, and tried to make friends, but it was difficult in that school where, as an English-speaker and a non-Catholic, she was always an outsider. And then when the blood began pouring from her, she thought it was punishment for hating her mother, for hating the girls who despised her, for hating Brussels, a place where she believed hypocrisy flourished. Here in Brussels, she acquired a visceral hatred of Catholicism and she grew to despise its attitudes towards women.

Julia's anti-Catholicism was felt rather than thought, taking hold when she was at her most vulnerable and unhappiest, in a state of shock still from her mother's desertion, living among people she did not know or understand, and unable to comprehend or articulate her emotions. An outsider, a stranger, among those schoolgirls of Brussels, Julia hated their whispering condescension. She scorned them for their beliefs, their lies, and their spite. Behaviour mattered to her, not prayers, not words. Her contempt for Catholicism and its symbols, the rosary beads and the statues, which she saw as pagan idolatry, was only fuelled by her grandfather's stories about the Sorells — French Protestants, known as Huguenots, who had fled to England in 1685 after recurring waves of persecution and, sometimes, slaughter by their Catholic compatriots.

She was not alone in her reaction to Catholicism. In 1842, just as Julia was leaving Brussels, Charlotte Brontë arrived to teach. She echoed Julia's feelings when she described the girls she taught:

> Whenever a lie was necessary for their occasions, they brought it out with a careless ease and breadth altogether untroubled by the rebuke of conscience … If they had missed going to mass, or read a chapter of a novel, that was another thing: these were crimes whereof rebuke and penance were the unfailing meed.

When, more than one hundred years later, the adolescent Dorothy Strachey was sent away to a small finishing school outside Paris, she, too, found the Catholic environment overwhelming with its *incessant talk about our Saviour's blood, the dreadful necessity of saving one's soul, the frightful abysses into which one might fall at any moment.*

But alongside her contempt, Julia was also developing an abundant compassion. Hating her position as an outsider, she grew to empathise with those who were different, who were shy, who were ill at ease. As for those who denied their background, who became what she saw as hypocrites, there could be nothing but loathing. Even in this dark time, though, her innate optimism, her fierce mothering of her siblings, and each small act of kindness she made worked their balm. Within the intimacy of her grandfather's house and the military circles in which he moved, Julia absorbed social and moral attitudes, she noted the roles of women, the various ways in which they reflected the men around them, and she observed the codes of femininity, the modes of fashionable dress, and the arts of social intercourse that prevailed. The result — a cosmopolitan vivacity, a quickness, a decisiveness — marked her, like her anti-Catholicism, for the rest of her life.

It took more than two years for her grandfather to arrange their passage back to Hobart, so anxious was he that they sail with Captain Chalmers, the same man who had captained the vessel that had brought them to Europe. The Captain was a delightful man, universally liked and regularly entertained by many of the old colonists who had sailed with him, and the former governor wanted to hand his grandchildren over to such a man. During that long voyage home, Julia grew to love the Captain — after he retired from the sea, she would sometimes stay with him and his family, and when she married, she took her husband to meet him. He, in turn, was utterly charmed by her. Many of the passengers knew Julia's story, and if at first they were drawn to her out of curiosity, it was not long before they, too, succumbed to her particular charm. She was interested in people. She had a decisiveness about her that inspired confidence. She had the gift of optimism, of looking ahead, never behind. And she had the gift of movement, always dancing from one person to another, never resting, always talking and laughing. Her gaiety and chatter, enhanced by the eloquent use of her hands — another characteristic she had picked up in Brussels — were infectious. She sparkled.

Julia loved being on the sea again. Each day placed a greater distance between her and those strained years in Brussels. She began to believe that once reunited with her father, no further disasters could possibly befall her. And then, on the very last day of the voyage, her eye had been caught by those two blackened bodies and she was immediately transported back to Brussels, standing before Mrs Kent. The woman was telling her that once she had returned home, it would be her duty to marry as soon as she could. That was what respectable young women did, she had said. But how could Julia be respectable when her mother had run off, and when even her grandfather and Mrs Kent weren't married? With such scandal clothing her, who would want to marry her? And her father — what would he expect of her? Would he, like Mrs Kent, want her to marry quickly and then find husbands for her younger sisters?

As the wind picked up and the bodies receded, Julia was seized with a sudden desire to turn the ship around, to sail on, to never dock, for on that little vessel, perched between her past and her future, there had been no expectations and no disappointments. Instead, the ship anchored, and Julia Sorell stepped straight into her father's arms and her new life. She was fifteen years of age, ignorant, yet strangely knowing, full of love and hate, skittish with excitement and energy, and always a lingering fear.

2

Entering Society

Sitting high on her father's carriage, Julia could barely recognise her home town. Yes, it felt quaint and primitive compared to the bustle of Brussels, but it had lost that bush feel that she had known. Its English trees were reaching as high as the church steeples and its soft-stone buildings were beginning to mellow. When the carriage turned towards the central area, Julia realised they were not returning to their old home in New Town. Instead, her father was taking them to a pretty, well-furnished cottage, in a strip of orchards and gardens along Sandy Bay. He had, he told her, moved house soon after they had sailed from Hobart. And he confessed that he had sold off most of the furniture, including the rosewood card tables, the carpets and rugs, the children's bedsteads, a small library of valuable books, and, to Julia's dismay, the square Broadwood pianoforte she had so loved playing. But it was not the time to argue with him. The house in Sandy Bay would be a new beginning for the reunited family. The piano could wait.

Julia remembered many of the places she passed on the journey along Macquarie Street. Government House was still standing behind its stretch of white fence and thick row of gums and there, too, was the high brick wall of the gaol. It was a stark reminder that Hobart was no ordinary town. It was still a gaol for England, or as she remembered her grandfather Kemp roaring, it was a dumping ground for home rubbish.

Just as the carriage reached the gaol, a chain gang, dressed in hideous leather caps and distinctive yellow pepper-and-salt clothing, shuffled its way with clanking chains across the street in front of them. Julia recalled such sights — so many of Hobart's population were convicts after all — but for the younger children, to see men chained was strange. And standing high above the gaol wall was the platform where prisoners were executed in full view of an assembled crowd. She had never attended an execution, but she remembered one of her cousins describing how he and his friend had played leapfrog and marbles while they waited for the execution to take place. It was no wonder that cruelty, like a darkening cloud, hung over the town.

Not far past the gaol were the soldiers' barracks. The military presided over this penitentiary town on the edge of the world, and its presence was pervasive. The drums of the military band regulated the town's movement, while the officers' dinners and balls provided an opportunity for the powerful and the fashionable to meet and mingle.

On the short journey to her father's home, Julia was momentarily struck by the convicts, the chain gangs, the soldiers, even the remnant number of the island's original inhabitants. However, she knew that before long she would not notice such things. Instead she would only see the shimmering surface, the beautiful harbour, the provincial English air. But there was much else that she did not know instinctively or otherwise about life in Hobart.

She did not know of the need to maintain distance between the free, the manacled, and the dispossessed. She did not know that the obsession with upholding rank and distinction prompted frivolous debates and slighted honour. She did not know that social ostracism was routine and privacy non-existent. Nor did she know yet how, in this community where men outnumbered women three to one, relentless scrutiny and gossip might be used with spectacular effect against women who transgressed the unwritten rules of fashionable society.

These were matters that the older and more worldly Louisa Meredith understood immediately when she settled in Hobart. Nowhere, she believed, were *the decent and becoming observances of social and domestic life more strictly maintained,* nowhere was the punishment of exclusion from society more effective, and nowhere were *people's past lives more minutely and rigidly canvassed, than in the higher circles of this little community.* The smallness of this community certainly intensified the impact of scrutiny and gossip, but Louisa felt it was also a result of *the frightful amount of snobbishness, which prevails here among those who might really well dispense with the feverish terror of being said or thought to do anything ungenteel or unfashionable.*

Julia made her entry into this dissembling, confined world in the sitting rooms of her many aunts and cousins. Eager as they were to nibble morsels of cake and sip tea with their vivacious young relative, few appeared willing to act as her mentor, to impart to her the feminine counsel she required. Julia felt this failure deeply. She struggled with her ignorance, years later telling her husband that *few families have been blessed with such a home training as yours, and very few in our rank of life have been cursed such as mine.* But the independence she had developed in her years in Brussels enabled her now to look elsewhere for support and for knowledge. She sought those women in her father's circle who were a little older than she was, who were able to proffer advice and to hold up to her the mirror that would reflect back the experience of being a woman, something that for all her closeness to her father, he could not give her. Female succour had begun in the close relationships she had forged in Brussels with her younger sisters, Gussie and Ada, and it would be an enduring thread in Julia's life. The Sorell sisters were not unusual in this regard. Confined for much of their time to the domestic hearth and with little opportunity to forge strong relationships with outsiders, sisters inevitably turned to each other.

Julia quickly found a rhythm to her life. As mistress of her father's house, she had first to learn the art of household management, an arduous array of duties that included keeping the household accounts, caring for the younger children, dealing with tradesmen, arranging functions and social gatherings, overseeing the garden and the cooking, and, importantly, supervising the servants. She found it daunting, as did her contemporary, the artist Mary Allport, who groaned under the weight of extra work caused by domestic violence and disarray among her servants. On one occasion she had all her *Saturday's work to do as usual owing to the gentle Wordsworth knocking down his wife, my washerwoman, and cutting her eye with the corner of the door.* The diarist George Boyes also experienced similar difficulties, but George, not burdened in the same way with domestic responsibilities as Mary, was able to adopt a more acerbic view, noting that after the 1840 Hobart Regatta took place, his servants *drank of course and the gardener gave Ann a thrashing in the kitchen to prove his love for her and enmity to a supposed rival.* Regardless of her mistakes and failings, Julia was never condemned or criticised by her father for her housekeeping. Instead, he praised her efforts and encouraged her, delighted that this whirlwind of a daughter was back with him.

And Julia's life was not all domestic duties. Women in the upper echelons of this society had concocted a world full of pleasure and activity to pass the time. Since her departure for Europe, there had been a burgeoning of cultural life in Hobart. Governor and Lady Franklin had become strong patrons of the arts and education on assuming their vice-regal role in 1837, and despite the bishop's wife, Mrs Nixon, believing that no one cared *a straw for the arts, or even for reading,* there was an abundance of cultural groups and organisations including a choral society, a piano-playing group, a library, two theatres, and a mechanics institute, in which a course of lectures were delivered weekly during winter. Julia quickly embraced this world and she passed her days in a whirl of visiting and receiving visitors, sketching, playing music, attending regattas, picnics, fetes, shooting parties, racing, cricket matches, and horticultural shows.

When she was not involved in the events that festooned Hobart's social calendar, Julia would join her father, whenever he could escape from his job, to ride with him in the government domain. It was, apart from music and dancing, her greatest pleasure, and she became a fearless, confident rider. In such a constrained and decorous world, riding was a release, a space where she could express her exuberance without fearing its effects. Julia was not exceptional in her enjoyment of riding. Louisa Meredith had been shocked when she first arrived in Hobart and found conversation was so laced with veterinary references among ladies that the first questions asked were *not enquiries after parents, sisters, brothers, or friends: no, nor even the lady-beloved talk of weddings and dress*, but almost invariably turfy, which she found unfeminine in the extreme.

Julia's days were full, as too were her evenings, which revolved around Government House and its dinners, concerts, dances, balls, soirées, and theatrical performances. She excelled at dancing and much preferred those evenings when the carpets came up and the military band came in rather than the *conversazione*-style evening parties the governor's wife, Lady Franklin, often liked to hold. Again she was not exceptional, as many of her friends were uniformly horrified at the idea of being *stuck up in rooms full of pictures and books, and shells and stones, and other rubbish, with nothing to do but to hear people talk lectures, or else sit as mute as mice listening to what was called good music.*

Julia loved the theatre too and was often among the crowd at The Victoria, although she much preferred to act herself, and when another governor's wife, Lady Caroline Denison, introduced *tableaux vivants* to Government House, she and Gussie and Ada were all keenly sought as actors. In one such tableau, *The Winter's Tale*, Julia took the role of Hermione, and she was, according to onlookers, a vision, lovely and motionless, on her pedestal, until at the words *'Music! Awake her! Strike!' she kindled into life.*

Not long after Julia's return to Hobart, Bishop Francis Nixon, a keen amateur artist and an avid collector, established an artists' group. It triggered a landscape and watercolour craze, and suddenly sketching materials, along with parasols, cushions, shawls, and cloaks, were added to picnic lists. The bishop's passion for art also caused a boon in commissions for professional painters, and William Sorell, like many of his peers, decided to commission a portrait. Curiously, it was not of his beautiful eldest daughter, Julia. Instead he asked the artist Thomas Bock to paint his eldest son, Percy. Julia, who was said to resemble the 'Aurora

Raby' in the annual *Heath's Book of Beauty*, may have reminded Sorell too much of his errant wife. Aurora is no pale English miss, but a dark-haired beauty with the robust and sensuous look of European ancestry. In truth, Sorell's reluctance was more likely caused by his unwillingness to have Julia sit for a convict artist who had been transported for seducing a young woman. When completed, Percy's portrait revealed a beautiful child with a cherubic face, but it was still not inducement enough for his father to commission a portrait of Julia. That would have to wait.

3

A Colonial Belle

Julia was not introspective. She much preferred to be *with* her family and friends, doing things, rather than writing about them, pouring fragments of her life and those of her friends into a diary. Others in her circle did keep diaries, and her name flits in and out of these pages. Chief among the diarists were George Boyes, the auditor-general of Van Diemen's Land and a contemporary of Julia's father, and Annie Baxter, the young wife of an officer stationed in Van Diemen's Land and a near contemporary of Julia. Boyes was deeply cynical about the people of Van Diemen's Land, believing they resembled the Americans in their presumption, arrogance, impudence, and conceit. He also thought them narrow, lying, slandering, envious, hateful, malicious, and incapable of any generous sentiments. Annie Baxter was a very different diarist to Boyes. She was given to spite and pride rather than cynicism, writing defiantly that *Plebeian blood is beneath my notice* when a group of young women behaved coolly towards her.

When Julia first met Annie at the Hobart Regatta in 1844, she immediately took her under her wing and introduced her to all and sundry, despite Annie being the older, married woman. From this initial encounter, Julia was subjected to Annie's relentless scrutiny and to her spite. The two young women mixed in the same circles, shared many of the same friends, and were courted by the same men — in Annie's case surreptitiously, due to her married status — but Julia's independence, her decisiveness, and her popularity aroused Annie's envy, and she took her revenge in her diary. When Julia took off her bonnet, Annie construed it as Julia wanting to show off her good hair. When Richard Dry, with whom Annie was secretly in love, paid marked attention to Julia, Annie described Julia as not pretty but good-looking, with *the Vixen* depicted in her eyes. There is something vivid and flirtatious in that word 'vixen', although it does not fit with another description of Julia as being very like the Waverley novels' illustration of Amy Robsart, a young woman with a challenge in her direct gaze and the suggestion of a laugh on her bow-shaped mouth.

Richard Dry, possibly the colony's most eligible bachelor, was one of Julia's earliest beaus. He had inherited Quamby, a 30,000-acre estate in northern Van Diemen's Land, on his father's death in April 1843, and he was a favourite with all. Julia met him when, not long after her return from Europe, she had accompanied her father, along with the rest of fashionable society, to Quamby for the wedding of Richard's adopted sister, Ellen. As a young, attractive girl of marriageable age, Julia's every movement was remarked upon, especially any exchanges with men, and without an ever-vigilant mother, she was able to give free rein to her lively, impetuous, generous nature. Inevitably a bevy of admirers gathered around her and the slightest suggestion that she admired someone would lead to wild speculation and gossip.

When Julia and Richard met, they liked each other, and they continued to like each other. It was enough to spark Annie's jealousy and to raise expectations that Julia and Richard would soon be engaged, the first of many occasions when this type of gossip, always carrying a hint of salaciousness, would engulf Julia. Sometimes she was rumoured to be engaged to several men simultaneously. At the same time that gossip raged about her relationship with Richard Dry, there were suggestions that she was engaged to her father's friend, the sixty-year-old colonial secretary, James Bicheno.

Julia was constantly cast in the shadow of her flamboyant, scandalous mother and never permitted to bask in the glow of her gentle, affectionate, and strictly honourable father. Subjected to an unremitting, remorseless gaze, her every action, no matter how trivial, triggered the same predictable response. When she was part of a large party visiting the governor at his New Norfolk cottage, she fell from a chair, and Annie Baxter noted in her diary that Julia was far from the first of her family to fall *through the machinations of Man!* But such judgements only made Julia more, not less, wary of men and marriage.

If gossip plagued her whenever she and Richard met, it went into a frenzy when she met Chester Eardley-Wilmot, one of the governor's sons, at Government House. Their friendship blossomed at fetes, dances, picnics, and in the drawing rooms of Hobart notables. It was not long before Chester trusted her not only to keep a confidence — he sent her a book that he had enjoyed reading and told her not to *tell anybody that I have lent it to you as it is not mine* — but to offer her his horse to ride when he could not accompany her to a picnic. Rarely, if ever, did a man offer his horse to another man, but to offer it to a woman bespoke a singular trust, a trust that went deeper when Chester eventually asked her to marry him — and Julia agreed. No formal announcement was made, yet only months later their relationship had foundered, smothered by colonial politics, the tightly bound, confined circle they inhabited, and Julia's own doubts about marriage.

Chester's father had been appointed governor of Van Diemen's Land in 1843 for a term of six years, and when he had arrived with his three sons but not his wife, his every action, his every judgement, and his every interaction with women was exposed to forensic scrutiny on the part of the colonists. At the same time, divisions were growing between Whitehall and the colonists over Whitehall's attempt to place the full burden of convict expenses on them. As the colonists saw it, transportation was British government policy and the British Treasury should pay for it. So when Governor Eardley-Wilmot sought to impose new and higher taxes, it not only made him very unpopular in Van Diemen's Land, but the unrest it provoked caused Whitehall to brand him incompetent, and his enemies in both the colony and in London began attempts to remove him from office. They would use any weapon to hand, and when a rumour began circulating that the governor had taken Julia to his cottage at New Norfolk where it was alleged they had remained alone for the night, Julia became caught up in these political manoeuvres.

The gentle William Sorell acted quickly and decisively to defend his daughter's honour and called upon the governor to denounce the story as untrue. When it transpired that it had been started by one of the governor's political enemies, the gossip about Julia subsided, but the story itself became another weapon against the increasingly beleaguered governor in his fight to remain in office. A climax came only months later when six members of the Legislative Council, known as the Patriotic Six, resigned and brought government in the colony to a standstill. One of the six was Julia's old beau Richard Dry.

In the midst of this turmoil, Julia and Chester Eardley-Wilmot decided to marry, although before any formal engagement notice was made, Julia sought reassurances from Richard Dry that he did not think that they had any prior commitment to each other. She had developed her own code of honour. There would be none of her mother's duplicity in any relationship she established. George Boyes's view on the relationship — he thought Chester a bold youth if he was aware of the risk he ran in making a connection with Julia — revealed yet again the prison of opinion her mother's behaviour had caged her into.

The politics surrounding the governor grew darker when Whitehall received details of the constitutional crisis caused by the resignation of the Patriotic Six, and he was dismissed immediately. His incompetence, the public explanation, together with his *fondness for the younger part of the fair sex*, the private explanation, had sealed his fate, and although his family, friends, and even the colonial press maintained his innocence, he died a broken man just six months later. In the wake of the governor's dismissal and death and the political furore that followed, the backbiting and rumours went into overdrive. Julia's alleged relationship with the governor re-emerged, and despite her love for Chester — some of his letters were still in her keeping at her death — she ended their relationship.

Julia's courage was depleted and knowing the gossip would only become more repugnant, she determined to leave Hobart immediately. Even the normally spiteful Annie expressed a rare sympathy for her, saying that Julia could not be blamed for breaking the engagement and declaring bluntly that had she loved Chester as much as Julia, then she would have done the same thing. Annie's sympathy went even further. She noted that though Julia was *very passionate in every way*, she had no mother to help her at this time, and *it would be well indeed if we could judge others as we do ourselves*. But Julia, not wanting sympathy any more than she wanted derision, fled Hobart to stay with a friend. There she nursed her bruised heart in private. Two years later, in December 1848, Chester married the sketcher and lithographer Jeannie Dunn. Annie had an opinion on that, too. She believed Chester was still in love with Julia and doubted the likelihood of happiness as Chester had told her that Jeannie *was old and ugly enough to marry*!

As a way of distracting her, of soothing her despair, William Sorell decided to commission Julia's portrait. He did not ask the seducer Thomas Bock to paint her, but turned instead to another ex-convict, Thomas Wainewright, an artist who had also established a reputation among prominent Hobart citizens. Wainewright was a mere forger, but curiously, it was Wainewright who was never allowed to be alone with the daughters of the gentry during sittings. This did not, however, deter sitters. Some critics of Wainewright deplore his maudlin sentimentality and his affected portraits of women, a style they argue that served to satisfy the sentimental family yearnings of the colonists, but others applaud his Regency discretion and simplicity. Whatever its artistic merit, his portrait is the earliest image that exists of Julia.

Following the conventions of the period, she poses facing the viewer. Wearing long pendant earrings and a richly decorated gown, which exposes her soft rounded shoulders, Julia reveals none of the French vivacity and the overflowing energy that she was so renowned for, yet those large dark eyes, delicate features, and bow-shaped mouth explain why she was the belle of Hobart society. Her famously expressive hands lie hidden from view. This

may reflect the artist's lack of confidence in painting hands —
none of his many portraits of Tasmanian colonists depict them
— but it might also point to the discomfort Julia felt at having
to sit still for any length of time. There is, too, a hint of sadness in
that rather pensive face, an acknowledgement that, at twenty-one
years of age, life had already bruised her.

If Julia thought the gossip might wane after the governor's
death, it did not. In September 1848, she was again the subject
of rumours, when Andrew Clarke, the governor's private
secretary, claimed that Julia had told him she wished to marry
Annie Baxter's brother, William Hadden. It did not matter that
William immediately denied it, despite thinking Julia was *very
fascinating and attractive ... and more*, still the rumours swirled.
Julia herself had no thought for romance. She and her family were
all in mourning for her grandfather, the former governor, who had
died in London. And her two younger brothers were enmeshed
in their own crisis which had caused an uproar in Hobart society.

Seventeen-year-old Percy had been expelled from his school,
Christ College in Hobart, for allegedly stabbing a fellow student,
as had his fourteen-year-old brother, William, who had run
away rather than face a public caning for defending him. Julia's
father may have been meek in the face of his wife's determination
to leave Hobart a decade earlier, but when his children's
reputations were at stake, he was a lion in their defence. Just as
he had demanded redress from the governor regarding the gossip
surrounding Julia, he now took on the headmaster of Christ
College, defending Percy against the alleged charge, questioning
the harsh treatment that both boys had faced, and demanding
that they be received back into the school. They were.

None of this induced a lull in the gossip about Julia. As soon
as one rumour died, another sprang up. When it became clear

she was not engaged to Hadden, nor ever would be, she was then allegedly tied to a Mr Elliott, giving rise to bets about its eventual outcome. When Elliott left for Adelaide, arguments raged as to whether he was in despair or relieved to go. But Julia was becoming increasingly weary of this constant unpleasant gossip. Only months later, in April 1849, she was reportedly engaged in another flirtation, this time with Captain Charles FitzRoy, aide-de-camp and son of the governor of New South Wales, who was visiting Van Diemen's Land. No longer bewildered, but certainly angered at the incessant noise around her, she decided to demonstrate her contempt for the gossips of Van Diemen's Land. Before leaving Hobart to stay with friends, she threw them a morsel, declaring that she was taking herself off to the country to rusticate as a punishment *for having gone on with FitzRoy in the way she had.* The gossip became even more frenzied.

This fixation on marriage was not something peculiar to Julia's circle. It was a universal preoccupation, one which drove the narrative of women's lives, determining with whom, where and how they would spend the rest of their lives. Julia's father loathed it. He had built a close connection with his children from the moment they had returned to him in Hobart, a closeness witnessed by the ever-observant Annie, who said of him that he was led *in the most extraordinarily unselfish manner, wherever his daughters chose to take him!* He thought the marriage market trivial and nonsensical, and the mothers of marriageable daughters utterly predatory. He was unwilling to push Julia into marriage and he was also concerned that she might marry simply because the society around her expected it of her. But he need not have worried. Julia knew the world wanted her to marry and would drive her to it, but she also knew about her mother's folly in marrying too soon. She knew about deception. And she knew, too, that her position was an enviable one and there was no strong imperative to change it.

She lived in comfort at the apex of her society. She was loved and supported by her father. She had the affection and company of her younger sisters and brothers. Occupying, as she did, her mother's place in her father's household, she had the independence and privileges of a married woman. At the same time, as a young and beautiful woman of marriageable age, she had the attention and devotion of every man who entered her circle. Why would she marry and surrender all her privileges for a possible life of uncertainty and regret? For Julia, it would require an unusual man to convince her to do so. Such a man arrived in Hobart at the beginning of 1850.

4

An Unusual Man

Tom Arnold's arrival in Hobart was always going to generate excitement. He had a famous name, he had a remarkably handsome face, and he stuttered. Even in this small, isolated community, the name Arnold was known, some might say revered. Tom's father, Dr Thomas Arnold, was the revolutionary headmaster of Rugby School, renowned empire-wide for the changes he had brought to English education. He was known, too, for his part in the drawn-out and fierce religious debates that dominated Oxford and English intellectual life from the 1830s. When his son Tom arrived in Hobart in 1850, Dr Arnold had been dead for only eight years, but such was his fame, a biography had already been published. Young Tom was dark, tall, and slim, with a fine, aesthetic face. It was the face of a dreamer, a word that also described his character. His stutter — or his hesitation, as he called it — had been with him since he was a child. It gave him a diffidence, a gentleness, that appealed greatly to those who met him.

Tom Arnold had arrived in Hobart to take up the newly created post of inspector of schools for Van Diemen's Land. He had been teaching in New Zealand when he met Governor Denison's secretary, Andrew Clarke, who on his return told Denison about the meeting. The governor was only too delighted to offer the position to the son of Dr Arnold of Rugby, no doubt hoping that some of the older man's glory might shine in Van Diemen's Land. It was not the first time that his father's name had opened doors for Tom, nor would it be the last. He was conscious of this, telling his mother that his father's name was *not only a source of proud and gentle memories, but actually and literally better and more profitable than houses and land.* With a salary of £400 plus travelling expenses, Tom had accepted Denison's offer immediately and made his way to Hobart.

When Julia entered Mrs Poynter's drawing room that evening in February 1850, she had no idea that something momentous was about to happen. Dancing had already begun and noticing a seat on the sofa next to Andrew Clarke, she made her way to it. Dressed in black — she was still in mourning for her grandfather — and wearing a single white camellia in her black hair, she passed the watchful row of matrons and chaperones ranged along the wall talking convict servants and ailing children. When Tom Arnold entered the room shortly afterwards, he was immediately struck by Julia's singularly refined and animated face. Clarke, noting Tom's interest, introduced him to Julia. For much of the evening, they talked and danced — to Julia's distinct advantage as she danced beautifully — oblivious to all the pretensions, the rivalries, the jealousies ebbing back and forth around them. It was clear to that row of matrons, and to all the young marriageable women in the room, that Julia Sorell had made another conquest. Tom Arnold only had eyes for her, so incensing one young woman that she declared she would never dance with him again for, instead of looking towards her, his eyes were always following Julia Sorell.

This was a match that no one could have predicted, least of all the two most concerned. Julia was all animation and emotion, a woman with a gift for happiness, her eyes full of fire, open to life, *seizing upon every variety of thought, feeling or pursuit which life had to offer her, and trying it to the end.* She loved society, dances, theatres, and parties. And her exuberance extended beyond people — it embraced the world around her. She loved colour, flowers, gardens, animals too. *A bundle of loves and hates: a force, not an organism.* When she came up against something she did not understand or something that instinctively repelled her, she accepted her aversion and did not seek to comprehend it.

Tom Arnold was none of these things. He was all inner life, by temperament a scholar, a spiritual wanderer, a man who was often silent, and who stammered when he spoke. And when Tom came up against something he did not understand, when he found mystery, he sought enlightenment and could never be content until he believed he had achieved this. Julia and he were polar opposites.

Born on 30 November 1823, Tom Arnold was three years older than Julia. He had been raised in a stable home, the third child of nine. It was a formidable family: his older brother, Matthew, would become a poet, critic, and essayist; his older sister, Jane, a German scholar; while a younger brother, William, would become an educationalist and a writer. The Arnold family moved to Rugby in Warwickshire in August 1828 when Dr Arnold became headmaster of Rugby School. Here he began his radical school reforms — introducing mathematics, modern languages, history, and pastoral care — that would make his name. The school grew rapidly under his regime, but, not content with his educational work at Rugby, Arnold increasingly engaged in the dominant public debates of the nineteenth century — that of religion in particular — preaching his notion of the national ideal, an Anglican theocracy where church and state were indistinguishable.

This immediately drew him into direct conflict with John Henry Newman, an Anglican priest and Oxford intellectual, who, as a leader of the Tractarian movement, wished to reassert the Church of England's Catholic heritage, in both theology and practice. The theoretical differences between the two men turned more personal when Newman ostensibly queried whether Arnold was in fact a Christian and Arnold denounced Newman as a fanatic. Arnold and Newman came to represent opposing sides in the drawn-out religious divisions that so dominated Oxford and other parts of English life. In an era when the shade of one's religion mattered deeply, men were revered or reviled for their religious opinions and practices.

After Arnold's death, Newman gained even more notoriety when he converted to Catholicism and was ordained a Catholic priest in 1845, the most famous and influential of Victorian English converts, but not the only one. Others included Henry Manning, later Archbishop of Westminster and eventually a cardinal, Robert and Henry Wilberforce — their brother Samuel would become an influential Anglican bishop — and the poet Gerard Manley Hopkins. Invariably, conflict followed such moves and often families were torn apart, including Newman's own. Such was the impact of conversion that it inspired even novelists, including Elizabeth Gaskell and Dr Arnold's own granddaughter, Mrs Humphry Ward.

In Julia's house, Dr Arnold was revered, not Newman.

While Dr Arnold was forging his name in education and defending the broad church, he and his wife were also rearing their large family. Tom was regarded as a delicate child having survived a near-fatal liver disease at the age of four. Whether because of this or his stammer, he was singled out by his father for special attention. In 1832, when he and some of his younger siblings were recovering from the measles, Tom asked his father to write him, in verse or prose, something to be his very own. His father responded by writing him a verse, part of which reads, *Now from thy little Bed thy Smile, How sweet it gleams when I draw nigh … Thy Father's Love, thou know'st it tru.*

When Tom's stammer continued to trouble both him and his father — Dr Arnold was a loving father, yes, but according to his son Matthew, he was also zealous, beneficent, and firm — a special tutor was employed to help Tom overcome it. It was a fruitless mission. In 1839, while Tom was bowing to Queen Adelaide on her visit to Rugby School, content in his stable, regulated world, controlled and dominated by his father, Julia was watching her own father's figure retreat as she sailed from Hobart with her mother into an unknown, tumultuous future.

If Rugby played a part in moulding Tom's character, so, too, did the Arnold's holiday house, Fox How, in the Lake District. Dr Arnold had taken a strong liking to the area when he visited the poet William Wordsworth and decided to build a house there, on a twenty-acre site suggested by Wordsworth. Julia delighted in Tom's stories of his life at Fox How, of the sailing and rowing, of the picnics and fishing, and of how on those wet days when the family was forced to remain inside this house overgrown with roses, they would produce the *Fox How Magazine*, a combination of word and image that described their holiday life.

Unsurprisingly, Julia concluded that Tom's upbringing was joyful in comparison to her own, but she might have hesitated in drawing this conclusion had she known that in 1831, on the occasion of his eighth birthday, Tom had written, *I think that the eight years I have now lived will be the happiest of my life*. It was a remarkable sentiment for a child so young, but Tom was always inclined to both the romantic and the dramatic gesture. This characteristic was noticed by his father when, in 1841 on a holiday in France with his children Matthew, Jane, and Tom, he noticed Tom walking up and down on the balcony singing into the night. Romance and idealism would prove a quixotic combination in Tom's life and many of his later decisions confirmed the acuity of Dr Arnold's observation.

A year later, while Julia was being reunited with her father in Hobart, Tom, now a student at Oxford University, was burying his. Dr Arnold had been in Oxford to deliver a lecture when he died suddenly from a heart attack. Tom was by his side. It was a deeply confronting death for the sensitive nineteen-year-old, and in an attempt to recover from the shock, he accompanied two of his sisters, Mary and Susanna, on a visit to their father's old friend Richard Whately, the Archbishop of Dublin. While he was there, Tom fell deeply in love with Whately's daughter Henrietta.

Although Tom's years at University College in Oxford appeared on the surface to be happy ones — he was popular, clever, a natural student — he wrote some time later to his sister that these were the unhappiest years of his life. It may have been that, for all its physical beauty, the atmosphere of Oxford was poisonous. In

1842 it was a closed Anglican community. On matriculation and again upon taking their degrees, undergraduates had to subscribe to the Thirty-nine Articles and otherwise testify *their loyalty to the established order of things, without much thought perhaps, but in very good faith nevertheless.* The religious dissension that had divided Oxford since the early 1830s, the divisions that had pitted Dr Arnold against Newman, erupted again while Tom was there.

William Ward, a fellow of Balliol, was accused of expressing ultra-Catholic sentiments in his book *The Ideal of a Christian Church*, and the University of Oxford was invited to censure the book and strip Ward of his degrees. On a day of pouring rain, a vast assembly crowded into the Sheldonian Theatre to hear Ward defend his position. Amidst cries for and against, the verdict was solemnly announced against him. Tom was in the thick of the drama, tramping up and down in Broad Street waiting for the verdict, and when Ward left the theatre, Tom saw him slip face down into the mud, his papers and pamphlets scattered in all directions. It was a physical humiliation for the poor man, a dramatic and vivid symbol of the consequences that pertained to anyone who sailed too close to Catholicism.

In this context, Tom, his brother Matthew, and many others in their circle, rejected established religion altogether, and turned instead to writers like Goethe, George Sand, Emerson, and Carlyle, each of whom explored materialism and individuality. Although they were attracted by the same writers, Tom and his brother read them very differently. Matthew, the extrovert, the rebel, the one who delighted to shock, developed a robust and sceptical attitude towards religion and read these writers with a sense of optimism, seeing in them a civilising influence. Tom, quieter, more inward, more emotional, sank into a form of existential depression as he sought something, anything, that might fill the void left by religion. His attraction to Goethe's young Werther — an appealing, generous, imaginative character, unfit to cope with life — was in part self-identification, but it was also an idealism that filled the void he so strongly felt. By the time Tom had finished his degree in 1846, both Ward and Newman had converted to Catholicism, and Tom had lost his faith completely.

Despite graduating with a first-class degree, the now faithless Tom could not become a fellow at University College where, as was the case in all Oxford colleges, fellows were expected to become clergymen and upon their marriage would move immediately out of college to take up parish life. Instead, Tom moved to London to study law at Lincoln's Inn. When he realised the law was not for him, his mother used her connections and his father's name to secure him a position in the Colonial Office. While Tom found this more congenial, he was increasingly depressed by his loss of religion and by a London full of squalor and poverty. Unlike Julia, whose life had been lived against a backdrop of clinking chains, marching feet, and the silent struggle of hanged and murdered bodies, Tom was, for the first time in his life, living away from the manicured serenity of Rugby and Oxford. Yearning for meaning and contentment in his life, he began helping the poor, and he asked Henrietta Whately to marry him.

She rejected him immediately. Religious doubts, she said, made him an unacceptable husband to her and an unacceptable son-in-law to Archbishop Whately. Tom was thrown into complete misery. His had lost Henrietta, he was distressed by English oppressions and English orthodoxies, and his benefactor in the public service, Lord Carlisle, considered him remarkably inefficient. Tom decided to flee England and try his hand at farming in New Zealand, a place that had been a part of his mental landscape since his father had bought 200 acres there in 1840. Tom now imbued it with freedom and beauty. It would be his salvation from despair, a place where a man *might mold his life afresh.*

Having made his decision, and despite his family's opposition, Tom now looked upon his New Zealand scheme as inevitable. Nothing would deflect him. His mother knew this tendency of his to see everything as black or white, to prefer dismantling rather than reforming. His siblings too knew this characteristic. They called it his stubbornness, but for Tom, changing his mind was akin to tampering with his conscience, and he would always choose his conscience over all else.

In May 1848 Tom reached New Zealand and using his Oxford degree and his father's name — a potent mixture in the web of influence that existed in imperial circles — he quickly established connections. Among them was Thomas Collinson, a young captain in the Royal Engineers, who would become a lifelong friend. Collinson has left one of the most vivid accounts of Tom Arnold at that time in his life:

> Naturally he was a studious, wide minded and large hearted man, of simple and gentle disposition; a character in short on which a strong impression would be made by the teaching of more powerful characters than his own. The result ... a vagueness in all. We all loved him; it was impossible not to love so amiable and openhearted a young fellow, who was so full of the best learning of the day, and straight from the society of the principal men of the day in art, science and politics. He became at once the representative with us of the advanced party in the philosophy of life.

Nothing in this description would suggest a farmer, but it took several setbacks before Tom himself realised his destiny was not in farming and that he was better fitted to teaching. Although he achieved some success when he established a school in Nelson — by March 1849 he had twenty pupils — he was often lonely and he began to consider the practical need for a wife. His highly respected name and good looks made him the object of some formidable attention, but despite his loneliness, he appeared unwilling to succumb to the temptations thrown his way. He had no intention, he told his mother, of plunging *into marriage with eyes shut*. His chance meeting with Andrew Clarke and the prospect of £400 a year would irretrievably alter this view.

5

Finding Love

From their first meeting in Mrs Poynter's drawing room, Julia's romance with Tom Arnold progressed rapidly. She had been immediately attracted by his difference. His background, and his passage through Oxford to Tasmania, was quite contrary to the official, military, and settler society she knew so well. In light of her mother's betrayal, the fact that Tom was *not* a member of the military, made him even more attractive to her. And her father, whom she loved deeply, had read and admired Arthur Stanley's biography of Dr Arnold, which only made Julia more intrigued to meet his son. Tom's stammer and his shyness added another dimension. She could never forgo rescuing people and animals from their misfortunes. She did not resist his overtures, but instead set out to enjoy the attention of this new man, a handsome adornment to Hobart society. It was not difficult.

Tom had no need to scheme his way into the houses, parties, and balls that she was invited to. His connections in the small world of Hobart — apart from his friend Andrew Clarke, he also had a cousin, John Buckland, the headmaster of Hutchins School

— and his position as inspector of schools made him a desirable guest in all the best drawing rooms of Van Diemen's Land. There, he assiduously pursued Julia. Tom had fallen in love with her at first sight and so overwhelming were his feelings towards her, he felt it was less a conquest than an annihilation. She was, he believed, his moral equivalent and it was this affinity that drew him to her. Such was Tom's intense pursuit of her — he was unable to *look at, or speak to, or think of, any other person but Julia Sorell* — their romance quickly became the principal *on dit* in Hobart. When the gossip reached an unprecedented frenzy, the Reverend Dr Bedford, who had christened Julia, felt it incumbent upon himself to question her about her feelings for Tom. He was satisfied with what she told him, and with his blessing, when Tom proposed, she accepted. It was less than a month after their first meeting. Julia had been, quite simply, swept off her feet.

Instead of abating, the gossip grew even more voluble and vindictive. The engagement had come so quickly, some in Hobart society believed Julia was pregnant. Annie Baxter certainly didn't believe this, although she did think, rather spitefully, that Tom needed rescuing from Julia who was *determined certainly to get somebody to marry her.*

But not all the opposition to the match arose out of spite or from ignorance. Tom's New Zealand friend Captain Collinson, who was passing through Hobart on his way home to England, thought they were so unsuited it would be a doomed marriage. He believed that Tom was incapable of turning the high-spirited Julia, the ruling belle of Hobart, into the Victorian ideal of a wife, someone of a faithful and modest nature. He also believed, as did others, that Julia could never be a poor man's wife. When Tom refused to listen to him, Collinson turned to Julia, endeavouring to make her see the wisdom of breaking off the engagement.

She was deeply touched by what he had to say about Tom's otherworldliness, his gentleness, and unable to ever hide her feelings, Julia wept at his words. But it changed nothing, except that Collinson, like so many others, fell in love with her, so much so that had Tom not been engaged to Julia, Collinson confessed to Tom that he himself would have asked her to marry him.

During their engagement Julia met Tom as often as her social calendar and his work allowed. His frequent absences from Hobart — his position required him to journey into all parts of the colony — did not hinder their relationship. Quite the contrary. Tom's literary skills were a far stronger weapon than his stuttering voice, and his wooing techniques on paper were formidable. In his letters to her he sang her praises, proclaimed her beauty, and expressed his jealousy of anyone she encountered. In one such letter from Launceston on Thursday 4 April 1850, Tom wrote:

> My own Julia, you cannot think how unspeakably happy your love makes me. The first thing in the morning, and the last thing at night, comes that sweet thought, my Julia is mine, and I am hers. I am prouder than if I was king of the world. And even as to ambition and the love of fame, 'that last infirmity of noble minds', what is there that a man need despair of effecting, who was sustained by the love of a being like you …

And on another occasion he wrote from Longford:

> O my own Julia, I shall never forget how beautiful and captivating you were that night; what a rage I was in

at finding you had gone home without me. After all, it was my chiefly own fault, for leaving my place by your side, where I was happy as a prince, in order to ask Mrs. Chapman to dawdle through an insufferable quadrille.

All this tender flattery was interspersed with humorous descriptions of his travels and his impressions of the island and all those he met.

Many women would have loved the writer of such letters, and Julia was no exception, but when Tom was in Hobart, she found him to be possessive and jealous. He wanted to spend all his time at her side, he found dancing with anyone else an ordeal, and he hated the young officers in their red uniforms bowing and soliciting the pleasure of dancing with her. Although irritated by it, Julia simply interpreted Tom's jealousy as an expression of his love for her. She was also irritated by Tom's desire to change her.

From the beginning, and despite his rapturous adoration of her, Tom found those very qualities that had so drawn him to her — her vivacity and her openness — deeply unsettling, as he did the whispers about her past. Julia, keen to assuage his anxiety, but not understanding the extent of his unease, suggested she absent herself from parties while he was away. Once challenged, though, Tom insisted she continue to go out if it would give her pleasure, providing she did *not overstep the limits which engaged persons ought to observe ... and act in all these things according to your own sense of what was right and fit, and you may be sure I shall be well pleased with whatever you do.* Already it was as if these two lovers actually loved one another more apart than together.

Julia did not take umbrage, or even warning, at Tom's lecturing tone, but simply consigned it to the basket marked 'jealousy'. Living with her gentle father and with no intimate model of married life before her, she had not observed the desire on the part of some men to master their wives, and could have no understanding of what it might mean for her own independent spirit. Surely Tom could not condemn her for the very warmth and animation that he found so enchanting, nor for the jealousy that her grace and beauty sometimes caused, particularly among women. She was only half correct in her surmise. Tom could forgive the jealously she triggered, believing that it was in great part because of her generosity, frankness, kindliness, and sincerity, but he had no desire for a spirited wife. That she did not perceive.

Julia shone brightly when she and Tom attended the ball given at the Custom-house by the Hon. Captain Keppell and the officers of the H.M.S. *Meander*. Many of her admirers were present, and as she danced to the music of the regimental bands in the flag-draped room illuminated by the two large sconces, Tom was sent into a jealous pique, his dancing partners into despair, and the Hobart gossips into a fever.

It was only at such social functions or in drawing rooms lined with chaperones, that Julia could meet Tom. Decorum demanded that they never be alone together, only adding to the intensity of their public meetings, as they tried to guess at the deeper meanings held in glances and words. They knew little of each other's ambitions, beliefs, fears, or follies. Julia did not know that Tom had abandoned religion altogether. She did not know anything of the despair that had caused it, nor did she know of his intransigence once his mind was made up. For his part Tom knew only a little of her life in Brussels, even less of her prosaic, practical religious beliefs — there had been no cause for her deep hatred for Catholicism to emerge — and he knew nothing of the curse that she felt was upon her and her family. They rarely, if ever, had any opportunity to discuss their feeling and thoughts, their expectations of each other, or their future married life. Such conversations could only be had afterwards.

For all the real and potential differences that were hinted at and then glossed over, this relationship had an impetus of its own. Tom may have averred that he would never plunge into marriage with his eyes shut, yet Julia had so blinded and subjugated him that he felt *he belonged more to her than to himself.* She was his first thought in the morning and the last at night. A future without this vivacious, beautiful girl was unimaginable even if in Tom's mind Julia was in need of a firm mind and a faithful heart to help her *overcome her temptations and become all that nature has qualified her to be.* Tom was being consistent at least. He was determined to have Julia — he would mould her into the sort of woman he deemed worthy of being his wife — and *nothing* would deter him.

Julia was equally determined to have Tom, an attitude that puzzled Annie Baxter. After canvassing several possible explanations, she decided that Julia was simply exhausted with the marriage game and tired of always being expected to marry. Annie believed that remaining unmarried was cause for anxiety and contempt, and Julia, at twenty-four years of age, could not be immune to the pressure to conform, each year counting against her. Annie's belief was reinforced when Julia's sister Ada told her that Julia loved Tom *quite as well as she can ever love anybody.* But, unlike Annie, Ada knew that Julia did not view marriage as an escape from a dreary life of duty, caring for her father and her brothers and sisters. Quite the contrary. She knew that any love Julia had would be fierce and irrevocable. Julia could love in no other way. So what was it about Tom that finally drove Julia to marriage?

For some time, and almost blindly, Julia had been searching for a deeper connection with life. She had no interest in dogma or institutional religion and had resisted the efforts of her dear friend Mrs Nixon, the wife of the bishop, to become more interested in religion, yet the yearning was still there. Then Tom appeared in her world of whiskers and swagger. Tom, with his earnest, sensitive nature, his deeply spiritual temperament, and his self-deprecating humour. Tom, the son of a good and religious man, one whom her father admired deeply. Surely there could be no one better than Tom to counter this growing unease she felt but did not understand. There was, too, the irresistible pleasure in snatching this desirable target from the grasping hands of Hobart's matrimonial matrons, who for so long had subjected her to their relentless scrutiny, their pious approval, their closeted unease. Marrying Tom Arnold would provide a sanctuary, an escape from these same women, and from any shame that might still linger from her mother's legacy.

Here was a perfectly eligible young man offering not simply love but adoration, an adoration that was so intense it was difficult to resist. And Julia did not want to resist. She, like Tom, believed in their *essential likeness and congruity of soul* and she loved him deeply. It was enough.

Julia Sorell became Mrs Tom Arnold on 13 June 1850 at St David's Cathedral in Hobart. Tom may have chosen the date — it was his father's birthday — but Julia insisted that the elderly Dr William Bedford, who had counselled her in the lead-up to her engagement, should marry them. The pews filled quickly. Many of those present felt, as Annie Baxter and Chester Eardley-Wilmot did, that unless they witnessed Julia marry with their own eyes, they would not believe it had taken place. Shortly before eleven, Tom and his best man, Andrew Clarke, arrived.

Tom was dressed in a *blue frock coat, with white waistcoat with lapels, light grey doeskin trowers, and a tie of brown and white silk, tied in large bows.* The groomsmen were Annie's brother Captain Hadden and Edward Bedford, the son of Dr Bedford, with whom Tom had struck up a strong friendship.

At eleven precisely, the wedding party entered the church. Julia was on the arm of her father and followed by her sisters, who acted as bridesmaids. Also in the bridal party were her two brothers, her grandfather Mr Kemp, and her aunt Mrs Jones. Tom thought there was nothing more beautiful than Julia in her muslin dress, high to the throat, with two deep flounces, richly trimmed with lace, and overlaid with a white lace mantle. A white chip bonnet with a small feather, a white lace veil, white satin shoes, and an ornate Indian gold chain round her neck completed her finery. She carried a bouquet of orange blossom and jasmine. In the language of flowers, a language which flourished in the Victorian era, orange blossom and jasmine translated as eternal love and sensuality. Julia was pale. It was not surprising. Marriage would determine the shape of her life. Would she reach a point in the future, when she, too, would wish to flee her marriage just as her mother had?

Annie Baxter's version of the wedding, while biting in its commentary — *the awful ceremony took place; & they are now 'One flesh'* … — exposed further bitter divides in this isolated Hobart community. Here it was not enough that white was against black, convict against free, settler against government. Difference of any sort was abhorred.

> We went into the Organ loft, and were congratulating
> ourselves on being so alone, when in walked Mrs Curll
> & all the family of Jews, i.e. Hortz & Cohens! Poor

Marianne! She said so quaintly 'I would give £20 gladly, to be out of this pew'! 'I will go home! I hate coming in contact with such persons'. I agree with her in all she said; excepting about the £20; - which I said, I would rather keep, myself.

Annie's agitation and horror were only exacerbated when she saw another outcast, *'Mad Paddy'! Poor soul! He was so cleanly dressed, with his hair so smooth, and looking so orderly.* Julia was always unwilling to cede to petty-mindedness and social convention and in her generous, frank way had invited the Hortz family, the Cohens, and Mad Paddy. It is little wonder her passionate nature was condemned, for any woman who strained against convention was considered dangerous. Yet Julia's tolerance in these matters only made her intolerance in other matters even more stark.

The service was short and when Julia and Tom left the church, they passed through several lines of onlookers, before driving to her father's house in Macquarie Street for the wedding breakfast. As soon as they arrived, Julia burst into tears — not, she claimed, tears of sorrow, but simply tears of relief that the wedding was over. She had always been expressive, unwilling to restrain her feelings, and in this instance those tears of relief were mingled with anxiety at what lay ahead. She had no mother hovering to offer advice and sympathy, to give her knowledge of what would come next. After the wedding cake *of ponderous dimensions* was cut and distributed, the colonial secretary, Mr Bicheno, toasted the couple's health, and Tom thanked the assembled party on his and Julia's behalf. At half-past one, after kissing her family, Julia left her father's house with Tom and went straight to their new home in New Town, about two miles from the centre of Hobart.

A shortage of funds and the demands imposed by Tom's inspection work prevented a honeymoon. Julia's married life began as it would continue. She had not married a rich man, nor an idle one.

6

A Woman's Destiny

New Town may have been on the outskirts of Hobart, but both Julia and her family were determined that neither her marriage nor distance would exclude her from their lives or from Hobart's social and cultural life. She and Tom continued to attend balls, parties, and dinners at Government House, and she often joined her sisters in the governor's box at the theatre. But Julia also loved those evenings when she was alone with Tom in their cottage, she sewing, writing letters, playing the piano, while he read or wrote reports for his work or letters to his family and friends. Sometimes he would read to her. And together they gardened and walked — Julia had quickly acquired Tom's love of walking — and Tom, on one occasion, like lovers down the ages, carved their entwined initials on the log they paused to rest on.

Julia's determination to accompany Tom on his travels only strengthened their closeness. It took some courage for her to undertake these journeys as the weather often made the roads hazardous and bushrangers were an ever-present threat. Although gentlemen often had pistols to hand, Tom did not carry arms, believing that New Town, so close to Hobart, would be immune from the terrors of assault. He was wrong. One evening, as the night closed around them on their return home from dining in Hobart, they were chased by a man intent on robbery. Julia was terrified, sobbing in fear, and only regained her composure when the frantic steps faded behind them. It was enough for Tom to determine that he would never go on that road again without arms.

When Julia and Tom travelled together for his work, they would stay with her large network of friends and family. Chief among them were Thomas and Catherine Reibey, who lived on the beautiful estate of Entally, near Launceston. Julia grew particularly close to Catherine and would turn to her when in distress, while Tom felt an affinity with Thomas, who had, like himself, been educated at Oxford. On his return to the colony, Reibey had become the rector of Holy Trinity Church in Launceston. They stayed, too, with various members of the Bisdee family — Julia had gone to school at Ellinthorp with James Bisdee's wife — and, always when they could, they stayed with her old friend Captain Chalmers and his family. Here Julia felt at peace, and in the Captain's large garden she and Tom played like children, the bright sunshine and the fragrant air of the bush elating her spirits and enveloping her and Tom.

When she was left on her own in the cottage at New Town, her sister Gussie would stay with her. They were particularly close, temperament as much as age drawing them together. Gussie, too, was a belle and shared Julia's flirtatious style and vivacious embrace of life — those same character traits that Tom was so wary of. Deeply in love he may have been, but he was relentless in his expectation that Julia change those aspects of her nature he did not approve of. During their engagement he had outlined the behaviour he expected from her, and now that she was his wife he was no less forthcoming about his expectations, one of which was obedience. Tom had learned from his own father that the man was the master of all that took place in his home. But unlike Tom's mother, Julia had never been gentle or yielding. Nor had she ever learned obedience.

Financial pressures arose early in Julia's marriage. Tom had disregarded all advice from his family and friends that he should wait until he was in a better financial position to marry. Instead, he had forged ahead and was from that moment

> always hampered with a heavy debt, the foundation of which was laid when we married, by my furnishing my house — the sodden ass that I was — on credit, and which the bad times which followed (bad for public officers, I mean, who could not dig for gold, and had nothing to sell) so far from permitting me to pay off, rather added to.

Julia had no understanding of what marriage to a poor man might entail. Her father was not wealthy, but his income as a civil servant had enabled him to sustain his household and rear five children in comfort. She assumed that her life with Tom would be similar. He held an excellent position, was on a good salary, and was destined for an honourable career in the civil service. Nor did she have any experience of running a household where her decisions were queried or criticised. Her father had been content with her management of his house, and she expected her husband would be also. She was wrong. Their first disagreement over money surfaced shortly after their marriage.

In Julia's era, married women were not recognised in law as having a separate legal identity, only the husband had legal status and only the husband could control financial matters. It was his duty to provide his wife with money for all the household expenditure and her own needs, unless he agreed that credit should be used, in which case he paid the bills either when they came due or, more often, when he saw fit. Wives could not make contracts or incur debts without their husbands' approval. Julia, unused to seeking her father's approval for her purchases and completely unaware of Tom's precarious financial position, did not think to seek his permission to use credit. When the bills arrived his anger and harsh words — *How dared you Madam* — poured over her, and they would remain with her all her life. She recoiled at the searing intensity of Tom's rage, but when her fright and anger at his outburst abated she determined to continue to manage the household as she always had. There was no other way.

With his characteristic burnishing of reality, Tom, too, was only too happy to put this confrontation behind him and not to concern himself with their debts. It enabled him to paint a very rosy picture for Collinson when he next wrote to him, and although he acknowledged that his old friend's advice to wait and save some money before marrying had clearly been wise, he told him that his debts were diminishing rather than increasing, and he was happy regardless, for he and Julia understood each other perfectly. Julia could not know then that Tom's inclination to borrow and her own sense of abundance and reliance on credit would become an enduring narrative in their marriage. Such knowledge only ever comes slowly, inexorably, and most often too late.

Despite the tension that simmered underneath the surface, marriage seemed to suit Julia perfectly, so much so that Annie Baxter noted that she looked remarkably well at the Government

House Ball. Within months of her marriage, Julia was pregnant, and she and Tom began planning as much as they could for this momentous change in their lives. Tom's preparation was relatively simple — he moved out of his study and into the dining room to make room for a nursery — but Julia found these months more fraught and difficult than most women in her condition. She was surrounded by friends and aunts, but with no mother to support her, her husband often away from her, and her sisters less experienced than she, she had to face, and then squash, her fears about the baby's welfare, her fears about her own capacity to be a mother, and, most terrifying of all, her fears about her own mortality. When Julia was facing childbirth the mean maternal mortality rate in England was estimated to be 4.6 in 1000. (Today that rate is calculated at being 0.1 in 1000.) Tom, too, was anxious, but he placed his faith in the gods — whoever they might be — and they did not let him down. On 11 June 1851, earlier than was expected, Julia gave birth. She survived the ordeal, as did her black-haired, brown-eyed daughter. Named Mary Augusta after Tom's mother and Julia's sister, the baby soon came to be known as 'Polly'.

If Julia expected the birth of their daughter to bind her more closely to Tom, she was mistaken. On the contrary it caused another fierce and divisive confrontation between them. Julia wanted Polly christened. Tom refused to give his consent. Julia was deeply shocked. She knew that Tom was sceptical about religion, but she did not understand that his scepticism not only denied Original Sin and its obliteration through the ceremony of baptism, but *all* religion. Why, then, had he married her in a church in a religious ceremony?

For Julia, religion was a framework, a set of rituals that she, along with most Victorians, adhered to — Sunday services, christenings, marriages, and funerals — rather like responsible citizens in a democracy today who vote in elections, pay tax, know the main issues of the day, and occasionally, if beliefs are disturbed, march in protest, but unless 'true believers', are unlikely to join a political party, stand for election, or volunteer for a substantive role in the polis. She had been reared in a Protestant 'scriptural' atmosphere and had been partly drawn to Tom because of his father's role in defending Anglicanism against encroaching Romanism in Oxford. Since their marriage, she had continued to observe the Anglican rituals despite Tom's own loss of faith.

Julia was not simply shocked at Tom's attitude, she was also very frightened by it. She may not have been deeply religious, but she did know that having an unchristened child beckoned divine retribution and threatened an eternity of fire for the child. She would not give in to Tom. This fierce confrontation over Polly's christening was her first real exposure to Tom's stubborn adherence to his beliefs and to his understanding of her role as a wife. Essentially, her beliefs were immaterial. He was master of the house, and she must do as he said. For three months, the battle raged between them — so much so that Julia began to believe Tom unstable — before he eventually surrendered, moved not by Julia's pleas or her fears, but by Thomas Reibey's intervention. This intense struggle, focused on belief and authority, became another thread woven into their marriage.

As the churning anxiety about her daughter's soul slowly dissipated, Julia began to delight in her new role as mother, even as her life changed dramatically, shaping itself to the needs of her child. She now only accompanied Tom on his inspectorate trips if she was able to stay with her closer friends, and she no longer rode, frightened of what might happen to her child if an accident occurred. She was learning that marriage and motherhood brought their own forms of containment, and nothing had prepared her — she was on a trajectory into the unknown.

Tom, too, had changed, following the birth of Polly. He began to voice a desire to return to England, in part prompted by his hatred for the prevailing transportation system, which he believed was putrid. He hated seeing the red flag flying at the signal staff, showing that another ship with convicts was arriving, and he decried its pervasive effects on the colony. He did not want his child polluted by it. He wasn't alone.

An intense campaign against transportation was underway among the colonists, a campaign that he wholly supported, as did Julia's father, grandfather Kemp, her uncles, and many more in their circle. Tom claimed that Julia shared his desire to leave Van Diemen's Land, despite the fact that she was pregnant again, despite her own very unhappy memories of her time in Europe, and despite her unwillingness to leave her close-knit family and wide circle of friends, particularly given her condition. But when Tom believed something, he expected that others would share his view, certainly his wife, and he asked his friends and family in England to keep an eye out for employment for him. When Julia gave birth to their second child, a son in September 1852 — they named him William after her father and grandfather — Tom's desire to leave Van Diemen's Land grew stronger.

With no money or a position in England to return to, Tom needed to find an alternative route home, so he proposed that the colonial government send him to England to examine potential candidates as teachers for the colony. Julia thought it unlikely that Tom's proposal would be accepted — she was always more realistic than he was — but she sensed his growing unease and encouraged him nonetheless. When the government rejected the proposal, she could not know that it would prove to be a pivotal moment in her marriage. Had Tom returned to England at this time, her life may have taken a quite different course. As it was, when news arrived later that year that transportation would finally cease, there was celebration in the Arnold household and Tom's determination to leave Van Diemen's Land abated.

Shortly after Willy's birth, and despite all his protestations to his friend Collinson that his finances were improving, Tom told Julia he could no longer afford the rent on their New Town house and they would need to move. Before they were forced to seek assistance from either her father or grandfather, Governor Denison offered Tom the former Normal School, a substantial stone house, at a reduced rent. It was situated on a spacious block of land, about half a mile from their current cottage, and Julia saw its potential immediately. She was an adept gardener and planted an orchard and grew vegetables on a scale that allowed her to sell the surplus. She also persuaded Tom to buy a cow, which supplied the family with butter and milk. It would not be the last time that her practical endeavours would ease their financial problems.

Julia was happy in this new house, with its bounteous garden, and with her cow. Years later, in the first of her novels — she called it *Milly and Olly*, code names for her brother Willy and herself— Polly used memories from her childhood to sketch her parents at this time, more particularly, her mother:

> Milly and Olly loved their father, and whenever he
> put his brown face inside the nursery door, two pairs
> of little feet went running to meet him, and two pairs
> of little hands pulled him eagerly into the room. But

they saw him very seldom; whereas their mother was always with them, teaching them their lessons, playing with them in the garden, telling them stories, mending their frocks, tucking them up in their snug little beds at night, sometimes praising them, sometimes scolding them; always loving and looking after them. Milly and Olly honestly believed theirs was the best mother in the whole world. Nobody else could find out such nice plays, or tell such wonderful stories, or dress dolls half so well.

Tom too appeared content. He was relishing his work, and having just read Joseph Kay's *The Social Condition and Education of the People*, he was infused with a messianic drive that absorbed, for the moment, his innate intellectual and spiritual restlessness. He no longer thought of leaving the colony.

But the idyll could not last. Tragedy struck on 19 May 1854, when Julia gave birth to their third child, another son. He was critically ill, and at Julia's insistence — Tom did not resist this time — the clergyman was called and the child was christened Arthur Penrose, after Tom's great friends Arthur Clough and Arthur Stanley. Not long after, his little body stopped breathing. Julia was heartbroken. In this era, when the death of a child was commonplace, women were expected to recover from the trauma in silence. They were expected to forget. But Julia could not, no more than the writer Elizabeth Gaskell, who wrote a sonnet to her dead baby, 'On Visiting the Grave of My Stillborn Little Girl', or Hannah Macdonald, the mother-in-law of the pre-Raphaelite painter Edward Burne-Jones and the grandmother of Rudyard Kipling, who, although she made no outward show of it, observed the anniversaries of the deaths of her three children every year. Silence, yes. Forgetting, no.

After she had buried her baby, Julia's health remained poor and her spirits, usually so ebullient, were low enough for both her father and Tom to express concern. Ever so slowly, she did what her nature demanded. She turned out to the world, hiding her grief in a growing frenzy of social activity. She went to more functions and events than she had done for years, the chatter, the sympathy, and the compliments all working to restore her confidence and her spirits. Her father was foremost among those encouraging her, noting, as did many others, that despite children and domestic vexations, she was *still the unquestionable 'Reine du bal'* whenever she made her appearance.

Little Arthur's death took its toll on Tom too, driving him to once more reassess his life. Essentially an intellectual man, without what his brother Matthew called *a still considerate mind*, Tom turned inwards, reflecting deeply and interminably about his son's death. His agonised soul-searching led him to a dramatic resolution. He would return to his Anglican roots, to the religion of his father. Tom would never avow that in mending the broken ties with his father, he hoped to remain connected to his own dead son. Instead, he claimed that he had led Julia astray through his agnosticism and that by returning to religion he could redeem her. Julia did not feel she needed redemption — she did after all attend Sunday services, and she had fought to have their children christened — but she was so delighted with Tom's return to Christianity, she did not challenge his rationale.

Even at their most divided, Julia and Tom had always shared an intense physical relationship, and it was not long before Julia was pregnant again. Despite little Arthur's death, she was relatively content throughout this pregnancy, knowing that her next child, whether dead or alive, would at least be christened with no resistance from Tom. She was right. When she gave birth to another son on the 12 April 1855, he was christened, without any arguments, Theodore, after Theodore Walrond, another of Tom's inner circle of friends at Rugby and Oxford. Less than three months later, Julia would sit down at her desk and write,

> I love you dearest Tom most deeply, and in separating from you I shall strike my own death blow, but as things are now it must be so.

7

An Impossible Choice

When Julia wrote those words, she was no longer in the frenzy of fear and fury that had drummed constantly in her since Tom had declared, without any warning or any discussion, that he had decided to become a Roman Catholic. She was in a quiet, sombre mood, exhausted by the futile struggle to comprehend how her life had been transformed in that moment.

When Tom first told her of his decision, she had reacted with a torrent of hate and despair. His words had immediately transported her back to Brussels, a girl abandoned by her mother, in the dark misery of that school where the corridors smelled of incense and sin. He could not possibly mean what he said. He knew nothing about the vileness of Catholics and the absurd things they believed in. He could not possibly ask her to live beside something she detested, something her very being revolted against. He would change into something she did not know or recognise. How could she ever trust him again? She would never have married him if he had been a Roman Catholic. Did he not think of her at all in this decision? Did he simply assume that as his wife she would dutifully follow him in his change of religion? He was no better than her mother in his deceit. He could not become a Catholic. She would leave him immediately. He needed to reconsider. He must talk to her father. He must talk to the Reibeys. He must write to his mother. The torrent eventually stopped. Nothing she said moved him.

Julia had been married to Tom for five years, and during that time she had experienced his stubborn adherence to what he thought was proper, what he believed was his role and what was hers, but this was the first time she had experienced his remarkable capacity for a complete volte-face — from no religion when she met him to a sudden adoption of Catholicism. She did not know, and certainly did not understand, that whatever philosophy or faith he adopted had to be followed to its extreme. And for her, there was nothing more extreme than Roman Catholicism. How could her husband have come to this conclusion? Even in his agnostic phase, he had displayed the deep-felt prejudices of his class and caste against Catholics, advising her not to take a Roman Catholic as a servant unless very strongly recommended — *altogether you cannot be too careful* — and scorning his friend and Oxford contemporary Gifford Palgrave, who had converted, thinking it absurd and Palgrave a goose, believing that if Palgrave fell *in with a pious Brahmin, who has still more of the 'religious life' than his Jesuit friends, I suppose he will take to Siva and Vieshnoo.*

After little Arthur's death had spurred Tom's return to his Anglican roots, he had appeared content and there had been nothing in his demeanour to suggest this was a mere stepping stone to something much more radical. Yet here he was, determined to become a Catholic, a religion his own father had deeply objected to and one that his wife despised beyond anything else. Had he gone mad? Tom would say not, simply that he was moved by various influences.

For a time, his all-consuming love for Julia and his work, with all the challenges it posed, had kept his restless mind and imagination engaged. But when Julia no longer accompanied him on his various tours across the island — and his travelling increased significantly in 1855 — his mind turned inwards to a soul fretfully searching for a deeper meaning to life. This same impulse had driven him to New Zealand and it was now working on him again. In his published memoir, written years later, he said very little about this decisive moment other than it had been a long time in the making and that it finally resolved itself after he was struck, initially by a passage from the first Epistle of Peter — possibly that description of the Christian inheritance as glorious in its incorruptible substance, in its undefiled purity and in its unfading beauty — and then by the life of St Bridget, a fourteenth-century Swedish saint. Tom had found St Bridget in Butler's *Lives of the Saints*, a copy of which was at the inn he was staying in on one of his tours of inspection. What it was about St Bridget that particularly attracted him he did not say, except that the impression her life made upon him was indelible.

The epiphany at the country inn may have gone no further had Tom enjoyed a coterie of intellectual and like-minded friends to discuss his theories and doubts with, but without such a group, his default position, the extreme response, was inevitable. If only his proposal to return to England after Willy's birth had been accepted, this dramatic leap of faith may never have happened. Tom had after all witnessed the trauma of converting to Catholicism when he was at Oxford. He had seen it, too, in the colony, for Van Diemen's Land was a society where all difference, including that of religion, was carefully calibrated. On one of his inspectorate tours, he had stayed with Charles Wilmot, brother of Julia's ex-fiancé and the youngest son of the former governor Sir Eardley. Wilmot had recently converted to Catholicism and Tom, though he scorned the colony's prejudice, had noted that Wilmot was now, *an object of great suspicion* to the locals.

In the absence of anyone to confide in, Tom began reading Dr Newman's *Tracts for the Times*. It was immaterial to him that Newman was on a different side of the religious divide to that of his own father, or possibly that would always be the most important element. Tom's friend Arthur Stanley observed of Dr Newman and Dr Arnold that not only were they like each other, but they were *of the very same essence*. In Newman's *Tracts* Tom found a justification for his action, a way of making the irrational appear plausible, the improbable appear routine. There was no one more likely to approve Tom's actions than John Henry Newman, a man who had traversed similar ground and had arrived at the same conclusion. He would be an ideal confidante and counsellor, and Tom wrote to him for advice. For his part, Newman, a man always surrounded by disciples, welcomed with open arms the son of his old foe, Dr Arnold.

Just as Tom's journey to New Zealand had been a work of faith, one that he could not interfere with for fear of tampering with the integrity of his conscience, so too now was his decision to become a Catholic. A martyr's compulsion drove his search for enlightenment and nothing — not a despairing wife, the bewilderment of friends, the contempt of men, even doubt as to whether truth existed — would halt that search.

Julia refused to accept Tom's decision, but how could she possibly counteract such single-minded belief? Once her initial bewilderment and panic had passed, she pleaded with him to do nothing definite until he had told his mother and knew her response. Julia believed, correctly, that Mrs Arnold would be horrified, and hoped that his mother would be able to convince Tom not to take this extraordinary step, even if Julia, his own wife, could not. Tom agreed to Julia's plea, but had she seen a letter he wrote to Newman at the same time, she would have been repelled. In it, Tom sought Newman's advice regarding the timing of his formal reception into the church, a ceremony during which he would profess his belief in the teachings of the Catholic Church followed by a public declaration of his acceptance by the church. Clearly, Tom had no intention of rescinding his decision, regardless of his mother's or his wife's reaction.

Julia also appealed to their friends Bishop Nixon and Thomas and Catherine Reibey to talk to him, but while they, too, deplored his decision, none could convince him to reconsider it. At the most, Catherine was able to extract a promise from him that he would not convert until he had heard from his mother. She also convinced him to see an Anglican clergyman and to read books in support of Anglicanism. All the while, Julia continued her arguments against his conversion and eventually she was able to wring from him a promise that he would not take any final step until he had actually *seen* his mother. She hoped that if he returned to England, his need for Catholicism might abate.

Despite his promises, Julia found no relief, as Tom sought constantly to have her and Catherine Reibey release him from them. Catherine eventually succumbed to his pleading — she recognised his stubbornness — and released him, but Julia would not. The roots of mistrust, once sown, are hard to smother, but she made one more desperate appeal, an appeal that exposed her depth of feeling and of thought. In the letter she found herself writing to Tom, those scant months after Theodore's birth, in which she explained her decision to leave him, Julia recognised the inevitability of Tom's conversion and that, despite all the promises in the world, his mind was made up. She wrote:

> So the fearful gulf between us is beyond redemption. God only knows what it cost me to feel this. How different were my first feelings on hearing that you had become a believer in Christianity, I thought (how utterly mistaken I was) that through you I, and our children would be led to God. But now for myself, I almost feel the utter impossibility of such ever being the case; a Romanist I cannot be, my whole soul revolts from a religion so utterly inconsistent with the true worship of Christ, and for our children I cannot but feel the prospects to be equally dreary.
>
> All I ask of you now is to try to view the question impartially, to ask yourself whether, as you were mistaken in your former views, you may not be mistaken now, and also to ask yourself if you cannot be content to live and die without joining the Church of Rome. If after you have heard from home … and having heard whatever may be urged against your present plans by anyone who has your welfare at heart, you are still in the same mood I will release you from your promise. But at the same time that I do this I will, I must, leave you.
>
> The fearful gulf that would be placed between us would be more than I could bear, and still live with you; for our children's sake as well as for ours it will be better for us to part. Of course as a true Roman Catholic you can never give consent to your children being brought up in the Church of England. I can never consent to their being brought up in the Church of Rome, and a division

of religion among children of the same parents would be frightful, if those children were to still live under the same roof. Do not think dearest Tom that it costs me nothing to feel this, would to God I could look upon it in any other way, but I could not live with you and feel at the same time so utterly separated from you. You tell me to pray to God, I cannot pray, I do not know how — and you who might have taught me have placed an unsurmountable barrier between us.

I love you dearest Tom most deeply, and in separating from you I shall strike my own death blow, but as things are now it must be so ... Your letter to me was the coldest I have ever received from you, you are rapidly losing all feeling of love towards me; you do not even at the end say, 'God bless you'. I do not remember ever to have received a letter from you that did not end with that sentence. I know I am not worthy, that God's blessing should be asked for me, but how bitter is the thought that you also feel this. I know that I am vile, God only knows how vile, but I cannot bear that you should think this. We are both young to feel that all our earthly happiness is blighted, but you have the fanaticism, the superstitions of the Church of Rome to take the place of earthly affections. *I have nothing.* Whatever I may say in moments of excitement (of excitement almost more than I can bear), that you may be happy even if I am wretched is the sincerest wish, I will not say prayer, of my life.

A shard of glass had ground its way into her heart. She knew divorce was impossible. It could only be granted by an Act of Parliament, which precluded all but the very rich, and certainly most women. If she left her husband, there was no guarantee that she would ever see her children again, unless he agreed that they could live with her. Abandonment. She had already lived that word and she knew instinctively — the only way Julia knew things — that without Tom's love, without her children, she would only have what she thought of as her 'vileness', her bitterness, and her anger as company. Even so she hoped he might be happy even if she was wretched. That was her penalty for loving him. But she could not, would not, become a Catholic, the thing she hated most. She knew when she married that her husband would be head of the household, but that did not mean he could control her soul. It was not something she could submit to.

In those dark months while she waited for Mrs Arnold's response, Julia continued her attempts to persuade Tom to revoke his decision. She knew she could not reason with him, so she tried to paint for him the loneliness of her position when his first thought would never be for her, but would always be for his own soul. Tom was moved by her desperation, telling her that he now knew how her whole nature revolted against Catholicism and that he realised he would deserve only contempt and loathing if he was *capable of sacrificing the fear, the happiness, the moral and religious growth, of the wife whom I love and who has been a true and faithful wife to me, to some morbid caprice or taste for spiritual luxuries* on his part. But this was no caprice, he said. It was his soul at stake and his religion should and would determine the religion practised in his household. There would be no divided Arnold house. If he converted, so too would Julia and all his children. It was not only his duty, but also *Julia's duty*, and *the duty of all* to submit to the Catholic Church.

Desperate appeal fought devout belief, but Julia could never meet or match this degree of conviction, particularly when rational discussion and emotional response were negated. The impasse was intolerable for these two lovers. Julia, all love and hate, *a force, not an organism*, and Tom, all conscience and belief. Something had to give.

Baby Theodore developed whooping cough, casting once more the shadow of death over the household. Julia was in a frantic state of mind, frightened by the baby's health and frightened, too, by the pain she recognised in the dark, frightened eyes of her daughter.

Polly was nearly five years of age in that house in New Town, watching silently as her mother became more distraught and her father retreated into stubborn despair. She heard friends and family trying to persuade her father that his conversion was unnecessary and trying to convince her mother to remain in the marriage. She observed the pain of her grandfather, William, as he reminded Julia of his grief when he lost his children and of the limbo he was in, neither married nor unmarried. And she witnessed her mother's friends Catherine Reibey and Mrs Nixon talk of the social censure and ostracism that Julia would face if she separated from Tom. Polly may not have understood the words spoken by the adults around her, but she absorbed the anxiety and she felt the pressure that was all the time building. This demonstrative, adventurous child — Tom thought her 'passionate' like her mother — did not resist when Julia sent her to stay with Catherine Reibey at Entally. Still, Mrs Arnold's response did not come.

In her later life as a novelist, Polly explored this deep fracture that developed in her parent's marriage, the conversations in novels such as *Helbeck of Bannisdale* and *Robert Elsmere* giving clues to the intimate exchanges that took place between her parents. Both novels explore the conflicts that arise between men and women when conscience and religious scruples are pitted against love, when a desire for independence is pitted against a demand for submission. Invoking Julia's sensibility, Polly's heroine in *Helbeck* tries to imagine her future in a dramatically altered landscape, in which she would be guided, loved, crushed if need be, by a man whose first thought could never be for her, who put his own soul before her. She asks her lover how they are to live together in this world and also in the next:

> I know you don't want to force me; but if, in time, I don't agree with you — if it goes on all our lives — how can you help thinking that I shall be lost — lost eternally — separated from you? ... And as far as I can see I shall reject it all — wilfully, knowingly, deliberately. What will you say? What do you say now — to yourself — when — when you pray for me?

And in *Robert Elsmere*, Polly turned to her father for inspiration, capturing his misery when she wrote of the hero Robert standing gazing at his home,

> the home consecrated by love, by effort, by faith. The high alternations of intellectual and spiritual debate, the strange emerging sense of deliverance, gave way to a most bitter human pang of misery. 'O God! My wife — my work!' ... There was a sound of a voice calling — Catherine's voice calling for him. He leant against the gate of the wood-path, struggling sternly with himself. This was no simple matter of his own intellectual consistency or happiness. Another's whole life was concerned. Any precipitate speech, or hasty

action, would be a crime. A man is bound above all things to protect those who depend on him from his own immature or revocable impulses. Not a word yet, till this sense of convulsion and upheaval had passed away, and the mind was once more its own master.

At the beginning of October, Tom received a letter from Dr Newman. It was all he wanted to hear, indeed he found it kind and comforting, but when Julia saw it she erupted. In frustration and fury, she sent off her own response to Newman, blaming him for all the ills that had befallen her. Tom was mortified by her action and wrote immediately to Newman begging his forgiveness for Julia's *unjust and half-frantic language*. He asked Newman to pray for her, as she was possessed at times by an evil spirit and had no knowledge of what she did or said. Newman destroyed Julia's letter, annoyed at the tone and anger conveyed in it. He was, according to some, a man who shrank from opposition. But after she had sent her demons sailing off to Newman, Julia recognised a new resolve in Tom, and she was forced to decide whether she would stay or go.

In the end, there was no choice. Impossible as it was to imagine her life with Tom if he became a Catholic, it was more impossible to imagine her life without him. What was more, the law held that after separation, children became the man's property. If there was no Tom, there could be no children. And there she stopped. She was still nursing Theodore, watching him struggle for breath as each cough racked his little body. She had just sent Polly away to shield her from the seismic change that was occurring in her world. She witnessed every day Willy's loneliness and his bewilderment at his sister's absence. Julia understood this language. She had seen it in her own younger brothers and sisters when their mother had abandoned them, and she knew she could never do that to her own children.

Her mind was made up. She would remain within the confines of her marriage, to conserve and preserve what she could of the life she had chosen. She did still love Tom, even if her trust in him was destroyed — a bleak truth to face, but too much had passed between them. She vowed then that she would never resile from her decision to stay, but could she reconcile herself to it? That she would not dwell on. Exhausted by the long battle between them, and wanting only peace, she yielded.

Her resolve to stay did not bring the peace she yearned for. Tom, no longer fearful of her desertion, reneged on his promise to wait until he knew his mother's reaction and decided to be received into the Catholic Church immediately. He blamed this on Julia, telling his mother that Julia

> was herself partly the cause of this, for she talked to
> everybody about the change in my opinions, and what I
> had done or contemplated doing, so that it was scarcely
> possible for me to stay where I was …

Julia's horror and distrust of the Roman Church and its attitude towards women was forcefully reaffirmed when Tom sought the advice of Robert Willson, the Catholic Bishop of Tasmania, who told him the promise he had made to Julia was a wrong one in itself, and that it was better to break it than to keep it because a promise that implies *we disobey the will of God, and fail to do what He has commanded, is not binding*. But Julia's humiliation was not at an end.

For months, now, she, along with her father and others in their circle, had tried to make Tom understand that his conversion could jeopardise his position as inspector of schools — a Catholic would be deeply suspect in a position of such influence — and threaten their fragile financial position. Sectarianism in Australia, affecting every aspect of life, from education and employment to friendship and marriage, reached its zenith in the mid-twentieth century when *so great was the social chasm dividing Catholics and non-Catholics in Australian culture that schools did not compete in athletics across denominational lines* ... Nothing would curb Tom's fervour. He simply would not countenance the idea that his religion could possibly threaten his job. He was wrong.

Anti-Catholic sentiment stirred as soon as his conversion became public and it roared to life on the morning of his reception into the Roman Catholic Church — 18 January 1856 — when one of Hobart's leading newspapers declared that Tom Arnold had *perverted* to the Catholic faith. It called upon him to resign his position. Tom's reaction was brutal. He immediately blamed it on Julia, claiming that the article was a direct result of *her having talked so much about the matter*. Reality was setting in and Tom did not like its guise. He knew that privacy was non-existent in this small community and that his conversion to Roman Catholicism was a matter of public knowledge and interest. He gave Julia no chance to respond to his accusation. Instead, he left for the church, intent on acknowledging the authenticity of his own inner experience.

Bitter at the injustice of his words, enraged that her soul should bow to his, Julia swept the flower basket from the table and ran into the garden, where she filled the basket with stones and hurried after him, indifferent to her dishevelled appearance, heedless of the glances and whispers she provoked, intent only on releasing the pain inside her. When she reached the church, she put her basket on the ground, picked up the first stone and sent it flying through the window, the crash and the falling shards of glass splintering the silence around her. She had done what she had to. The vehemence, the physicality of her action, stood as a memorial to her anger and humiliation. She left the basket, the rest of its mute stones gaping at the sky above, and returned home to her children.

8

Between Two Worlds

In the weeks following Tom's conversion, Julia came to dread the newspapers as the campaign to remove him from his position as inspector of schools gathered vitriol. *The Courier* argued that a pernicious bias, though it might be an imperceptible one, would inevitably result from his conversion. Private individuals might have personal religious liberty, but the inspector of schools, as holder of a post which influenced *the future training of youth in this Protestant community, did not have the same liberty*. That the system of public education in Tasmania was non-sectarian and disavowed religious instruction or that Tom had made every attempt to ensure that religious conflict was kept to a minimum — it had been his idea to form a Board of Inspection representing Anglican, Presbyterian, and Catholic interests — mattered little to *The Courier*. Quite simply, a Catholic could not be the inspector of schools.

Tom did have some support. The *Tasmania Daily News* and Launceston's *Cornwall Chronicle* both defended him, although the *Cornwall*'s defence was hardly overwhelming:

We confess that deplore as we certainly do, the change in Mr Arnold's sentiment, and disposed as we are, to deprecate any sinister influence incompatible with the unsectarian character of the government schools ... we cannot for all this, acquiesce in the justice of making Mr Arnold pay the penalty of forfeiture of office for his religious opinions ... We might indeed, from the fact of his CHANGE — from the circumstance that a religious persuasion substituted for one cast off, is more apt to evince a proselytising energy — we might from the particular complexion of that belief itself — be inclined to a suspicious watchfulness upon his official acts; but that is all ...

And even the governor himself, Sir Henry Young, expressed his support, confirming that there was no contractual obligation on him to resign from his post and while he continued to perform his duty impartially, there could be no issue. And in another clear signal that his position was safe, he was, in January 1856, granted a further pay rise to more than £679 annually.

Julia was not blind to the effects of Tom's conversion. She knew from her father and others that various members of the Legislative Council were angry about his action and were determined that he should resign, but when Tom himself began talking about resigning, she was mystified. He seemed determined to fall on his sword as he became increasingly unwilling to continue in his position *without* promoting his new faith. As with his previous epiphanies, he needed to manifest his change of faith and he seemed utterly indifferent to their financial position, simply saying that God would look after them, a view that Julia could not share. Unbeknown to her, Tom had already written to Newman asking if employment could be found for him in a Catholic institution, in the event of his being forced to leave the colony, and he had discussed with Bishop Willson his capacity to continue in the role as a Catholic without promulgating his new faith. The bishop, a strategic thinker, was determined that Tom remain in his post, as no doubt were Julia and their friends, although for different reasons to those of the bishop.

As the loud and colourfully expressed cries for Tom's dismissal grew rather than abated, Julia felt them drawing closer to the chasm each day. She knew that day had arrived when the colonial secretary called Tom to a meeting. As several members of the Legislative Council believed Tom's religion should preclude him from his position as inspector of schools, the colonial secretary proposed that Tom either take leave of absence and go back to England with an understanding that he not return, or alternatively, exchange his current position for another. To Julia's great relief, Tom chose to exchange his position, and although they would have to leave the old schoolhouse she had grown to love, at least he still had a secure position. And now the newspapers would surely stop hounding him. As she packed up the house, she felt the dread inside her begin to dissipate. That feeling did not last.

Within a month of taking up his new position, Tom declared it *impossible* and on 8 May 1856 he formally applied for eighteen months leave of absence, on half-salary, to enable him to *proceed to England upon important private business*. His application was granted to take effect from November of that year with the tacit understanding that there was little possibility that he would ever return. Tom had cast himself adrift, and with him, his wife and their children.

Julia was devastated. She was being forced to leave her family and her home, probably forever, her husband owed money, and he had no prospect of work. Their position in Tasmania had been an enviable one. Tom's salary was more than £600 a year, they lived in a comfortable house at reduced rent, they had a productive garden and a cow provided all their milk, butter, and cream. How could they possibly fare as well in England? But Tom appeared oblivious to the consequences of his decision: *divine providence*, he said, was all that mattered. He would not listen, no more than he would hear. He ignored everyone's advice, even that of his own mother and brother, who told him that with responsibilities as a husband and a father, to return to England without definite work awaiting him *would be wild & very wrong*. Tom's mind was made up. They would leave Hobart in November 1856.

Julia could do nothing. She was pregnant again. An insistent thread of desire continued to exist between her and Tom, a desire that was stronger than anything that separated them, and in the tormented days since he had declared his intention to convert, Julia yearned for tenderness, unable to resist loving. Polly drew on her mother's stormy but constant feeling for Tom to explain Laura's inability to resist Helbeck even when she was at her most miserable and exhausted:

> The storm of feeling through which she had passed had exhausted her wholly; and the pining for his step and voice had become an anguish driving her to him.

Although Julia no longer had strength enough to even throw stones, she did have the strength to insist that she would not give birth at sea with all its associated risks. She had lost one child and the prospect of losing another was always with her. But if she thought that her pregnancy might delay their departure, she was wrong. Instead, Tom decided they should leave immediately.

Julia had no time to lament. While Tom was on a busy round of public farewells, she dealt with all the practicalities, packing up the house, organising the sale of the furniture and the cow, and moving the family into lodgings near her father's house in Macquarie Street. For her father's sake, she tried to be cheerful and hopeful, but she dreaded that moment when, once again, she would watch his figure disappear across the water. Amidst the chaos of their departure, those closest to Julia did all they could to support her. They were concerned and uncertain as to how she and Tom could continue living together. They knew that Julia was neither reconciled to his actions nor, since her stone-throwing, was she at all inclined to behave in a wife-like manner. She was too forthright, too rebellious, too unwilling to take any advice.

These characteristics particularly concerned her friend Bishop Nixon. He decided to make his farewell gift a letter that she could keep beside her when she no longer had her friends and family to guide her. In it he detailed her duty as a wife. She must be, he said,

> uniformly gentle, loving, and considerate, with your dear husband — for indeed he is a very noble fellow — Let him feel that his wife's face always brightens at his return home — that her tones are always those of wifelike duty, and wifelike love and desserts. Make him love his home, for its peace, its comfort, its rest. Give him no temptation to see happiness elsewhere. You will be rewarded.

The bishop, unwilling to witness the protest his advice might cause, handed his gift to Julia just as she embarked on the *William Brown*, on 12 July 1856. On the back of the envelope he had written, *Not to be opened, Ma'am, if you please, until you are fairly out to sea.*

In an era when letters took little more than eight weeks between England and Tasmania, the voyage on the cramped *William Brown* took nearly fourteen weeks. It was difficult and interminable. From Hobart until they had rounded Cape Horn, nearly six weeks later, the weather was cold and stormy and, as Tom observed, the ship tossed *like a cork up and down the great rollers.* No relief was provided by stopping for reprovisioning or fresh water. The boat did not land anywhere during the voyage and it was more than two months before another ship was sighted. The food was uniformly poor — the beef was hung up in the rigging till it turned black — and sometimes completely indigestible. Even the children found the voyage far from adventurous. Both Polly and Willy were disgusted by the swarming and voracious rats, and they hated being plunged shivering into huge barrels full of sea water on the deck. Tom, meanwhile, was delighting in shoals of flying fish, splendid sunsets, long moonlit nights, and his imminent return home after nine years on the other side of the world. He was ecstatic at the prospect of seeing once more the familiar stars of the northern sky, to breathing native air, and to setting foot again on English soil.

Julia was sick for most of the voyage and rarely managed to leave her bed. Adding to her distress, little Theodore developed a disturbing inflammation on his thighs, and she developed a painful abscess on one of her fingers. When they reached the tropics, she found the heat and humidity almost intolerable, and although she gained some relief when the captain rigged up a tent so she could have a bath, she was left to wonder what form of hell she had arrived in and to pray that this interminable voyage would end.

As the Southern Cross, the glory of the Australian heavens, sank beneath the horizon, she was torn between resentment at having been uprooted and hope that the move to England would mute Tom's devotion to his new religion and allow them to lead a new, less divided life. She was anxious too at the prospect of meeting his family and was dreading that moment of first inspection. How would she appear, eight months pregnant and trying to find her land legs? From the young woman who Tom Arnold had fallen in love with — someone who loved horse-riding and dancing — she had become a woman whose body was battered by five pregnancies, whose back was racked with pain, and who now needed a permanent truss.

In this transition between her old world and new, Julia had the time and the privacy to rail against her fate, to mourn her youth, and to understand at last — a truth she had refused to acknowledge before — that for a woman, marriage was destiny. Nothing more and nothing less.

9

Facing Reality

When the ship finally docked in England at the end of October in 1856, Julia was so weak she did not notice the grimy inn that Tom took her to, but Polly did, and its dingy ugliness and barred windows remained, for years, a vision of horror to her — a vision in striking contrast to Tom's eldest sister, the brown-eyed, graceful Jane, who rescued the family from this squalor. Polly thought her *an angel of help*. Thanks to her father, Dr Arnold, Jane was an extremely well-educated woman, a scholar of Latin and Greek, a speaker of German and French, and, before her marriage, a teacher at a local night school near her mother's home. She married the wealthy Quaker manufacturer William Forster in 1850 and was living with him near Bradford, where they would remain until his election to parliament in 1861, after which they lived for much of the time in London. The Forsters immediately took the family to London, where Julia was able to obtain the medical attention she required following her ordeal on the boat. After several days of treatment and rest, she was able to begin the final stage of their long journey to Fox How, the Arnold house in Cumbria. There, Tom's mother and his youngest sister, Fan, awaited their arrival.

Julia found the journey very tiring, but as they approached the house and the garden came into view, a faint wind fluttering the red leaves on the lawn, she felt her heart lighten. It was a similar reaction to that of Charlotte Brontë when she had first seen the house several years before. Then it had been twilight, but Charlotte was moved to write that it *looked like a nest half buried in flowers and creepers; and, dark as it was, I could feel that the valley and the hills round were beautiful as imagination could dream*. Here was a lovely place for her child to be born, and it was exactly as Tom had described it with the little stone pier running out into the water, and beyond it, the old green-and-white family boat rocking gracefully. Julia was comforted by the tranquillity and by the truth of Tom's words.

The serenity of Fox How's exterior was matched by the quiet dignity of its mistress, and the attractive confusion that prevailed indoors, the tables covered with letters, drawings, dictionaries, needle books, and flowers from the garden. After the tiny cabin of the sailing ship, the house felt immense — it did have three sitting rooms and ten bedrooms — but it also felt embracing and safe, and Julia, now so much in need of comfort and care, warmed immediately to it, and to Mrs Arnold, whose soft brown eyes radiated sympathy and welcome.

The Arnold family had gathered — the only one missing was William in India — to welcome Tom home and to meet Julia. There were Tom's sisters: Jane, who had accompanied them on their journey from London; Susy, married to another prominent Quaker, John Cropper, the son of a philanthropist and abolitionist campaigner; Mary, already widowed once and now married to a clergyman; and his youngest sister Frances, or Fan, still at home with their mother. And she met his brothers: Matthew, already a published poet and now a school inspector; Edward, a fellow of All Souls College; and Walter, studying Arts at the University of Durham. They were all eager to see this colonial belle with whom Tom had fallen so deeply in love. And Julia, equally eager to see these almost mythological creatures she had been hearing of and writing to for years, enjoyed meeting them all. She was always at ease with people, and her delight at finding herself off the high seas and in such an attractive place added sparkle to her face.

Of all Tom's family, Julia was most drawn to his sister Mary Hiley, a forthright, independent woman with a keen sense of humour. Mary had been something of a rebel in her youth — her family nickname was 'Small Wild Cat' — and her *generous impetuous character ... her passionate Liberalism, her natural love of equality* were traits that appealed to Julia. Mary was also the one most able to understand and empathise with Julia's own lively, open nature. An immediate bond was forged between these two women, drawing them into a lifelong friendship. Since her marriage to the Reverend James Hiley, Mary was living at Woodhouse, a small estate in Leicestershire. Julia also grew close to Susy Cropper, and in the years that followed she would often stay with Mary at Woodhouse or with Susy at her beautiful home Dingle Bank on the River Mersey in Liverpool. Along with Fox How, these houses would all become havens in her now uncertain future.

Despite the pleasure of meeting Julia and the excitement felt amongst the family at Tom's return, the fact of his conversion was immediately and harshly felt. He refused to join the family in their routine of evening prayers because *the Catholic Church forbids her members to hold religious communion with those who do not belong to her*. For the first time, Tom's family began to realise some of the more intimate implications of this conversion. Mrs Arnold's tolerance towards her son was sorely tested. She felt his absence from family prayers a cruel betrayal of the moral precepts that she and her husband had lived by and had so carefully instilled in their children. It was, she thought, all the fault of Newman, her husband's arch rival, laying hold of her son, when her husband himself was no longer there to fight him. Jane Forster had already expressed herself very clearly in a letter sent to Tom while he was still in Van Diemen's Land. In it she had written,

> I was understandably astonished by the contents of your last letter to me for I believe the adoption of Roman Catholic opinions was the only change which had never entered into my contemplation with regard to you. And as you knowing something of my conviction — or knowing at least the moral and intellectual principles in which we have all been trained — you would not believe me, dearest Tom, if I were to pretend to deny the sorrow with which I hear of your embracing a creed opposed equally (in my firm belief) to both the one and the other. If there is one belief wrought into the depths of my moral convictions it is that of the personal, individual responsibility of each human soul to God — & to Him alone — the whole Roman system from its lowest & most vulgar forms of priestly power up through the claims of infallibility to the invocation of saints & worship of the Virgin — seems to me one vast device to escape from this responsibility — from this awful but blessed truth of a direct intercourse between God & the individual conscience, in which no third — be it saint, angel or Church — can have a share.

Tom's other sisters and brothers were also astonished and crushed by his conversion, and, while Matthew was pointedly silent on the matter, his younger brother William, in India, was not. He expressed his intense distaste, saying there was something unsocial and alien to genuine life in Roman Catholicism. Tom took immediate umbrage at this, and although he wrote a long defence of his position, he believed that William would only think him a fanatic. He was right.

Settled at last, and with Julia now in the care of his mother, Tom finally turned his mind to finding employment. He wrote to Newman, asking him if there might be any work in Dublin, possibly preparing pupils for the Catholic University there, of which Newman was now the rector. Newman responded immediately. He realised the Arnold name would be a drawcard for potential students, and he was thrilled at the prospect of having Dr Arnold's son at his university, particularly considering how energetically Dr Arnold had opposed him and Catholicism. He offered Tom a temporary position as Professor of English Literature at £200 a year. As an added inducement, he told Tom he could also tutor youths at £10 a head. Tom hesitated. Even the tantalising prospect of actually working with Newman could not outweigh the unease he felt about his stutter and the impact it might have on his capacity to teach. But with no other employment in sight, he decided to go to Dublin. Julia encouraged him to go, although the thought of his being with Newman repulsed her. And she hated his leaving her at such a crucial time — her child would soon be born — but they would all be destitute if he did not secure a position quickly.

Julia now found herself alone in the midst of his family, and although she felt embraced by them, she struggled with life in the quiet house. There was a strong religious atmosphere — daily psalms and lessons were read aloud — and there was a sense of discipline quite unlike anything she had known. It was such a different world to that of Hobart, where she had been at the centre of a large social circle, prominent among it her laughing, energetic sisters and her ironic, placid father. Once more a stranger in a foreign place, Julia felt this difference more strongly with each letter from Tasmania, particularly when Gussie wrote of her fiancé James Dunn's election to the parliament and the visits and parties that she and Ada had made and attended. In an attempt to escape the pain of their absence, Julia retreated regularly to Mrs Arnold's garden. Its wild strawberries and raspberries, its birch trees, its rhododendrons growing like weeds on mossy banks, and the long silky grass in the parts left to go wild, filled her with a sense of abundance.

As the weeks passed, she grew to like and trust her mother-in-law, despite their very different temperaments and their very different attitudes. They were certainly bonded in their opposition to Tom's conversion, but for all Mrs Arnold's sympathy for Julia and her disapproval of Tom's actions, she was uncomfortable with Julia's overt opposition to Tom and to his change of religion. Mrs Arnold, like Tom, held a firm conviction that a wife must support her husband, regardless of her own views. Julia found this tolerance baffling, and, instead of finding the vocal support she had believed she would, she found that Mrs Arnold's apparent reasonableness made her seem all the more unreasonable. Her reaction was to straighten her back and set her mouth in defiance of Tom even more. It was she and her children Tom was hell-bent on converting, not Mrs Arnold, and she knew that Tom would stop at nothing to achieve this. She was right.

In Dublin, Tom had already discussed Julia's conversion with Newman, who was keen to keep Julia away from Tom, concerned that she might temper his devotion to his new-found faith. He told Tom that if Julia were to live in Dublin with him, she would in all likelihood become intimate with the Anglican Archbishop of Dublin, Dr Whately, an old friend of Dr Arnold's, thereby hindering her likely conversion. Tom, eager that Julia join him in Dublin, was sure that any intimacy between Whately and Julia was improbable, as Whately would never excuse or think well of those who, like Tom, *have been educated in full Protestant light, and have then fallen away.* As it was, they were both wrong. Julia had no intention of ever converting to Catholicism, and her resolve in this matter did not depend on any relationship she might or might not develop with Archbishop Whately.

With letters now the sole source of communication between them, Julia found their differences abating and the deep attraction they held for each other surfacing. The humour and intimacy between them was palpable once more. She used her letters to describe to him her drives and visits in the neighbourhood and to express her wifely concerns, among them, whether Tom had flannel drawers. He, on the other hand, recounted all the university gossip, the attempts being made to entice aristocratic and wealthy Catholics to it, and the pleasure of finding himself unexpectedly among an Oxford and Cambridge coterie of men who, for various reasons, had found themselves part of Newman's great Catholic experiment. He talked of the possibility of making £300 a year, still insufficient to maintain his family in the manner they were used to, and he expressed concern about his stammer, but, most importantly, he reassured Julia that he would be home for the birth. It was a promise he kept.

On 15 December 1856, when she gave birth to another son, Tom was at Fox How. They named him Arthur, despite their first Arthur having died only a day after his birth. It was a common practice at the time, but it might have given Julia pause had she known that her own mother, Elizabeth, gave a daughter by her lover Major Deare the name of Julia.

When a few weeks later, in January 1857, Julia finally set out for Dublin, the last leg on the journey that had begun in Hobart more than six months before, neither Polly nor Willy accompanied her. While she had been waiting for the birth of Arthur at Fox How, pondering her future and that of her children, she had finally confronted what remaining with Tom would mean. She knew she had no choice but to join him — she had not come this far to separate from him now — but what of her children? The prospect of them being raised as Catholics in Dublin was now imminent. She wanted none of it nor did Tom's mother, so, at first delicately, and then more openly, Mrs Arnold talked of the possibility of little Polly remaining with her and being educated in England, thereby keeping her safe from Catholicism. Julia was receptive to the idea — so desperate was she that her daughter not be tainted by Catholicism — and together with Mrs Arnold, she worked to convince Tom to allow Polly to remain with his mother, at least until the household was established in Dublin. He finally agreed.

It was not Julia's intention to also leave young Willy behind when she journeyed to Dublin. Her health dictated that decision. She was still very weak after Arthur's birth, and, knowing she had to set up house in a strange city where she knew no one, with her husband earning what she regarded as a pittance, and with four children under six to care for, she asked Tom's sister Susy if she would care for Willy until she had regained her health and established a home in Dublin. Leaving Willy at Dingle Bank at least reduced the burden on the household and it meant, too, although Julia did not hold this hope strongly, that Willy would be, for the moment, protected from Tom's Catholicism.

When Julia had left Hobart she knew that her future might be difficult and uncertain, but even she would have been daunted had she known the struggles to come. She was young, though, and despite all the trauma and the upheaval, she and Tom did still love one another fiercely, even if they wanted to change each other completely.

10

A New Beginning

Julia's arrival in Dublin in January 1857 signalled a new beginning. The parameters of her life had been dramatically redrawn, and she would now have to find a way of living within them. She had married Tom and, despite his conversion, she had remained with him. She was now confronting the consequences of those decisions. Living in Catholic Ireland with a Catholic husband was not a destiny she had ever imagined for herself. It was not one that she had freely chosen, nor was it one she wanted. It had required all her natural optimism, her verve, her feistiness, to go where his conscience had taken her. Yet it was these same characteristics that compelled her to constantly resist his choice and to rebel against his overtures to lay claim to her soul and to those of their children.

Like Hobart, Dublin in 1857 was an outpost of Empire, a colonial city where many of the privileged occupations were filled by outsiders; where social life focused on the vice-regal court based at Dublin Castle; where the streets were filled with the colours and bands of the infantry; and where its imperial military officers were the mainstay of vice-regal social functions.

But unlike Hobart, Dublin was a city in decline. Its Protestant Anglo-Irish ascendancy was diminishing just as its buildings were decaying. Its dark, disease-ridden slums were the worst in the United Kingdom. It was a city deeply divided by religion and class. It was haunted by its past and exhausted, not by a black war or a convict stain, but by the ravages of the recent famine. It was a place Julia did not want to be.

Her reality was, from the beginning, fraught and messy, and her first impressions of Dublin were complex and ambivalent. She was living in temporary accommodation, separated from her two oldest children, recovering from childbirth — her back was causing her extensive pain — and she was consumed by domestic woes. Her first priority was to find suitable accommodation that would enable them to take in students and boarders — this, Tom believed, would form another financial stream — and she was having difficulties finding reliable servants. It was a common problem. Another émigré, Elizabeth Grant, who lived in Dublin between 1851 and 1856, recorded in her diary the constant need to replace *unreliable housekeepers, alcoholic butlers and light-fingered cooks*. Even Dublin's weather took some getting used to. Julia hated its cold, bleak winter. It was too like the misery of Brussels.

Her domestic woes were in part allayed when she found a house to rent in Rathmines, a middle-class area within walking distance of the Catholic University. Like many new suburbs being developed, its drainage was suspect, its water pressure inadequate, and its refuse collection intermittent, but in the heavily sectarian climate of nineteenth-century Dublin, this was one suburb Julia felt comfortable in. It was favoured by the Protestant professional classes. Utterly repelled by the vast assemblage of Catholicism against which she had to somehow protect herself,

Julia determined from the beginning that she would never fall into the ways, habits, customs, manners, or opinions of those she lived among. She had remained separate in Brussels and she would do the same in Dublin. In Brussels, though, she had been a child, unable to express her thoughts freely, but here she was an adult and could, if she chose, say exactly what she wished. It was a freedom she gave rein to and it was a freedom that her mother-in-law feared.

Mrs Arnold had witnessed Julia's outspoken opposition to Tom's religion at Fox How, and when Julia continued to voice this opposition in Dublin, Mrs Arnold put aside her usual diplomacy and, in the strongest words possible, reproached Julia for her bitter opposition, setting out in almost doctrinal tones the position of a wife in Victorian society:

> Your letter ... gives me great anxiety for what you say of pain given you, and even horror by seeing the Roman Catholics crowding round the Cross with passionate devotion makes me fear that your position in Ireland may be full of unhappiness for the present & future for both you and to Tom ... I am in great anxiety that you should consider what you owe to your husband, and how much you add to all his difficulties if home irritations & want of consideration for him meet him where he might most hope for rest. I do not hesitate to say this dear Julia for you know how truly we all feel for you, & how far we are from agreement with Tom, but I could not but see how much more forbearing he has to you with regard to these painful religious differences than you were to him and in Ireland I know the bitterness is so great between Protestants & R. Catholics, that I dread unspeakably

the effect this may have upon your domestic happiness and peace. Nothing can secure this, unless you resolve steadily to avoid all accusations — all hard speaking or thinking — all conversation with others which can create irritation between you & your Husband. This he owes to you on his part and you to him — and I know it will be hard, but dear Julia look to God for help remembering the bond between you, & then by his strengthening & softening & guiding spirit, you may make your husband's home a blessed one to him. The other side of the picture I cannot bear to look at.

To soften her forthright language, Mrs Arnold signed herself *your affectionate mother & friend*.

Julia had never been good at heeding advice — she had not listened to her Hobart friends Bishop Nixon and Catherine Reibey — and she had never been able to adopt a serene view. She knew and understood the world instinctively, not conceptually, not rationally. She knew she had been banished from the centre of Tom's universe, replaced by his Catholicism. Full of repugnance, but without any weapons or tools to counter it, she could only rage against her perceived exile from his world. In her wilful choice of ongoing resistance, she made her marriage a battleground. She refused to remain silent if she noticed Tom losing weight as he fasted through Lent. She remonstrated fiercely when she heard him reciting his prayers as she walked past his study. She rifled through his books, drawn and repulsed by them, wondering why they were better friends to him than she was, looking for clues as to why he had chosen Catholicism. And when his Catholic friends came to the house she felt an outsider, a pariah, believing that there was a door shut between her and a whole side of his life. She felt submerged and eclipsed and reacted with anger, resentment, mockery, never tolerance or understanding. And then, when the anger was spent, she was full of deep regret and self-abasement, wondering at her own resistance, at her own perceived evilness.

As Mrs Arnold foresaw, in this deeply mannered world where the display of any type of passion on the part of a woman was censured, Julia needed to control her involuntary horror of Roman Catholicism. But she seemed incapable of achieving this and she certainly had no desire to achieve it when it came to Newman, the man whom she believed was responsible for all the troubles that she was facing. Their relationship was, from the beginning, cold and unforgiving — on both sides. She saw him as the source of all their problems. He thought her a carping irritant. When he had received her abusive letter from Tasmania, he had branded her a shrew, and her continuing antagonism to him simply confirmed him in his belief. He had done all he could for Tom — not only had he shown him the way to God, but he had also provided him with employment when no one else would — and the argumentative, vituperative Julia was ungrateful. Her dislike and fear of him fed into her struggle to live with and beside Tom, but in the event, she did not have to deal with Newman's physical presence for long.

Only a year after her arrival in Dublin, Newman effectively resigned his rectorship, deeply frustrated in his attempts to develop his ideal university and thwarted by the government's refusal to grant a charter to the university to grant degrees. He returned permanently to the Oratory in Birmingham, there to establish a school for Catholic boys on the same lines as the English public schools so that English Catholics would no longer be forced to send their sons abroad or tutor them at home.

Julia considered Newman's departure a blessing, but Tom regretted it and began to reconsider his position at the struggling university. He had enjoyed working alongside his mentor and believed that Newman had been a victim of the distrust felt by some in the Irish Catholic hierarchy towards educated converts, particularly English ones. He also believed that one of the telling flaws of the Catholic University was the ill-educated Catholic clergy and their intellectual inferiority to the Protestant clergy. Such inferiority did not encourage Catholic gentlemen to attend the university, nor would it encourage European Catholics to send their sons there. But with no better prospects and while the university had students, Tom decided to remain in Dublin.

Once the household was settled in Rathmines, it was time for Polly and Willy to return home. It was no coincidence that at precisely this moment, Mrs Arnold wrote to Tom and Julia, pleading to keep Polly at Fox How. The child was, she said, well and happy, she had their undivided attention, and they would be delighted to keep her there. Most importantly, a former governess in Dr Arnold's family, who had married well, had offered to pay for Polly's school fees in England, this last observation a deliberate ploy to sway Tom. It took Julia some time to persuade him, but eventually Tom agreed that Polly could remain at Fox How. Willy, on the other hand, must return to the family. Julia had to be satisfied that her daughter, at least, would not be stigmatised as a Roman Catholic — she knew only too well the effects of being branded by the action of a wayward parent — and Tom had to be content that his sons, at least, would be reared as Catholics.

From the very beginning Julia was determined that her daughter's absence would not cause any emotional distance between them. She often sent Polly gifts and clothes, and wrote to her regularly. Polly, for her part, was mostly happy with this arrangement, but she missed her family, particularly her parents and her brother Willy, and was always eager, when she could, to meet those siblings born in her absence. Both she and Julia would have been far less content with this arrangement had they known that she would pass her whole childhood separated from her mother and her family. But if Julia was able to shield her daughter from Tom's religious fervour, there was no escaping his right to have the boys brought up as Roman Catholics, and with Willy's return to the family, the question of his baptism arose. Although she was no more reconciled to Tom's religion than she had been in Hobart, Julia did not send any stones through the windows of the Rathmines Parish Church when this event finally took place and Willy, aged seven, was baptised a Roman Catholic in October 1859. As to Willy? This event marked his entrance into the world of adult discord, and he finally understood why his older sister was no longer living alongside him.

It was not in Julia's nature to stay despondent for long, and as soon as Willy returned, she began to embrace life in Dublin. Tom had been given an introduction to the Viceroy, Lord Carlisle, by the Arnold's Fox How neighbour Harriet Martineau, and when they were invited to the annual St Patrick's Ball at Dublin Castle, nothing, not even a painful back, could keep Julia from dancing. She quickly made friends, her eager, sympathetic temper drawing people to her. Among the first were Archbishop Whately and his family, disproving immediately Tom's prediction to Newman that Julia would have nothing to do with the Whatelys. It was always a likely friendship as Dr Arnold and the Archbishop had been very close friends — so close that Dr Arnold had christened his youngest daughter Frances Bunsen Trevenen Whately Arnold — and the Archbishop went out of his way to welcome Tom and his young wife to Dublin, despite Tom's conversion. In a very short time, Julia had developed a close friendship with Mrs Whately and her daughters, particularly Mary Louisa and Elizabeth Jane. Julia had always been attracted to strong and determined women, and the Whately women were no exception.

Mrs Whately wrote religious and travel texts, and her daughters were among those intriguing Victorian women who defied the boundaries of their lives and set out to fulfil themselves in unexpected ways. Only two years older than Julia, Mary Louisa Whately was, according to her sister, an impulsive, hot-tempered, and generous woman — characteristics that Julia warmed to immediately. Educated at home by her parents, and only recently returned to Dublin from her first visit to Cairo, Mary Louisa was assisting her father in his educational programs and other philanthropic works. In 1860, when her mother and younger sister both died tragically in quick succession, Mary Louisa would return to Egypt, where she established schools for Muslim girls — she later did the same for boys — and then a medical mission. She lived mostly in Egypt and in addition to writing an autobiography of sorts, she also wrote fiction for the Religious Tract Society. Her sister Elizabeth Jane had a similar trajectory, although her evangelising work was based mainly in Madrid. Elizabeth wrote biographies of both Martin Luther and her father and also wrote fiction, much of it anti-Catholic in tone. Julia may have been closer in nature to Mary Louisa, but it was in Elizabeth Jane that she found a spiritual ally in Dublin. Another sister Henrietta, Tom's first love, had married in 1848 and was living in England.

Julia also formed a close relationship with the Benison family from County Cavan in the north of the country. James Benison was a Protestant Anglo-Irish landowner who had married a Catholic woman, but was bringing up all his children, sons and daughters, as Protestants. In this he was defied, however, by his oldest and youngest daughters, Josephine and Emily, who, in 1853 when Josephine was twenty-two years of age, converted to Catholicism. Five years later, in 1858, the Benisons arrived in Dublin with their daughters Tomasina and a very ill Emily. Looking for lodgings in Rathmines, they were immediately attracted to the Arnolds' large house in Leinster Street, and to Julia's gregarious nature. Emily thought Julia, *such a nice person, but far from worldly wise*, an observation borne out when Julia blithely told Mrs Benison that her husband was a Catholic Professor at Dr Newman's university, information that caused Mr Benison to continue searching for accommodation elsewhere. However, when the Benisons could find no other satisfactory lodgings, Mr Benison put aside his prejudices and returned to the Arnolds where the family took lodgings for £5 per month.

Julia was deeply touched by their plight when she discovered that Emily had been diagnosed with consumption and was dying. She paid every attention to them, ensuring that special treats were given to the patient to entice her to eat a little — *today, cook has told me Mrs Arnold ordered her to have a nice little rice pudding at Emily's dinner hour* — and giving her books to amuse her. Despite the tragic circumstances of her sister's illness and death — Emily died in June 1858 — Tomasina enjoyed the days she spent with Julia and was intrigued by the way in which the religious divide affected the household. The cook had told her that, initially, when Catholics came to dine with Tom, Julia would not join them, but that slowly she had come to like Catholics, although she could not abide converts. Julia was growing so tolerant of the Catholic society around her, the Benisons believed she would eventually be won over, but she was no closer to accepting Tom's conversion. She continued to see this as a deep betrayal of her, but she might have gained some comfort had she known that her aversion to converts was something she shared with Dr Arnold himself, who had thought Roman Catholics a fair enemy, but converts a treacherous one.

When Josephine Benison, Emily's older sister, arrived in Dublin to spend some time with her, she, like Tomasina, was immediately drawn to Julia, only five years her senior. But Josephine was also strongly drawn to Tom, and Tomasina's sketch of him revealed his attractiveness as a thinker, a philosopher, a dreamer, devoid of any practical trait:

> There was an obstreperous lock here that Mr Arnold came down to fix but failed in the attempt and afterwards sat with us for a good while. He is very quiet and gentlemanly but has a hesitation in speaking partly from nervousness. I think it is a great disadvantage.

After Emily died, the Benisons returned to County Cavan, but they did not forget Julia's compassion and friendship in those dark days in Dublin, every few months sending country produce to the Arnold house.

The relentless pressure of child-bearing continued, and each pregnancy was more fraught than the last. When Julia gave birth to her sixth child and her second daughter, Lucy, in July 1858, she was so ill Tom was forced to take her to his sister Mary Hiley at Woodhouse. There she slowly regained her strength — being with Mary suited her more than being with Mrs Arnold or any other member of Tom's family, and with its beautiful avenue of lime trees, on the edge of Charnwood Forest near Loughborough, Woodhouse was an ideal place to retreat to in times of illness and unhappiness. While she was recuperating, she and Tom wrote to each other often. Their letters expose the love they had for each other pitted against their division over religion, a constant refrain, sometimes spoken about in anger, at other times in frustration, bitterness, or bewilderment.

On Tom's part, his desire for Julia was often repressed because of her resentment and hatred of his religion. He felt he could not speak freely to her — she would call it cant, he said — and without friends with whom he could discuss his ideas, he was *like a tree exposed to the sea blast, one side of my nature which ought to be most expansive fresh and vigorous, is withered crushed and shrivelled up for want of sympathy.* Her lack of sympathy and encouragement meant he no longer knew what he felt, what he thought, or what he wished for, causing him to question whether he even loved her. It was a cry of anguish from a clearly bewildered and distraught man who, having delivered his agony up to her and blamed her for it, then pleaded with her that she not let it pain her. But it did.

Julia was full of remorse and self-reproach at the way she behaved towards him — she understood the fault line of their relationship — but she too struggled both within the context of her marriage and in Ireland. She found it, she said,

> very hard to think of your going through life without finding the sympathy from your wife which if you were not married you might find from friends; to me also this has been and is I am afraid likely to be a bitter trial, you

know dearest that you can no more enter into my feelings and wishes with regard to Protestantism than I can into yours with regard to Catholicism. Still it must surely be a comfort to you to feel that you are living in a country where you can sympathize on Religious matters at all events with the majority of the peoples now in Ireland. I feel that I have no sympathy with the religion of the people and very little with the Church of England as it is there. The sense of loneliness, of intense longing for sympathy is sometimes almost more than I can bear & this often makes me when in my heart I love you most dearly behave towards you as if I had no love for you, but this you know is not the case. Surely it will not always be so there is much in which our natures can sympathize.

Julia's reflections were also a cry for help. She was, she believed, one of those unhappy people whom God had abandoned and it was an awful thing to despair about one's future. If only Tom were less reserved, more open, then she might feel he cared for her more. She yearned to be back with him and she longed for him to *pet her*, their sexual appetite for each other having remained constant.

On her return to Dublin, Julia was determined to modify her behaviour towards Tom, to be more gentle and sympathetic towards him and his Catholicism, but it did not happen. Instead she continued to lash out at him and his religion.

Like most women of her class, Julia lived a busy life, a messy mosaic of children, friends, servants, pets — the children had a pet dog, Fury — morning calls, letter-writing, even jam-making and baking, but always, in the background, was the relentless pressure of child-bearing and an ever-increasing financial strain. By the time she gave birth to her seventh child, another son, Francis (known in the family as Frank), in May 1860, the family had moved to a smaller, cheaper house in Kingstown in Dublin's port area.

Like Rathmines, it too had poor sanitary arrangements and no proper water supply, but it did have the advantage of the sea. Julia loved taking the children to the pier, there to watch the boats and listen to the seagulls, and, in the winter when they could not walk, she could hear from the house storms lashing against the seawall. The smell and sounds of the sea brought her solace in her exile, as did the arrival of the yearly box full of gifts from her Tasmanian family, but nothing, not even her innate optimism, could blind her to their increasingly impoverished life. Julia knew that Tom's meagre salary had forced the move to Kingstown, but even she was dismayed at just how precarious their situation had become.

The Catholic University, which occupied an imposing eighteenth-century mansion on the south side of St Stephen's Green, was small and struggling, and Tom had been desperately trying to supplement his income: tutoring private pupils, writing reviews and essays for various journals which paid, writing a textbook — his *A Manual of English Literature, Historical and Critical*, published in 1862 became an enduring, standard textbook — and doing intermittent examining work for the Civil Service Commission, which was work his old friend Arthur Clough had found for him, and which paid well.

Julia, too, was doing all she could to supplement Tom's income by caring for the lodgers and student boarders living with them. And both their families were assisting them, particularly Jane and William Forster and, after her marriage, Julia's sister Gussie and her husband James Dunn, the managing director of the Commercial Bank in Hobart. But it was not enough.

Tom borrowed money from Clough and then, when that ran out, tried to sell his father's land in New Zealand. This came to a standstill — the land could only be sold at his mother's death — so he asked his brother Matthew, and his friends in England, to keep an eye out for possible positions that might suit him. He was, he said, *living on starvation pitch*.

Conscious of Tom's financial incompetence and despite knowing it would be ignored, members of his family continued to proffer advice. Mrs Arnold expressed herself most eloquently, and often, on the fact that his income and expenditure needed to meet. She did not mince her words, telling him that his circumstances were not exceptional, that living without debt was practised every day by numerous families who, like Tom, were bringing up and educating children. Quite simply, he had to adjust his expenditure to his income, and if he did not, he would always be in trouble, *always more or less dependent*. She also stressed the need for unanimity between him and Julia if the necessary self-denial and good management was to be achieved. Matthew was also critical of Tom's incapacity to live within his means, and although he knew that Tom was unable to face reality and adapt to it, he had also come to the conclusion that Julia was equally financially unrealistic. He advised them to live in lodgings rather than a house as that would at the very least spare them the expense of both servants and furnishings, items which swallowed up small incomes.

Julia thought it utterly provoking that Matthew, with £1600 a year and fewer children, should preach to them about living more carefully, but her position was difficult. She was completely dependent upon Tom to provide her with the money she required for all the household and her own expenses. Even if she had money of her own, as a married woman, she could not control it.

And Tom would not cede her any control over their affairs. It was, he said, his duty, and his alone, as the head of the household, to manage their finances, just as it was his duty to determine their religion. The result was a constant cry from Julia. It was there like a moaning wind that intermittently gusted into a roar. On one occasion when he was visiting England, she pleaded with him:

> You must send me some more money as I have none left and the servants' board the wages and the washing runs away with a good deal besides which I have been buying both bread and butter and some meat. Sarah McCabe came down yesterday bringing with her a pair of splendid ducks for which I am to pay 2 shillings 4 fowls for which I am to pay 10d a piece 2 dozen of fresh eggs at 9 pence a dozen 2 lbs of butter at a shilling a lb and 12 quarts of gooseberries at three half-pence a quart. I shall have to pay for these on Tuesday so I wish you would send me a cheque. You will I am afraid think that I am writing a good deal about money but I really cannot help it.

With little or no cash in hand, Julia purchased on account or credit, a pattern of payment that she had begun surreptitiously in Hobart, and which she now continued in Dublin. Tom inveighed against it, but he provided no alternative, and although Julia could find no protection from his fury at what he called her 'extravagance', she had not yet reached the point of wishing that she and her children were in their graves. That was the desperate conclusion reached by one of her contemporaries, Mrs Karl Marx, who was struggling with her husband's financial insecurity. Marx was, like Tom, juggling accumulated debt and insufficient income and constantly appealing to others to support him. There was one singular difference, though. Marx was aware of the suffering this caused his wife and could not blame her for feeling as she did, for as he acknowledged, *the humiliations, tortures and horrors that have to be gotten though in this situation are in fact indescribable.* Tom would not acknowledge the same to Julia.

At the end of 1860, while she was still nursing Frank, Julia received a letter from her brother Percy informing her of her father's sudden death in Hobart. Having always held onto the hope of seeing him again, she was almost maddened by the thought that she would *never look upon his dear face again in this world.* She and her father had shared a particular closeness, forged in part by her assumption of her mother's role, and her father had felt her absence with a sharp poignancy when she had left Hobart four years earlier. Even Gussie had remarked upon it, saying how much he missed Julia and her children *particularly of a Sunday when instead of going out to see you as he used to do he sits by the fire reading & we can't get him out for a walk which I am sure would do him good.* Reading Percy's letter, Julia felt her exile deeply, believing she would never be happy again and only wanting to be with her younger brothers and sisters to share her grief with them.

Although Percy's description of her father's last hours was heart-rending, Julia was able to derive some comfort from knowing that Ada had been with him when he died. And she felt consoled, too, by the way in which the Hobart community had revealed the enormous respect and love they felt for him. All the Public Offices and many of Hobart's shops had closed for his funeral, and the Roman Catholic bishop had asked his family for *permission to toll the bell for the death of one so esteemed.*

Julia's own vulnerability at this time was subsumed by her distress for Ada, who had neither husband nor children to comfort her, and who was now without a home, the grim prospect facing many unmarried daughters when their fathers died. William Sorell had died intestate and so his estate was to be divided among all his children, which meant the house had to be sold. With no means to establish her own home and with little or no opportunity to become independent, Ada was completely beholden to her family. She, at least, was among the fortunate, for Gussie and James insisted she live with them, a prospect that delighted her. William Sorell's estate was not a large one, and Julia was left about £170. That, and a lock of his hair.

Leaving Tom to look after the children, Julia went to England, in the hope that it might distance herself from her grief. As a way of further diverting her, Tom wrote her long reports about the Yelverton case, which was enthralling the whole of Dublin, and Tom in particular. Clearly, he imagined that Julia might find some comfort in its riveting exposition of the religious intolerance between Protestants and Catholics. Theresa Longworth, an English Catholic, and the Hon. William Charles Yelverton, later 4th Viscount Avonmore, an Irish Protestant, had been lovers since their meeting in 1852. They had neither married nor lived together, as Charles had promised his family he would not marry a Catholic, and Theresa would not live with Charles without a Catholic marriage ceremony. Eventually, Charles reneged on his promise to his family, and he and Theresa were married secretly by a Catholic priest in August 1857, although, as the law stood, any marriage between a Catholic and a Protestant performed by a Catholic priest was considered null and void. One year later, Theresa had suffered a miscarriage, and Charles had met Emily Forbes. When Theresa refused Charles's plea that she give up her status as his wife and emigrate to New Zealand, he proceeded with his plan to marry Emily in Edinburgh, prompting Theresa to sue him for maintenance in Dublin.

In one of his letters Tom told Julia that

> Nothing is talked of here but the Yelverton trial, such interest and excitement did not exist even, I was told by a gentlemen yesterday, at the State trial of O'Connell. The gentleman is an unprincipled rip, and the lady an artful schemer, who, I confess I think, (at least unless his evidence is a tissue of lies) has over-reached herself and been ruined in the endeavour to hook him. They are both very clever people, and that makes the trial all the more interesting. The popular sympathy on her part is unbounded; crowds assemble every morning round the Gresham to cheer her as she goes down to court; and Yelverton was one day hooted out of Jude's; yet I doubt if, in the present state of the law, the Judge will not be obliged to direct the jury to find for the defendant.

Although Tom may have thought William Yelverton *an unprincipled rip, and the lady an artful schemer*, neither he nor any of the interested spectators could know as they soaked up the hysteria surrounding the case, that it would lead, only ten years later, to legalising mixed marriages in Ireland. Nor did Tom acknowledge — it was something that Julia already understood — that beyond exposing the bitter landscape of religious intolerance in Dublin, the Yelverton Affair also revealed the precarious state of women, regardless of their religious views and regardless of their marital status.

Responding in kind to Tom's interest in religious matters, Julia wrote of her own experiences, saying she was a happy participant in religious ceremony providing none of it was Roman Catholic or had any vestige of Roman Catholicism. On one of her Sundays in London, she told Tom, she attended three church services: the Vere Street Chapel to hear F.D. Maurice, the controversial English theologian and Christian Socialist; a service at St Paul's; and, in the evening, a service at All Saint's Margaret Street, a newly built High Anglican Gothic Church. Although she found the latter the most exquisite thing she had ever seen in her life, and the music very beautiful, she thought the clergymen were evidently Roman Catholics in disguise as they all bowed to the altar when they came in and made signs of the cross.

As Julia began to recover from the shock of her father's loss, she started writing to Tom in a playful, yearning manner — *I hope all the darlings are well and that I will find you looking none the worse for Lent. I am longing to see you again. Kiss the chicks for me and with much love to your dear old self* — which, in turn, caused him to express his regret that he was *not to have my darling back till Saturday: well I must 'grin & bear it'*. If only these two could have lived and loved apart, they would have had the perfect marriage.

But the past, with its spectres of her mother's abandonment and her misery in Catholic Brussels, was not quite ready to release Julia. Her step-grandmother, Mrs William Sorell, the former Mrs Kent, made a morning call with one of her daughters while she was in London. Julia had not seen Governor Sorell's widow since she had left Brussels as a young girl of fifteen to return to her father in Hobart. Strangely, the meeting did something to soothe her memories of that time, and she came away from it puzzling over Mrs Sorell's reputation for being a fascinating woman, somewhat bemused by how old age had changed her into something *almost childish*.

It was fortunate for Julia that her encounter with the past had been in the form of her step-grandmother. Shortly after she returned to Dublin, her own mother, Elizabeth, arrived in London. Since her escape into the arms of her lover George Deare, Elizabeth had been living with him in India, where she had had four children with him — Louisa, George, Elizabeth, and Julia. With the death of William Sorell, Elizabeth and George, who had risen to the rank of Lieutenant-Colonel, were now free to marry. The service was performed at St Martin in the Fields on 19 August 1861, a few weeks after their arrival in London. Had Julia wished it, she could have reconnected with her mother at any time — the sweep of her extended family and the concentric and ever-moving ex-colonial circle of which she was a member would have allowed her to know where her mother was and how to reach her. Instead, Julia remained silent.

11

Adrift

Even in Julia's relatively carefree days in England, the stress of
the family's financial position was ever present, and on her return
to Dublin, she threw caution to the wind and sought help from
her brother-in-law James Dunn. She wanted James to lend her
£200 to buy furniture, in the belief that renting an unfurnished
house would be much cheaper than renting a furnished one. Julia's
desperation, and her humiliation, leap from the pages of her letter
to James. *This is the first promissory favour I have ever asked from
any of my relations, and I have been a long time before I could make
up my mind to do this, but it is so very difficult with our small means
to make the two ends meet.* She wanted James to understand that
any loan would be just that, and not a gift. At his mother's death,
Tom could expect to have £2000 — at which point they could
easily repay the loan. In a distraught tone, she told James of her
desire to educate her children and her expectation when she had
married that she would have the means to do this. She also told
him that it would be very likely that Polly would, like her siblings,
need to turn her education to account at some future time. Julia

had learned that marriage was an inadequate path to economic security and she was clearly determined that her daughters would not make the same mistake.

On her return home, Julia had also recognised immediately how unhappy Tom had become with his life there and her anxiety rose in parallel with his eagerness for change. His numerous job applications — he had even applied for a Factory Inspectorship — had come to nothing and her fear of where Tom's restlessness might take them hardened into dread when he received a letter from her old nemesis John Henry Newman. Industrial unrest had hit Newman's Oratory School in Birmingham when the headmaster, Nicholas Darnell, resigned in protest after clashing with Newman. The bulk of the staff followed Darnell, leaving Newman with no masters, only one matron, and a school of more than fifty boys. Instead of seeking a compromise, Newman decided to replace the departing staff. Knowing the advantage of the Arnold name for his beset school, he asked Tom to become the Classical Master at the Oratory, offered him £150 for the term, and said he would organise three months' leave for him from the Catholic University. As a further inducement, he offered a place for his sons in the Oratory School and the use of a pretty four-bedroom home — *all nice on a small scale* — if Julia and the children came with him. There was a rider, though. Tom would be required to pay his substitute lecturer at the university. Even so, in their impecunious state, a rent-free house for several months was irresistible. Tom did not hesitate and left Dublin for Birmingham in January 1862 with his three older sons.

Julia, left with her two youngest children, Lucy and Frank, began packing up their lives in Dublin. She was well practised in the art of moving house, but this time it was even more difficult. Tom had left her without any money, and she could do nothing but write letters to him detailing the expenditure involved and pleading for the money she required. She hated writing these letters — and she knew Tom hated receiving them — afraid that he would think she wrote about nothing but money *but indeed dearest I cannot help it.* Eventually the money arrived, and Julia was able to leave Ireland. She went first to Fox How, where she was greeted with the news that Newman had offered Tom a permanent place at the Oratory, and he was struggling with the dilemma it presented him. He preferred working in a university, rather than a school — his stammer was more of a curse in the schoolroom — and he was puzzled as to which might be the better option.

Julia was practical and realistic, urging Tom to think beyond what suited him to what might be best for them financially and for their children. She asked him to consider whether his wage would cover the cost of living and the house rent, whether he would be able to continue doing his Civil Service work, which paid well and which he enjoyed, whether he would be engaged in work that he liked, and, crucially, whether he would get on permanently with Newman. She felt everything else could be dealt with if Tom answered yes to both these last questions. She knew Newman was desperate for the Arnold name, and she was anxious that Tom understand this and negotiate himself into a position of strength. Mrs Arnold agreed with her. Together, the two women proposed the minimum terms he should seek — £350 a year and a house, with the addition of the boys' schooling, which would take his whole package to about £400 a year — a much more attractive salary than the one he had in Dublin.

As to her own preference, Dublin or Birmingham, Julia was almost indifferent. Apart from the awful prospect of an ongoing and close proximity to Newman, she liked the promise of the economic stability that a permanent position at the Oratory offered. She liked the prospect of living in England. It would bring her so much closer to Polly. And she preferred her sons be raised in England for although

> it is and always will be a source of bitterness their being … being brought up as Roman Catholics but if this is inevitable of course I would much rather that they go to a good school where they would be associated with the sons of gentlemen than that they should go to such schools as they would be likely to go to in Ireland, and your means are never as far as I see likely to enable you if you live in Dublin to send them over to England. And certainly if they are to be brought up by priests at all I should much prefer their being brought up by English priests, who would be likely to be gentlemen.

On the other hand, she had grown accustomed to Ireland, she had made many friends there, and if Tom wished to return to Dublin, she would not object. She was happy for him to make the decision, but she did want to see the house and discuss the offer with him more fully before he gave Newman a final answer. Tom, fearful that she might dislike Birmingham and the house, did nothing to encourage her to come, nor would he be hurried into making up his mind.

Julia was unusually gentle with him while he grappled with yet another life-changing decision, despite being deeply unhappy herself — unusual because Julia was never gentle when she was unhappy. She missed Tom and the boys, she was anxious to know where she was to live, and she felt stranded in Fox How with her two youngest children, but she was gripped by a more profound malaise. Her instinctive *joie de vivre* had deserted her, as had her fortitude. Staying with Mrs Arnold, free from all domestic responsibilities and free, too, from Tom's religion permeating the house, Julia had the time to confront the deep fracture in her marriage and her role in its creation and continuation. But her despair went beyond this. It was as if, for the first time since her marriage to Tom, she looked at her life and found it utterly daunting:

> God knows dearest Tom I wish as ardently as you that there was not the difference of opinion between us that there is, but I cannot see any prospects of its being done away with. I often feel that I am not happy myself and that I certainly do not make you happy, & I also often think that it would be for your happiness eventually and for the children's good if I were to die. I feel bitterly that I am not fit to be the mother of a large family, and I know not how to become so.

When her weeks of uncertainty ended with Tom's decision to remain in Birmingham and to accept Newman's offer of £400 a year — she and Mrs Arnold had clearly done their sums — Julia was so overcome with relief and with apprehension, she went straight to her room and prayed to God. She prayed for help to conquer what she saw as her wicked temper. She prayed for help to make her home a happier one, and she prayed for help to set a better example to her children. When she had finished her pleas to God, Julia poured out her heart to Tom. She acknowledged a little of the turmoil and insecurity she felt and asked him why, with the love they had for each other, they could not be happier. She revealed, too, how his often-expressed view that her unwillingness to follow his chosen religious path set a poor example to their children found fertile ground. This sense of unworthiness, an abiding disquiet, had settled in her core and would not be stilled. If she was unfit to be a wife or a mother, what purpose did she have?

> I often feel when I see mothers with their children how much I lost as a child in having no loving, gentle mother to guide me and teach me to love God, and how unless it should please God to change my heart, I am utterly unfit to be a mother myself. I have been very unhappy for some months past. I cannot help seeing that my example has done the children harm, and unless God's goodness enables me to do differently for the children's sake I hope I may not live long. It is the feeling of my own unworthiness often makes me so irritable and violent, anything seems better than calm.

She felt so rudderless in the great sea of motherhood she believed that even God could not hear her pleas.

It was not surprising that Julia's expression of pain at her mother's absence and her lack of confidence in her own capacity as a mother should emerge while she was staying in Mrs Arnold's peaceful household. At Fox How all orders and commands emanated from a woman who was in control of her own destiny and from a mother who was at the centre of a deeply unified family. It presented a stark contrast to Julia's own domestic landscape where she had no authority, where she was wretchedly divided from her husband, and where her daughter was separated from her. Polly was now the same age that Julia had been when her mother had abandoned her, making Julia feel like an orphan in the maternal cosmos. She no longer had any maternal guidelines. She was on her own and she was daunted.

She kept grappling with what a 'good mother' might be, restlessly examining her own behaviour and its impact on her children. The boys squabbled and Polly, when home, bullied the younger ones and was increasingly impertinent, but was this because of her behaviour? Julia was the disciplinarian in the household — Tom always retreated rather than confronted — but why did this cause her to always turn a critical gaze inwards, to label herself a 'bad mother' when Tom never doubted his own capacity as a father? It diminished her confidence and built her resentment. And the religious divide in the household only exacerbated matters. Tom had insisted that while the boys were in the nursery, she had to choose a Catholic nurse. He did not want a Protestant servant confusing their young minds. But now that Lucy, at four years of age, was the oldest child in the nursery, she hoped that he would allow her to employ a Protestant nurse, and she couched her request in practical terms, arguing that it was almost impossible to get good Catholic servants in England.

In what could not have been a coincidence, while Tom was equivocating over Julia's request, he received a letter from his mother asking if he and Julia would allow Lucy to live with her at Fox How. It was an exact replay of her request to have Polly live with her six years earlier. Mrs Arnold even used a similar argument saying that Lucy would get the attention she needed, attention unlikely to be obtained in a crowded nursery. When Matthew also urged Tom to agree to their mother's request, it was clear that Tom's family were eager, as was Julia, to do all they could to shield his daughters from Catholicism. Tom refused his mother's request, but when he was approached later in the year by his sister Susy and her husband, John Cropper, he agreed to Lucy going to live with them at Dingle Bank. Julia had lost her second daughter to Tom's conscience and her own ongoing resistance to it.

If Julia's resentment was growing, so, too, was her fear when a widespread furore erupted over the case of Edgardo Mortara. An Italian Jewish boy living in Bologna, Edgardo became seriously ill and was baptised a Catholic by one of the family's domestic servants, who believed that he was dying. Papal States Law forbade non-Catholics raising a Catholic, so when the Papal authorities discovered that Edgardo had been baptised, he was immediately removed from his parents, made a ward of the state, and taken to Rome. His parents were not permitted to take him home until and unless they converted to Catholicism. They refused to convert, and despite several audiences with the Pope, they were unable to retrieve their son. An international outcry ensued as prominent people, organisations, and governments protested against the continued confinement of the child. Even Tom expressed *a certain amount of involuntary sympathy* towards the parents. But the case reverberated deeply inside Julia. She was a non-Catholic parent with no rights over her baptised sons and forced to send her daughters from her.

When Julia eventually left Fox How for Birmingham in March 1862, she did so with a troubled heart. She was thirty-six years of age and had been married for less than twelve years. She had given birth to seven children. One was dead, one was living apart from her, and another would shortly follow. The house in Birmingham — a house she had never seen — would be her eighth home since her marriage. Before she began her journey, she had her photograph taken, a rare *visual* pointer marking her journey through life and the impact of her twelve years with Tom. Gone was any comparison with Aurora Raby. Her portrait sent a pang to Tom's heart and would, she knew, shock Gussie and Ada. She looked twenty years older than she was.

12

A Dark World

Julia was delighted to be with Tom again, and he with her. If nothing else, their lengthy time apart had caused them both to recognise the strong bond between them. He had been deeply grateful for her temperate, loving tone in their discussions about his future in Birmingham and he had yearned to be with her:

> I suppose this will be the last letter I shall write to you, my own darling, and it seems to me that when I have once got you back I shall not let you be parted from me again in a hurry. I hope it will be long before we have such another lengthened correspondence. How sweet it is to have some one whom one can love with all one's heart, and to feel, in spite of all things, justified and borne out in such love … Oh my darling wife how I long for you.

He acknowledged her life with him might not be one that she would have chosen:

My thoughts travel back to certain morning walks taken years ago with one Julia Sorell, when she and I had all our troubles before us, and she thought more hopefully of her marriage than experience has borne her out in, poor dear!

But he was grateful that she was with him and he loved her all the more for it. And she responded with love. *I count the hours until I see you again my darling…* A few weeks after her arrival, she was pregnant again.

Birmingham was, after London and Liverpool, the third largest city in Britain, with a population of more than a quarter of a million people and growing. Its abundant employment opportunities and its religious tolerance acted as a magnet for hopeful immigrants, whether they were escaping the limitations of rural life in England, the ravages of famine in Ireland, or the violence of pogroms in Europe. It was a booming place, blessed and blighted by its industrial base.

Ten years earlier, Matthew Arnold had visited Birmingham and had been very impressed, describing it as, *next to Liverpool the finest of the manufacturing towns*. It was not a view widely shared. The artist Edward Burne-Jones, who grew up there in the 1840s, remembered the ramshackle slums, the crude and ugly townscape caused by too rapid industrial development, and the badly nourished inhabitants. *Blackguard, button-making, blundering, beastly, brutal, bellowing, blustering, bearish, boiler-bursting, beggarly, black Birmm*, its brashness driving him to despair. It seemed not much had changed since fifty years earlier when the poet Robert Southey had been dizzied with the hammering of presses, the clatter of engines, and the whirling of wheels, his head aching with the multiplicity of infernal noises, his eyes burning with the light of infernal fires, and his stomach sickened by the filth which fills the whole atmosphere and penetrates every where, spotting and staining every thing, and getting into the pores and nostrils.

Abraham Lincoln's consul, Elihu Burritt, thought it black by night and red by day, and even Julia's own sons complained of never seeing the sun because of the coal smoke.

By the time Julia arrived, extensive poverty, widespread employment of underage children, and overcrowded and slum-like conditions co-existed with an expanding suburban area peopled by the prospering middle classes, public lighting, sewerage, a library, a museum, and an art gallery. It had the air of a vigorous, enterprising, tumultuous, noxious place, focused on the future, not on the past. Julia was immediately captivated by it, exhilarated by the sheer mass and complexity of the industry that took place in the thousands of small workshops, which seemed to match her own animated, vivacious nature.

She liked her neighbourhood. She liked the Botanical Gardens at the end of her street. Edgbaston was the most desirable suburb in Birmingham and their neighbours included many of the city's notable families, such as the Cadburys, the Chamberlains, and the Kenricks. She liked, too, Birmingham's reputation for openness. This was the place that had seen men such as James Watt, Josiah Wedgwood, Erasmus Darwin, and Joseph Priestley meet to discuss social and scientific subjects, and it had shaped Joseph Chamberlain, the social reformer and politician. And she liked, above all, the city's religious diversity. Unlike Dublin, it was not dominated by Catholics — here they constituted no more than one per cent of the population — and Julia was drawn to the style and substance of the nonconformist approach to religion and to ministers like George Dawson, who regarded fixed creeds as productive of mischief and who believed that religion should be judged by its effects on practical conduct.

For all that she liked Birmingham, Julia did face problems adjusting to life in her new home. Prominent among these was her proximity to Newman. His presence was material and constant, and she felt suffocated by it. She was not only living alongside him, but her husband was employed by him, her sons were being educated by him, and, because of his influence on Tom, her daughters were banished. She hated Tom's adoration of him, which she thought blinded him to the fact that he was being exploited in his teaching position at the Oratory. Julia believed *£400 a year is as little as the master of such a school ought to receive*. Her antipathy towards Newman was so strong — she would cross the road rather than meet him — and her distrust of his influence on her children was so intense that even they would shrink from him in childish resentment, understanding him to be the cause of their family misfortunes. It was a sentiment shared by her mother-in-law. When Willy performed well in his first examination at the Oratory School, Julia had written to Tom expressing her gladness and adding,

> although I must confess the thought of our son being examined by Dr Newman carried a pang to my heart. Your mother I found felt it in the same way; she said (when I read out to her that part of your letter) with her eyes full of tears oh! to think of his grandson dearest Tom's son being examined by Dr Newman so you see

my own dear husband other people feel these things as well as me.

But Birmingham was large enough to contain both Julia and Newman, and with the name Arnold, she and Tom were quickly welcomed into its social and cultural life. One of their first friends was Sebastian Evans, the manager of the art department at a glassworks company near Birmingham. His window design for the International Exhibition held in London in 1862 was the reason Julia and Tom visited the exhibition. A Cambridge graduate, Evans was a friend of Matthew Arnold, and he and his wife, Elizabeth, introduced Tom and Julia to their wide circle of friends, including the novelist William Makepeace Thackeray, the scientists Charles Darwin and Thomas Huxley, and the artists Edward Burne-Jones and John Ruskin.

As was her custom, Julia quickly developed strong friendships with the women in this circle. Two in particular, Charlotte Kekewich and Emily Tyndall, both near neighbours, responded immediately to her warmth and gaiety, and became enduring friends, Charlotte even naming one of her daughters after Julia, and Emily providing a refuge for her on various occasions in the future. They were both there when Julia gave birth to her eighth child in December 1862. Julia's third daughter was christened Julia, but was immediately dubbed Judy to avoid any confusion with her mother.

Aside from Newman, Julia's major difficulty in Birmingham was constant illness. If she herself was not ill, then it was one of the children or Tom. Despite having promoted it to her as a suitable place to live, when he succumbed to a severe attack of lumbago only eighteen months after his arrival even Tom was no longer able to ignore the harsh, cold wind that brought *sooty smoke and acid vapours.* He began referring to it as *that Dismal City,* an apt description when first little Frank became very ill with erysipelas, a bacterial infection, and then he himself relapsed, this time with a severe case of scarlet fever. Julia acted immediately and decisively. She sent all the children, with their nurse and one of the servants, to Fox How, she sent another servant to the hospital to be treated, and she took on the task of nursing Tom herself.

During that long and bitter winter of 1863 she was often up before dawn to light the kitchen fire, to meet all the household calls of the day, and to nurse Tom, whose condition deteriorated when he had a sharp but transitory attack of the same rheumatic fever that he had previously suffered in Hobart more than ten years before. Her Christmas was utterly forlorn, but matters only worsened in the New Year when she received a notice from the Oratory informing her that because of the scarlet fever, Tom could not return to teaching for several months. Consequently, £50 would be deducted from his salary to pay for a substitute teacher. It was a devastating financial blow to a family already under stress. The three boys — Willy, Theodore, and Arthur — were also barred from returning to the school as they were likely carriers of the scarlet fever infection. Julia was utterly dismayed that the Oratory would treat them in this cavalier manner, but Tom was furious and threatened to resign, an unusually aggressive response from this shy, diffident man, and one that so surprised Newman, he reinstated his full salary and agreed to the boys returning to school.

Tom, in particular, was relieved. His peace was being increasingly disturbed — not by Julia — but by the boys. They were becoming difficult. A year earlier, when he had expressed concerns about his sons' behaviour to Matthew, his brother had advised gentleness and patience. Neither had had the desired effect. During Tom's illness, eight-year-old Theodore and seven-year-old Arthur had misbehaved badly while staying with their grandmother at Fox How. To Julia's dismay, Tom's solution was that they should board at the Oratory rather than live at home. Tom was a scholar who yearned for peace in order to pursue his own exploration of matters spiritual and intellectual. The material world was always a puzzle to him, and he often found his wife and his children unsettling. Boarding school would remove at least one of these puzzles, but instead of improving, the boys' behaviour only worsened.

In March, Theodore was sent home from the Oratory. Only days later, Arthur broke his leg above the knee, and he, too, was sent home. Arthur's banishment was temporary, but Theodore's was not. Newman categorically refused to have him back at the school, believing his behaviour would not improve. Routine boyish pranks would not have drawn such a draconian response from Newman, particularly given his regard for Tom and his desire to have him as a teacher in his school. It was something more offensive. Theodore, who had reached the age to take first communion, had begun to rebel in his own childish, stubborn way against his father's religion.

Children observe, they imitate, they react. Willy and Theodore, and now Arthur, talked on their way to and from school. They knew the reason Polly was sent away from home and only returned for holidays. They knew why Lucy had gone to live with their aunt at Dingle Bank. They observed their sisters reciting different prayers. They heard their parents argue and they saw their mother cross the road rather than meet Newman. These differences were not philosophical. They were material, at the core of life in the nursery and in the household. Unlike his younger brothers, Willy was well-behaved and making excellent progress at the Oratory, yet he, too, determined to give up Catholicism as soon as he could. Theodore had formed the same determination, but, being of a more rebellious nature, was unwilling to wait. When Newman expelled him, Tom had to find another school for him, and quickly. His choice was revealing.

Allesley Hall was a boarding school near Coventry, some 40 kilometres from Birmingham. The principal was Thomas Wyles, who had established the school in 1848 and had developed what was perceived as a progressive curriculum. He believed that incessant failure often produced a stolid ignorance, a kind of mental paralysis, and claimed that when he dealt with such cases, he had seen intelligence rekindled. Tom was hoping a similar miracle might happen with his sons — he had decided to enrol Arthur there as well. More revealing was the fact that Thomas Wyles was an advocate for unsectarian education, believing that it promoted more intelligent, religious, and happy people. But when the Arnold boys arrived at Allesley Hall, even this advanced educator found them difficult, particularly the madcap Arthur, whom he declared *a perfect dare-devil*. Arthur was building a reputation for restlessness and mischief, and his behaviour would become more rather than less bewildering as he grew older.

Polly, too, had grown increasingly miserable at her school at Shifnal, and Julia decided that while Tom was enrolling Theodore and Arthur into their new school, she would go looking for another school for her daughter. She found one at Clifton, but when she sought Tom's agreement to move Polly, he refused, arguing that it was too expensive. Julia did not give up. She sought the support of Mrs Arnold, who told Tom she would assist with the fees on condition that she should choose the school. But Tom declined his mother's offer, unwilling to be dictated to by either his wife or his mother. Mrs Arnold reacted uncharacteristically to Tom's rebuff. Instead of retreating from this marital disagreement, she entered the fray, reminding him that while he could choose how his sons would be educated, he should defer to his wife in matters that affected their daughters. Polly was sent to Clifton. The change wrought its desired effect, and Polly loved her new school.

It was a small victory for Julia who was now able to turn her attention to Tom. She knew he was struggling both mentally and spiritually. It manifested itself in his increasingly fragile temper, which even he acknowledged was *not often what it ought to be*. But the vehemence of his outbursts, even after the children were more settled, was new and disturbing, and Julia could only hope, as did Matthew and others in their circle, that Tom would find another position quickly, and they could escape from what had become an intolerable environment. Matters worsened when Julia contracted measles, an alarming diagnosis at any time, but even more so for a pregnant woman, which Julia was once more. She fled in terror to Mary Hiley at Woodhouse, where she knew she would be carefully nursed, but while she was there, Tom's unhappiness, his increasing difficulties with the Oratory, and his growing religious doubts began to manifest themselves more openly.

13

Returning to the Fold

Julia did not know it, but while she was recovering her strength at Woodhouse, events were unfolding in Italy that would have a direct impact on her life. At first, these events played out as reports from a distance always do — they were read about, thought upon, and then put aside. But slowly through the year they coalesced with her family's constant battle with illness, with Tom's feelings of resentment at his treatment at the Oratory, and with his constant, tortured desire for a belief that would unite head with heart, and body with spirit. The struggle for Italian unification, the discord surrounding papal authority, and the continuing fallout from the infamous Mortara case all fed into a growing coolness on Tom's part towards the Catholic Church. Possibly not even conscious of his own trajectory, he began slowly moving away from the Oratory, yearning all the while for a new landscape. And when Tom was in doubt, he was in great distress.

As a liberal Catholic, he was directly opposed to those in the Catholic Church who believed that the authority of Rome, the Pope, was unquestionable in all matters, ecclesiastical and temporal, an issue that was, in the face of the secular demands for Italian unification, dividing Catholic from Catholic. If he was looking for signs to confirm his growing disenchantment with Catholicism, Tom found them everywhere. Pope Pius IX's Encyclical in 1864 had branded modern religious and political trends as secular attacks on the church, a position Tom disagreed with, and, instead of soothing Tom's growing despair, Newman only fed it when he rejected Tom's decision to award a book by Ignaz von Döllinger as a prize to one of his students. Tom interpreted this as a sign of religious oppression at the Oratory, as von Döllinger, a German priest and theologian, was one of the loudest voices within the church against a more substantial definition of Papal Infallibility and against the temporal sovereignty of the Pope.

During this critical period, Newman was utterly absorbed in writing his now renowned *Apologia pro Vita Sua*, a detailed history of his religious opinions and how they had developed. Unwilling to interrupt his mentor, Tom did not discuss his growing doubts with him. Had he done so, events may have played out differently, but when the *Apologia* was published, and Tom thought he might approach him, Newman was equally as busy responding to the acclaim his work brought. Its richness, its eloquence, and the power of life and spirit it conveyed, demonstrated Newman's intellectual breadth and his charisma. It explained why Tom and so many others — Edward Burne-Jones had said that he would have gone wherever Newman had told him to go — were so drawn to him. It also explained why Julia feared him so much.

Julia had never been able to talk civilly to Tom about his religion, so it was inevitable that instead of turning to her for comfort, he turned to their Irish friend and his fellow convert

Josephine Benison, hoping that her unwavering faith might strengthen his. It did not, and when Julia, recovered, returned to Birmingham from Woodhouse, she knew that a fundamental shift had taken place in Tom, a knowledge born of *the insight of long habit, so much more reliable than love.* She had witnessed his decision to send the boys to a non-Catholic school and she had watched his dissatisfaction with the Oratory grow, but even she was startled that it was something as prosaic as a pay dispute that caused the final rift with Newman and Catholicism.

Tom had discovered that his equivalent at Rugby received a remuneration in the vicinity of £1600 per annum as opposed to his own package of £400, accommodation and his sons' tuition. With Julia's wholehearted support, he felt perfectly justified in applying for a pay increase. Newman's response to the application was a quick and unambiguous *No*! Tom's reaction was equally definitive. He told Newman that he would have to end his connection with the school and would give due notice. Newman naturally assumed this was a resignation from the Oratory and told Tom that it would take effect from April 1865.

Tom wasted no more time agonising. He decided to return to his Anglican roots. His mother's response was ecstatic: *My own precious Tom. If you knew how your mother's heart is full of joy too big to be expressed.* Julia's response was more complex. She felt not only an emotional release, but also a physical one — a letting go. Her step became lighter, and she began to imagine a different future. Now that this profound rift with Tom had dissolved, there could be no further cause for bitter argument. Her daughters could return home, and her sons would no longer be raised in an alien culture. But she had no time to relish this new unity with Tom. Her baby was due, and she left for Fox How to await the birth. She was confident that this physical separation could not dampen the newfound intimacy they both felt. She was again his *own dearest darling love* and nothing could possibly come between them again.

A few weeks later, just before Christmas 1864, Julia gave birth to her ninth child and fourth daughter, Ethel Margaret, but this latest birth and the events leading up to it, took an immense toll on her. She was very fragile and she wanted only to be with Tom. She knew he would be overwhelmed by what he had done, and she was fearful that he might be drawn back into Catholicism. She was also desperately worried about their immediate future. Their house was attached to his employment with the Oratory, his contract was about to be terminated, and he had not found an alternative position. And she wanted to escape Fox How. She had always found its sober atmosphere alienating and she was finding her relationship with Polly, now fourteen years old and with her at Fox How, increasingly fractious. She simply longed to be with Tom again, and told him,

> you are worth your whole family put together, in my eyes
> at all events...Do not think me ill-natured or that there
> had been anything in the slightest degree disagreeable,
> but I must unburden myself to you or I should explode.

Explode. One simple word conveying the toll extracted in balancing her need to speak against the dictum to be silent.

Julia was right to be fearful about Tom's state of mind. In his restlessness, he took precipitous action. He decided he would become a tutor in Oxford, preparing young men for entry to university. The idea had been planted in his mind a year earlier when Newman had put his name forward as a possible head for a proposed Catholic college at Oxford. Newman's rationale was straightforward. Tom's name and connections were good, he was *a perfect gentleman in his manners and bearing towards young men and boys*, and although he was *not a good disciplinarian* and was a liberal Catholic, he had *a simple faith and spontaneous devoutness which was most edifying.*

Although plans for the college did not proceed — the Roman Church did not permit Catholics to enter English universities until the end of the nineteenth century, although some did — Tom decided to seek Newman's agreement to his going to Oxford on half-pay to explore the idea further. He had still not told Newman that he had returned to his Anglican roots, nor had he turned his mind to how he was going to care for his family on half-pay, when he already found it so difficult to manage on full pay. He was simply desperate to leave Birmingham. As was Julia desperate that he should. She preferred him anywhere other than at the Oratory and near Newman during this fragile period of disengagement. She encouraged him to leave immediately.

If Julia and Tom were highly unrealistic about their situation, others were not. Matthew was furious. He believed Tom had abdicated all responsibility by effectively setting up his own dismissal at the Oratory and that he lacked the drive to make the tutoring business work. It was an uncertain occupation, paid a pittance, would be a most unpleasant life, and Julia would detest it, he told Tom. He should think instead about a public appointment in the colonies. At the very least, it would provide a secure and stable income. Queensland was the obvious place to look for such an appointment because the governor of Queensland, Sir George Bowen, was an Oxford man who would know who Tom was and would be interested in him. But

Matthew insisted that until the Queensland matter was resolved, Tom should stay at the Oratory. *Are you absolutely demented that you want to cut adrift before that?*

And when Tom told his brother-in-law William Forster of his plans — he needed Forster to provide a further £500 loan from the family trust fund to start his tutoring business — he, too, was sceptical about Tom's likely success in Oxford and would only agree to Tom's request if he could show that he had *a satisfactory prospect of pupils*. He reiterated Matthew's advice that he not leave the Oratory until his proposed plan was effectively in place. But Tom brushed aside this concerted opposition to his Oxford scheme, insisting that neither Matthew nor William Forster understood the tuition market as well as he did. Besides, he would be able to get on much more quickly with the book he was working on, and Julia had an extreme distaste for going to Queensland. Tom had clearly forgotten that Julia had also expressed a distaste for going to Dublin. When he was all conviction, nothing, certainly not reality, could divert him.

Tom may not have obtained a positive endorsement for his tutoring scheme — although in his autobiography he recalled *having received some encouragement to settle in Oxford* — but he certainly did expect validation when it came to his change of religion. He did not receive that, either. There was none of Julia's relief or Mrs Arnold's ecstasy. Instead, Matthew and Forster were cool, almost embarrassed that Tom would become, once more, an encumbrance. Matthew told him curtly to *keep an absolute silence on the whole subject, to everybody* while the Queensland proposal was being investigated. In the meantime, he should apply as a Catholic for one of the assistant commissioner positions being established by the new Schools Commission, *on the chance that they may take one Catholic for the sake of getting access to the Catholic Schools.*

Matthew had one further piece of advice for his younger brother. Do not have any more children. It was a blunt assessment of Tom's unworldliness and his general incompetence in the art of living. When Tom failed to obtain any of the assistant commissioner positions, even Matthew's more worldly outlook was tested. Until that moment, he said, he had not understood the extent of the antipathy towards employing Catholics in education, and he now believed that Tom's employment prospects in England were virtually non-existent. Despite all the advantages that had accrued to him as Dr Arnold's son, and even if he publicly renounced his Catholicism, his chances of employment were precarious precisely because he had been a Catholic. In fact, changing his religion again would only cause further scandal. If Matthew understood the precariousness of Tom's position, Tom himself seemed incapable of doing so, and Matthew's frustration, vented from a distance, mirrored the anxiety, the anger, and the bewilderment that Julia had lived with for years.

On this occasion, though, even Julia did not want to face the reality that Matthew was painting, so anxious was she to remove Tom from Newman's orbit and so convinced was she that Tom's rejection of Catholicism would not only still all his doubt and rage, but would also solve their financial troubles. She did not want Matthew or Forster painting another future, an even grimmer one, and she encouraged Tom to go to Oxford as soon as he could. She agreed to stay in Birmingham to deflect the curious who might wonder at his absence, but even she was left speechless by his quixotic nature when she asked him how she should fend off any queries and scotch any rumours about his alleged defection from Catholicism. His unfathomable response was to *do what is immediately best seems the best rule to follow under such circumstances, without paying regard to inferences which people may draw, and even without drawing any oneself.*

As Julia knew it would, the gossip began immediately on Tom's departure and it surged when she took Willy from the Oratory School and placed him at Rugby, where the headmaster, Dr Temple, had agreed to accept him on the basis that he would now *be brought up as a Protestant.* Tom had equivocated — the word Protestant stuck in his throat — but agreed that if Willy himself felt no moral repugnance with it, then he would agree. Willy chose Rugby. As soon as she had settled her son at his new school, Julia journeyed to Oxford to visit Tom. It was the first time she had been to this university town and she fell in love with it. And she fell in love with Tom again. Together both spiritually and physically, their relationship was reignited and his letters to her on her return to Birmingham read as if he was courting her again. *Your visit was a pleasant little gleam of light, a rent of blue sky between two great cloud banks.*

Back in Birmingham, Julia knew she would not have to dissemble for much longer. After six months, Tom was becoming entrenched in life at Oxford and his tutoring business was growing — he now had seven pupils — as Benjamin Jowett, the Master of Balliol, and the wider Arnold and Oxford networks directed pupils to him. Tom had assured her that he had definitely finished with the Oratory and that his departure from it was an immense gain. She believed she could face anything now, even Newman, who had already challenged Tom about the rumours circulating in Birmingham that he had rejected Catholicism. In a quandary — he was anxious that the Oratory might withhold his cheque, something he could ill afford — Tom told Newman that the rumours were false, although he could not guarantee that his opinions might not change in the future.

That public change came sooner than either he or Julia had imagined when several weeks after Julia's return to Birmingham, a notice appeared in the papers, including *The Times* and the *Bristol Daily Post*, to the effect that Tom Arnold was no longer a Roman Catholic, that he had returned to the Church of England, and that he was now living in Oxford. In this era, it was newsworthy that Tom, precisely because his name was Arnold, had effectively renounced Catholicism and returned to the religion of his famous father. Newman was stunned, particularly in the context of Tom's recent denial, and he blamed Tom's defection entirely on Julia.

She was, he believed, not only responsible for Tom's rejection, but also for his unmanageable children. She was *a Xanthippe*, a shrewish wife, and Tom, although *a very good amiable fellow*, was *weak and henpecked*. Newman remembered the abusive letter that Julia had sent him from Hobart, and he remembered all her other faults: how, when Tom was received into the church, she had thrown a brick through the church window; how she was still unmitigated when he gave Tom a professorship at Dublin; how, when they came to Birmingham, she used to *nag, nag, nag* Tom, till he almost lost his senses; how she preached against Catholicism to her children, and made them unmanageable; and how, despite Tom's *large salary, she took care to make him feel he had nothing, and was out at elbows*, and had forced him to request a salary increase. But for all his dislike of Julia and his determination to blame her entirely, Newman did concede there may have been other factors at play in Tom's decision — from his poor instruction in Catholicism in the first place to his sons being offered splendid berths at Rugby — but amidst the blaming game, Newman held that Tom was, if anything, *a non-practising Catholic*. A fine distinction, but would it be a telling one?

Julia would have been bemused had she known that Newman held her responsible for all Tom's actions. She knew, with deep regret, that she held no sway whatsoever over his actions or his conscience. Fortunately, not everyone reacted like Newman. Polly, now fourteen years of age, was, like her grandmother, ecstatic. She could hardly contain her excitement and wanted immediate confirmation that it was true, writing to Julia, *My darling Mother, how thankful you must be!*

And Julia was deeply thankful. Now that it was public, there was no need for her and Tom to remain apart, and she could move to Oxford. As she began packing up the household and farewelling friends, she hoped this might be her last move, but if she hoped for Tom to return to Birmingham to help her, he did not. Nor did he return to farewell Newman. Tom wanted the approbation of those he esteemed, not their condemnation.

Julia was finally ready to move to Oxford at the end of summer in 1865. She was going to live in one of England's most beautiful towns, an ideal setting in which to renew her relationship with Tom. It was a place where he felt embraced, and where Tom was embraced, surely she, too, would be. Julie needed embracing — she was exhausted. She had borne Tom nine children, eight of whom still lived; she had travelled so far and moved so often; she had fought for her own soul and those of her children. With no cause for vehement disagreement between them, a more harmonious relationship, like that of their early years together, would surely re-emerge. It was a seductive thought.

14

A Landscape of Desire

Oxford was a landscape that lodged in people's minds, not as a vivid memory, but as an abiding presence. Its honey-coloured colleges, its church towers, its bells, and its meadows all cast an indiscriminate spell. The artist Burne-Jones had thought, as he walked around the colleges under the full moon, that it would be heaven to live and die there. The novelist Elizabeth Gaskell thought that nothing lovelier could be conceived and she would never forget its beauty. Even Mrs Arnold remembered well the enchantment that she had felt on her first visit there. And Tom, too, from the moment he returned, was once more captivated by *its memories, its libraries, its stately, imperishable beauty.* Enchanting as it was under sunlight and moonlight, in the winter, Oxford could be quite different. Surrounded by miles of frozen floodwater, its air was fog-laden and penetrating, and when at last the floods subsided, *the meadows were strewn with rotting river weed and little dead fish, which gave out sickly effluvia in the spring sunshine.* Julia was fortunate. She arrived in the summer and she fell in love with it.

Tradition, religion, learning were inscribed onto this landscape, regardless of season. They were attributes that appealed to Tom, but would they also appeal to Julia with her love of dance and music and gaiety? Oxford was a largely provincial, clerical community where the deep division between religion and secularism, between belief and reason that had in part underscored the schism between Julia and Tom, was now being confronted. The Arnolds arrived only a decade after the *University Reform Act* had opened up the university to students outside the Church of England, thereby loosening the Anglican hold on Oxford. It was the beginning of what was a very gradual embrace of a more inclusive and secular structure, although another twenty years would pass before non-Anglicans could take up fellowships and university offices, and even longer before women could fully enter its hallowed halls.

It was only five years since the publication of Charles Darwin's *On the Origin of Species* had prompted the famous public debate in Oxford's Natural History Museum between the Bishop of Oxford, Samuel Wilberforce, and the biologist Thomas Huxley — the first time Christianity and science were ranged against each other in a public forum. One witness evoked the extraordinary impact this occasion had on its audience when she recorded how the bishop rose to assure the audience in a light scoffing tone, that

> there was nothing in the idea of evolution; rock-
> pigeons were what rock-pigeons had always been. Then,
> turning to his antagonist with a smiling insolence, he
> begged to know, was it through his grandfather or
> his grandmother that he claimed his descent from
> a monkey? On this Mr Huxley slowly and deliberately

arose. A slight tall figure stern and pale, very quiet and very grave, he stood before us, and spoke those tremendous words — words which no one seems sure of now, nor I think, could remember just after they were spoken, for their meaning took away our breath, though it left us in no doubt as to what it was. He was not ashamed to have a monkey for his ancestor; but he would be ashamed to be connected with a man who used great gifts to obscure the truth. No one doubted his meaning and the effect was tremendous. One lady fainted and had to be carried out: I, for one, jumped out of my seat.

And it was only five years, too, since the publication of John Parker's *Essays and Reviews*, an explosive volume of seven essays on Christianity written by a collection of men who ranged on the more liberal side of the Church of England. Among these men was Benjamin Jowett, the renowned Master of Balliol College. At this point in his career, Jowett was the Regius Professor of Greek at Oxford University, and in his essay, he had pleaded for greater freedom of scholarship, arguing that the Bible should be treated like any other book and not with unnatural reverence. He was to pay for his views. The Church of England threatened all seven essayists with the ecclesiastical courts for heresy, and although such moves were eventually squashed, Jowett was hounded for some time for his beliefs. Oxford was demonstrating that nowhere was immune to the enormous social and cultural changes wrought by the industrial revolution, the growth in scientific knowledge and the extension of the franchise. Julia would meet Jowett both formally and informally over her years in Oxford, sometimes in her own home and those of her friends

Julia Sorell. Portrait painted by Thomas Griffiths Wainewright, c. 1846

Tom Arnold during his term as inspector of schools in Hobart between 1850 and 1856

*The house in New Town occupied by Julia and Tom
immediately following their marriage in 1850*

*Tom likened Julia to this version of Aurora
Raby by W.P. Frith in* Heath's Book of
Beauty, *1847. Aurora Raby was a sixteen-
year-old to whom Don Juan in Byron's
satiric poem is greatly drawn.*

*Tom also likened Julia to this version of Amy
Robsart in the illustrations of Sir Walter
Scott's Waverley romances. Amy appeared
in Scott's historical romance* Kenilworth.

Julia's father, William Sorell, Hobart

Tom's mother, Mrs Mary Arnold, at Fox How

Tom's father, Dr Thomas Arnold of Rugby

John Henry Newman

Fox How, Lake District

*Laleham, the house that Tom built in Banbury Road, Oxford,
is now part of Wycliffe Hall Theological College.*

Charles Dodgson (Lewis Carroll), 1857

Benjamin Jowett

Judy and Ethel Arnold.
Photograph taken by Charles Dodgson

Mary Humphry Ward (Polly).
Photograph taken by Charles Dodgson
several weeks after her wedding to
Thomas Humphry Ward in 1872

William Arnold (Willy). This photograph was used as the frontispiece for Polly's biography of Willy published in 1907.

Theodore Arnold before his departure for Australia and New Zealand in 1879

Judy, with her son Aldous Huxley, in 1898

Ethel Arnold in New York, just prior to her 1910 lecture tour of the USA

Julia, 1875. Photograph by Charles Dodgson

and sometimes at the dinner parties he held regularly at Balliol. She would come to enjoy a quiet friendship with him and in his turn, Jowett developed both a great sympathy and a great respect for her.

When, at the end of 1865, Polly, Willy, Theodore, and Arthur all arrived from their respective boarding schools for Christmas in Oxford, the family appeared united at its core for the first time in more than ten years. Polly was ecstatic, writing to a friend that the family was happier in Oxford *than we have ever been before*.

In this mood of contentment and optimism, Tom decided to build a house. He wanted a large one to lodge not only his family and servants — a cook, a housemaid, a nurse, and sometimes a manservant were the norm for families like the Arnolds — but also his pupils, so sure was he that they would increase in number. Julia had never, in her sixteen years of marriage, lived in her own home and she had come to loathe the relentless moving, the need to make new friends and say goodbye to old ones. Owning their own home might signify a halt to this. She believed, too, that Tom had finally 'come home' — that this was where they would be for the rest of their lives. She did not concern herself with how they would pay for it — that was Tom's business — and instead submerged herself in the domestic realm. Four children were still in the nursery, and she had to care for Tom's students who boarded with them and the servants. The house-building would be Tom's project. She also knew that he was determined to build. Nothing would deflect him from it, certainly not the question of how, in the insecure and speculative profession of tutor and scholar, he would finance this project. As with so much else, that would be a matter for the gods.

A year after the house-building began in Oxford, Julia chose Devon for the family's summer holidays. It was here that Polly wrote her first notable fiction. *Lansdale Manor — A Children's Story*, is about fourteen-year-old Edith Lansdale, the eldest of a large, somewhat fractious family, who yearns for her father's approval. Mrs Lansdale is an invalid *full of gentle tender sympathy* and love for everyone in the household, her blue eyes shine and her voice is at its sweetest for her husband. Likewise, Mr Lansdale's manner towards his wife is full of tenderness, with an undercurrent of strong feeling. Like most first attempts at fiction, *Lansdale Manor* contained numerous autobiographical elements — but fiction is often distorted and exaggerated, stretched this way and that, constructed solely to meet the author's demands. Writers, even very young ones, probe their desires as much as their reality. The Arnold family on holiday, and Julia and Tom in particular, were something other than their counterparts depicted in *Lansdale Manor*.

Tom had borrowed extensively to build the house and to landscape the grounds. And he was not holding back. On its completion, Laleham — Tom named it after the village in Surrey where he had been born and where his father lay buried — was described by *Jackson's Oxford Journal* as one of the largest private buildings in the city. Matthew often alluded to the forest destroyed to build it and always referred to it as the palace or the barracks. On that family holiday in Devon, Tom, preoccupied by the slow pace of the house-building and by the riddle of how he was to pay for it, was extremely bad-tempered, and when he decided to return to Oxford early to take on another pupil, Julia erupted into a passionate tirade. All restraint had dissolved in an instant.

Tom, incensed and deeply resentful at her behaviour, left. When he reached Oxford, he sat down and wrote her a long letter in which he admitted that he had been more cantankerous than the situation warranted, but he brushed that aside and compared the burning devotion he had for her with the mere affection she had for him. Why, he asked, did she not think of his anxiety and worry, and why did she not consider the impact of her behaviour on the children?

> Does it never strike you that many of our children have come to an age at which things that happen in their home remain vividly impressed in the memory, and are recalled, either with pleasure or pain, pride or shame, in after life?

Now that religion no longer separated them, a deeper, more pervasive division was finally exposed. Tom wanted Julia's submission in *all* things. It was central to his definition of marriage, and of himself. Such a view of marriage and a wife's role was not unusual and Tom was like any other man in his circle, even the most progressive of whom understood the limitations placed on women, yet believed that they must be adhered to. Mandell Creighton, interested in women's education and one of the first to admit women to his lectures in Oxford in the 1870s, wrote to his future wife Louise that while he would always have enough to do — *the practical side of life* he called it — which would be out of her reach, her whole sphere would always be within his reach and knowledge, and she must *take on trust many things that I do: if I am wrong, you can slowly convince me; but it will not be wise of you to lay orders on me to desist.*

What was unusual, and the cause of this deep rupture between them, was not Tom's attitude to marriage, but Julia's. She was simply unwilling to submit to her husband. No amount of advice would change her attitude. Both Bishop Nixon and Mrs Arnold had spoken to her deliberately, and strongly, about her wifely duty to make a peaceful home and be content under Tom's guiding spirit. She might have succumbed had Tom been a wise and humorous teacher, but from the beginning, he had tried to change her, to make her something she was not. And when he demanded that she convert to Catholicism, her antagonism towards him had turned to steel. She felt her own soul was threatened, and now, even when religion did not divide them, all she heard was a demand to mask herself, to always echo his voice. It was something she could not do.

Now in their early forties, Julia and Tom were who they were. There was no possibility of changing, only the possibility of accepting each other.

If the arguments between them had a remarkable intensity, so too did their reconciliations. By the beginning of 1867 Julia was pregnant again — her tenth pregnancy in fifteen years — but she faced this one with more equilibrium than previously. Tom's tutoring scheme appeared to be prospering, the house-building was progressing, the children seemed settled, and there was much to occupy her in the last months before the birth. When misfortune struck, it was not Tom's conscience that caused it, but one of his pupils, who had contracted scarlet fever. Fearful for her unborn child, Julia fled immediately to her friend Emily Tyndall in Birmingham, but it was too late. The baby died at birth. Julia was desperately ill and, for a time, near death. Somehow, she survived, but her battered body would carry no more children. She now had another date to remember alongside that of little Arthur whose body was buried on the other side of the globe.

While Julia was absent, Theodore returned home in disgrace from his school, and Polly took on the task of tutoring him. Julia was away when the family was plunged into further grief with the sudden death of Matthew's twenty-month-old son, Basil, in January 1868. She was away, too, for the final move into Laleham, further marking the house as Tom's project rather than a joint one.

Months later, when she finally packed up her grief and returned home to Oxford, Julia walked into a storm. Laleham had become another of Tom's ill-fated schemes, the debt so large that it now appeared there was no alternative than to sell it. She was both devastated and mortified. Unable to extract any more money from his father's estate and feeling he could not turn to his mother or to Matthew for assistance, Tom did as he had done so often before and sought help from his brother-in-law.

When William Forster examined Tom's finances, it became immediately apparent that Tom was incapable of managing his tutoring business. He had not even instituted a payment system, simply content that his students pay if they could and when they could. It was inconceivable and unacceptable to Forster that Tom could be so cavalier with a wife and eight children to support, a large house under mortgage, and servants to pay. Sympathetic towards him, but determined that his brother-in-law should better manage his affairs, William Forster only agreed to organise a second mortgage on the house when a student payment system was established. The family was able to stay in Laleham.

Before the year was finished, death once again visited the Arnolds — this time taking Julia's grandfather Anthony Fenn Kemp and another of Matthew's sons, his eldest and Tom's namesake, only sixteen years of age. Young Tom's death was particularly tragic for the Arnold's coming as it did only months after little Basil's death. Delicate from birth, young Tom had become more so after he had fallen from a horse whilst staying at Fox How in the summer of 1868. When he became ill, no one was unduly concerned for him; he had so often been very ill and rallied again that hope was never abandoned until his last breath. Matthew grieved almost as much for his wife as for his son and for the blank it would leave in every day of her life. But even in his grief, Matthew took the opportunity to remind Tom that his namesake had a horror of debt, and was precise to a hair's breadth in all his accounts and money transactions. Matthew was hoping, like Forster, like his mother, and like Julia, that Tom would learn from his recent crisis, that he would stay clear of debt, and that he would begin to understand, and assume, his financial responsibilities.

With the house safe, the children settled, and Tom seemingly free from distress, Julia felt content and if, at times, she heard ominous sounds coming from Tom's study — was he chanting a Latin prayer? — she overcame her fear and moved on. She was particularly delighted when, in 1869, she was advised that her grandfather Kemp had left her a bequest. She immediately thought of buying Tom some books, but he graciously rejected her suggestion, telling her to instead invest *at least £100 of it* and use the rest as she pleased. He told her to go to either William Forster or John Cropper or their Birmingham friend Mr Tyndall for advice, and he assured her that she would be certain to get at least five per cent interest, which would be pleasant for her to have coming in every year without any trouble. Even such a modest windfall felt generous.

In the spaces given her amidst the domestic minutiae of her life, Julia quickly established a wide circle of friends and acquaintances, just as she had done in Dublin and again in

Birmingham. Through Tom's name, his connections and his work, she entered the social life centred upon the university. Her lively and generous nature — or as Tom described it, her *distinct and charming versatility* — ensured that she made friends quickly and Laleham enabled her to receive callers in comfort, hold drawing-room parties, host musical evenings and performances, and most delightful of all, have visitors to stay. Matthew had not exaggerated when he said of Julia that she was *hospitality itself*. This feeling of connectedness and reciprocity had always been a key part of her character and for the first time since she had left Tasmania she felt able to fully express this side of her nature.

Among the many abiding friends Julia made in Oxford was the novelist and activist Felicia Skene, who was only a few years older than her. Felicia had been born in France and, as a child, had travelled extensively in Europe, Turkey, and Greece until her family eventually settled in Oxford. When cholera broke out in Oxford in 1854, she had quickly organised a band of nurses, which brought her into contact with Florence Nightingale, and when the cholera abated, some of Felicia's nurses went with Nightingale to the Crimea. This was the beginning of Felicia's social work — she visited prisoners and worked with prostitutes — and in her spare moments, she wrote novels, articles, and short stories, and edited the magazine *The Churchman's Companion*. Her friendship with Julia and her many kindnesses to the Arnold children were enduring — she helped publish one of Polly's first attempts at a short story — and Polly remembered how much Julia *loved and reverenced her*.

Julia also became very close friends with her neighbours Georgina and Max Müller. Georgina was among the remarkable band of women who helped galvanise university education for women in Oxford and her husband Max was an orientalist and a philologist, a fellow of All Souls College, and the first professor of comparative philology at Oxford. The Müllers's place was considered one of the pleasantest social centres in Oxford, and Julia was often in their shaded garden during the summer or at their weekly 'at home' in the winter, a privilege that allowed her to be among those who first saw Graham Bell's telephone, which was on display at the Müller house. Julia's daughters, Lucy, Judy, and Ethel, became great friends with the Müller's daughters, Ada, Mary, and Beatrice, the girls coming and going between the two households. Max Müller became a great favourite with them and other local children, as did another man who entered their world — the Reverend Charles Dodgson.

At the end of Julia's first year in Oxford, Dodgson had published his book *Alice's Adventures in Wonderland* under the pseudonym of Lewis Carroll. A mathematician as well as a writer, Dodgson, like Tom Arnold, was afflicted with a stammer and this formed part of his attraction for Julia and her daughters. From the moment of his initial meeting with the girls in The Parks in 1871, Dodgson became a familiar presence in the Arnold family. Ethel remembered their meeting occurring on *a typical Oxford afternoon in late autumn — damp, foggy, cheerless*. A number of little girls, including Ethel and Judy, were dancing along one of the paths, a staid governess bringing up the rear, when they spied a tall black clerical figure in the distance, swinging along towards them

> with a characteristic briskness, almost jerkiness, of step. Spotting the opportunity for enjoyment, the children joined hands and formed a line across the path; the clerical figure, appreciating the situation, advanced at the double and charged the line with his umbrella. The line broke in confusion, and the next moment four of

the little band were clinging to such portions of the
black-coated figure as they could seize upon.

When Edith and Judy hung back, seized with shyness and awe
at this tall, dignified gentleman in black broadcloth and white tie,
Dodgson shook off the clinging, laughing children, and instead,
took the hands of the two little strangers, who in no time at all,
were *chattering away as if they had known him all their lives.*

Julia instantly warmed to this shy, stammering man, just as
her daughters had done, and he quickly became a regular visitor
at Laleham, spending time sketching and photographing both
Judy and Ethel — it was in this period that Judy became one of
his most photographed models — lending the children books,
taking them for walks, and encouraging their love of dress-ups
and private theatricals, an interest they had inherited from their
mother, who had enjoyed doing exactly the same as a young
woman in Hobart. Julia grew to love her amusing new friend, and
he in return would provide great support and comfort to her and
great amusement and pleasure to her daughters. On one of his
many visits to the house, he entertained Julia and her daughters
by inventing a game, which he would name Doublets and which
became an instant craze in London when it was first published
in *Vanity Fair* in 1879. The game involved transforming a given
word into another by changing only one letter at a time to form a
new word with each letter change. Years later, Ethel recalled that
Dodgson was *a bringer of delight* and that she saw *the hours spent in
his dear and much loved company as oases of brightness in a somewhat
grey and melancholy childhood.*

For the moment, at least, Julia was satisfied as her life unfolded
in this large house in Oxford, with the neighbourhood children
traipsing in and out of the house and garden, and Fury the dog

monitoring the many guests who came to the musical evenings and dinners she hosted at Laleham. She was also satisfied on those quiet evenings when the family gathered in the lamp-lit room, she embroidering, Polly or Lucy playing at the piano, Frank sprawled on the sofa reading a magazine, and the two younger girls puzzling over the latest word game created by their friend Mr Dodgson. Tom was usually working in his study, while, downstairs, the cook and the parlourmaid chatted quietly, sometimes irritably, about the demands of the student boarders and their unsatisfactory habits, or the latest talk that had been overheard upstairs. Even the absent boys, Willy, Theodore, and Arthur, were doing well. Arthur was finally demonstrating he could behave himself, Theodore had become more diligent at his new school, Cheltenham College, and Willy was continuing to do well at Rugby — he would go on to become the head of school — although Tom expressed a wish that Willy was *not quite so silent and glum … rarely opening his lips at table to answer when he is spoken to*. It was a peaceful household.

In the summer of 1867, when Polly finished her schooling and returned to Laleham, it marked the first time since they had left Tasmania that Julia and her eldest daughter were living together. They were strangers to each other as women. Having grown up in the Fox How atmosphere of her father's family, Polly had no need to decipher what drove Tom — his scholarly gifts and his passion for learning — but she had had no real context for knowing her mother or even understanding her. This changed as they spent more time in each other's company.

Polly, like Julia, was dark-eyed and dark-haired, though striking and elegant, rather than pretty. She had inherited her mother's love for novels and poetry and her passion for music. She had also inherited Julia's quick-tempered and forthright nature. Polly initially filled her days studying music under James Taylor, the future organist of New College, helping Julia with the younger children, and assisting Tom with his research work. But she was not content with this life. She wanted to be a scholar and a writer herself.

Tom did not share this ambition for her. He was happy that she should do some research or copying for him or tidy his room, or read the same books he was reading, but he believed she required no further education. Julia reacted to her daughter's ambition quite differently. She encouraged her writing, and, through her friendship with Felicia Skene, helped Polly get her early fictional work published — but she was ambivalent about Polly's ambition to be a scholar in the strictly gendered world of higher learning. Determined not to be deflected, Polly quickly found herself in the circle surrounding Mark Pattison, the rector of Lincoln College, and his art historian wife Francis, a fascinating couple, reputably the models for George Eliot's Dorothea Brooke and Edward Casaubon in *Middlemarch*. They both encouraged her ambition to research and write, Pattison most particularly by enabling her to gain access to the Bodleian Library, an unheard-of privilege for a woman and one that remained so for decades.

On the other hand, Francis, who had already established herself as an art writer, editor, and critic of some renown, an excellent conversationalist, and a hostess, provided Polly with an exemplar of how a young woman might live and achieve distinction in her own right. Opinions varied on this dynamic, interesting woman, as one near-contemporary, the scholar and feminist Janet Hogarth Courtney, noted:

> By the young she was adored; by some of the more conventional her manners were thought too free and

> her way of life too daring … She gave Sunday supper-
> parties, she wore unconventional garments, she was
> even said to have fencing-bouts with her men friends
> on Sunday mornings instead of going to chapel!

A prudent mother of a young, unmarried daughter might have been nervous of such behaviour, but Julia recognised enough of herself in Francis — her gaiety, her impatience with decorum — to feel comfortable about her daughter spending time with her. Polly may not have recognised this familiarity, but she did respond to it.

Julia wanted her daughters educated, aware that they might have to turn their education to account, but she also understood that a comfortable marriage was still the ideal for young women in Victorian England. And although neither herself, nor her sisters had demonstrated an unseemly rush into marriage — Ada had only just been married in Hobart at the age of thirty-eight — Julia was anxious to see Polly, and indeed all her children, settled, in case Tom's conscience might once again jeopardise their futures.

With this in mind, she chaperoned Polly through the array of social requirements demanded of a young woman, guided her, drawing her out of herself, holding up a mirror to her. Julia was in her element. She sparkled. Her warmth was reactive and her vivacity, a strength. Polly finally understood something of her mother's nature and during this hectic period of chaperoning, they developed a strong bond with each other, one that would endure to the end of Julia's life.

When, towards the end of 1870, the tall, fair-haired Thomas Humphry Ward (known as Humphry to all his friends), a fellow and tutor at Brasenose College, began courting Polly, Julia immediately warmed to him. She liked his liveliness and she responded to his more liberal, secular views. She thought him an excellent husband for her daughter. As did her friend Felicia Skene, who, when Julia could not afford to buy Polly a ticket to the Commemoration Ball, took on her guise as fairy godmother and obtained the ticket. While Felicia's intervention had its desired outcome — the engagement between Polly and Humphry was sealed at the ball — it did point to the financial constraint that Julia confronted while raising her children. Her grandson, Julian Huxley, recalled his mother, Judy, talking of how she and Polly *had to go to parties in turn, as there was only one pair of best shoes and one evening dress for the two of them*. And while this memory cannot be accurate — Judy was only ten at the time, not going to balls and certainly not fitting into the same shoes as Polly — it points to the *felt* experience of the family's poverty.

Tom did not share Julia's view of Humphry. When asked to give his approval to the match, he refused. He liked Humphry's cleverness, always an appealing quality to Tom, but he did not like his secular outlook, nor his financial status. Humphry's fellowship at Brasenose carried with it a stipend of approximately £600 a year, an amount Tom believed was insufficient for the young couple to live on. He only agreed to the engagement when Julia and Polly pointed out to him that this was a similar income to his own — and he had a wife and eight children to support — but he grasped the opportunity to express his views about marriage and women's work. Polly, he said, would *have to look to her housekeeping very closely* as she was not naturally thrifty, and her housework would always need to take priority over her intellectual life. He warned her in the strongest words he could find, how it was her *duty to postpone literature & everything else to the paramount duty of keeping a straight and unindebted household*. In Tom's mind, conscientious housekeeping, not an adequate income, was the key to staving off financial disaster.

Julia did not hold these views, nor did Polly, who kept working, despite her father's dictum to postpone her academic work and the numerous social demands caused by her engagement. In October of 1871 her first academic piece, on the Spanish *Poema del Cid*, was published in *Macmillan's Magazine*. And as if to demonstrate that she had found a husband who, unlike her father, believed in the importance of her work, one of the first things the young couple did was write a joint essay, *A Morning in the Bodleian*, which Humphry had privately printed. Polly did not share her father's religious views, either. Although she was intellectually interested in both religion and religious history and would have loved to discuss such matters with him, she refrained, believing that they would agree too little and that Tom would in fact be shocked by her own more pragmatic religious framework. Polly had come to share her mother's attachment to Christianity without a belief in miracles.

Julia was particularly lighthearted as 1872 dawned. Not only was Polly now safely engaged, but news had reached her that her dearest sister Gussie was coming to live in England with her husband, James Dunn. Julia had always tried, in the various places she had lived, to replicate the female companionship she had known with her sisters, and now, finally, after nearly sixteen years apart, she would have one of them close. It was a moment to savour. On her way to London to welcome Gussie personally, she went to Matthew's house in Harrow, and walked straight into another tragedy.

Matthew's second son, eighteen-year-old Trevenen — known as Budge — had died suddenly and swiftly. From no trace of illness at the beginning of the week, he was dead by its end. This death hit all the Arnolds — it had only been four years since the deaths of Matthew's eldest and youngest sons — but staying as she was with the family, Julia felt it deeply. Budge had taken greatly to both Julia and Tom when they had joined Matthew's family for a holiday, and she had the hard task of telling Tom. Weeks later, as Matthew emerged from the shock, he told Tom how kind Julia had been in those sad days. Her kindness was one of those traits that people often noted. She did nothing in halves. Like her anger, Julia's empathy was felt.

15

Coming Adrift

When Polly married Humphry Ward in April 1872, Julia was determined that her daughter would have a lovely wedding. Financial distress would be no impediment although even a modest trousseau required some outlay and took some time to create. There was something still from her grandfather's bequest, so throwing all caution to the wind, Julia ensured that the bride and her three bridesmaids — Lucy, Judy, and Ethel — were exquisitely robed, from the flowers in their hair to their elegantly shod feet. Only weeks after the wedding, Julia received a letter from Tom presenting her with a draconian choice. He was so agitated, he could not bring himself to speak to her directly, so wrote instead. There was no 'Dearest Julia' or even just 'Dear Julia', his usual greeting in his letters to her — unless he was furious with her. And that was exactly the case. Tom was furious with Julia. She had, he told her, brought them to the brink of financial ruin.

Quite simply, they had no money. He would need to borrow immediately, but before he did this, he wanted to come to an understanding with her. She was clever and an expert in household management — a capacity, he said, that was *well-known, and could not easily be surpassed* — but she was utterly incapable of keeping accounts and balancing income against expenditure. As a consequence, she must henceforth consult him over every expenditure she wished to make, because only he, as the controller of funds, knew what they could afford. If she did not consult him and they fell further into debt, he had two courses of action. He could sell the house, which would not only destroy his tutoring business as he could no longer house his students, but would also render the family *homeless and bare before the world*. Or he could publicly notify all the Oxford tradespeople and merchants that her credit was unacceptable unless she had a note to that effect from him. If she wished to avoid this humiliating, public indignity, she must do as he asked. If she refused, then he would declare his necessary tight control over her credit and subsequently expose her role in their financial debacle.

Julia was stunned. She had had no idea their situation was so grim. Her role had always been to calculate how a diminishing income might meet all the demands of their large family and his student boarders, but surely her domestic expenditure could not have brought them to this state, even with the added expense of the wedding. Her instinct was correct. Tom had failed to tell her that his tutoring business was in terminal decline and had been for several years. Benjamin Jowett and others in Oxford had seen the decline, but Tom had persisted in believing he earned a tolerably large income. And now, while he acknowledged that his finances were in disarray again, he refused to acknowledge the root cause. He was simply not earning enough to support his family in the manner in which they, and their circle, lived.

Tom's brother Matthew, with far fewer children, earned more than £1600 a year. The scientist Thomas Huxley calculated that he needed at least £900 a year to survive with four children. Polly's friend Louise Creighton reckoned £600 as the lowest income on which a young couple, with no children, could set up house, yet Tom, with eight children, was barely earning that. Still he concluded that it was Julia's spending and her extravagance that had caused their financial ruin. William Forster, who probably knew most about their finances, had always encouraged her to help Tom by economising, but no amount of economising would help if there was insufficient income.

On the one hand, poor accounting, on the other inadequate income. Marriages come asunder under such stress. Julia, with her generous nature and her love of abundance, should have listened to their friend Collinson when he had advised her not to marry Tom. It was sage advice. Instead, she had married him and embraced the conventions that doomed so many women to frustration, to submission, to despair. When Tom himself appeared indifferent to his income, trying to balance this income against expenditure would always be a fine, if not impossible, art, but if she and Tom were to continue to live as their class dictated, then Julia would need to achieve that skill, and quickly. It was one way of addressing their increasing poverty. The other was for Tom to understand what was required to maintain a wife, eight children, and a household in comfort. Other men, such Charles Dodgson, had chosen *not* to marry precisely because it would have required them to find *an occupation sufficiently lucrative to support a wife and family in reasonable style*, but Tom had married, and it was incumbent upon him to find that occupation. Was that possible?

Disaster was once again averted when William and Jane Forster came to their rescue. Julia was grateful for their intervention, but she could not forgive or forget Tom's threat to publicly humiliate her, and the tension between them remained intense. It only began to thaw when, in September 1873, Mrs Arnold fell ill, and within weeks was dead. Julia's anger dissolved immediately and, as they assembled for the funeral, she felt only love and a protective concern for Tom, who had shared a special connection with his mother.

Julia was anxious that this death might trigger another battle between Tom and his conscience, just as the death of his son had done in Tasmania. She had good reason to be afraid. Tom's feelings were dark. He felt his mother's death as a young child might, grieving for a home that in his mind had been *the abode of manly compass, of the purest female worth, of reasonable liberty, of blessed harmony*, a stark contrast to his own domestic hearth, so often full of friction and strain.

Julia's own feelings towards Mrs Arnold's death were more complex. Certainly, Tom's mother had always felt for her, yet there had never been a natural sympathy between them. They had shared the intimacy of birth and death and together they had connived to distance Tom's daughters from his Catholicism, but Mrs Arnold had never really understood the difficulties that Tom's equivocating, controlling nature and his financial incompetence had caused for Julia. But Julia also knew that with Mrs Arnold's death, a protective presence had gone, for while she had lived, Julia had believed Tom would never return to Catholicism. Her sense of foreboding increased in the months following her mother-in-law's death as Tom's fears about his declining business, his anxiety in the face of his inability to find a stable position, and his troubled conscience cast a dark shadow. Julia felt her worry gnaw away at her, knowing as she did that there was nothing she could do to protect herself and her children from Tom's conscience.

In 1873, Polly, along with her two friends, Louise Creighton and Charlotte Green, established the Lectures for Women Committee in Oxford, and Polly's house in Bradmore Road — she and Humphry had bought a house just behind Julia and Tom — *became a centre of modern ideas where the daring new schemes for women were discussed.* Julia's near neighbour and friend Georgina Müller was also a part of this push to respond to the growing demand among the women residents of Oxford for more serious instruction.

The audience for the first lecture in the early spring of 1874 was so large that the original room had to be abandoned for a bigger one, and the lecture's success and that of the following series of lectures led the women to expand their work. They formed the Association for the Education of Women, with Polly as its first secretary, and before the end of the decade this remarkable group of women had established two women's halls in Oxford — Lady Margaret Hall and Somerville. The push for women's higher education would never be turned back.

As part of this momentum, Oxford parents began school classes for their daughters, which culminated in the foundation of The Oxford High School for Girls in 1875, a pioneering institution in the field of girls' education in England. In addition to enrolling her younger daughters at the school, Julia carved out her own role in this historic change. When the advance of women's education collided with the need for women's accommodation, she grasped the opportunity and offered accommodation to students coming to the newly established high school, to the women who had come to teach them, and to the young women wanting to attend the lectures being organised by Polly's group. She knew if her scheme filled the void left by Tom's disappearing student clientele, then she could not only supplement the family's ever declining finances, but free Tom to find other, more substantive employment. For her scheme to succeed, Julia had to commit to it full time. In addition to accommodation, these young students would require chaperoning, a duty that only she, as a married woman of a good family and connections, could provide.

When Julia, full of excitement and purpose, took her proposal to Tom, he was dismissive. He was the breadwinner not her. But she ignored him, and slowly, the house began to fill with female boarders, both teachers and students. Unwittingly, and with the best of intentions, she had created another divisive thread between them.

One of Julia's first student boarders at Laleham was Gussie's niece, the young Violet Eardley-Wilmot, whose father Charles, the brother of Julia's old beau, Chester, was married to Gussie's sister-in-law, Grace Dunn. Violet recalled her days there as *the happiest period of her life*, in part because Julia was *always so cheery & bright & kind & taking such an interest in all one's small doings*.

Violet also observed the intense pride Julia took in her children, particularly her two eldest. Polly had developed into a determined young woman, using her intellect and her energy in her own research and writing, and in her drive for women's higher education. Willy, who had also inherited Julia's dark eyes and black hair, had grown into a self-contained, decisive young man, unafraid to make his own choices and go his own way. He had won a scholarship to University College where he was completing his degree, and was described by one of his best friends as a very stimulating personality, with a vivid interest in knowledge generally, a lightning-like way of seeing the interesting points in things new to him, whether be it art or poetry, and with a strong sense of moral dignity and a savage hatred of brutality.

Eighteen months earlier, Willy had met and fallen in love with Henrietta Wale, the daughter of Tom's first love, Henrietta Whately — the woman who had rejected him because of his unsteady religious sentiments. Despite the young lovers' wish to marry quickly and the families being delighted with the connection, all parents believed that at twenty, they were far too young, and no engagement had been allowed. Mrs Arnold's death changed that. Julia hoped that an engagement now — a turning to the future — might distract Tom from his increasingly fretful soul-searching. He was eventually convinced, and with their parents' permission, the young couple's engagement was announced.

Julia was even more hopeful for Tom's state of mind when, in the New Year, Polly announced that she was pregnant. Surely becoming a grandparent would turn Tom's thoughts outwards. It seemed to work. Julia sent her younger daughters to their Aunt Fan at Fox How so she could concentrate on caring for Polly and was with her when Dorothy was born in July 1874. With her mother so near at hand, Polly continued to write and agitate for women's education. She even turned motherhood itself into an educational topic and wrote a leaflet entitled 'Plain Facts on Infant Feeding', circulating it in the slums of Oxford. It triggered Polly's lifelong and groundbreaking campaign for better maternity care and for early childhood development.

If Polly and Willy were settled, it was not the case with Julia's two wild boys, Theodore and Arthur, who had now both left school. As they grew older, the waywardness of Arthur and the incompetence of Theodore had assumed a darker note, their behaviour reflecting a deeper fault line in this household where the tone of the boys' education had been determined by their father's conscience. Ever ready to denounce the impact of Julia's behaviour on his children, Tom had been oblivious to the impact of his own. Unlike Willy, neither Theodore nor Arthur had demonstrated any academic prowess, and although Tom had done what he could to find positions for them, they had failed to obtain any. The alternative in such circumstances remained the colonies. As the most difficult, Arthur was sent away first, and by the end of 1875 he was in New Guinea prospecting for gold. Theodore, for the moment at least, remained in London looking for work. Julia's youngest son, Frank, located as he was among the girls, and having been spared the consequences of Tom's see-sawing conscience, was not as yet causing any anxiety.

Only after the upheaval of Arthur's departure had begun to subside did Julia become aware of just how fragile Tom's allegiance to the Anglican Church was. Even the younger children had noticed his restlessness as they accompanied him to church — nudging each other when they heard him muttering Latin prayers under his breath — but habituated as they were to religious tension in the home, they kept their silence. Julia only took notice when Tom began reciting the same Latin prayers and chants in his study. She could feel the coil begin to wind in her and the anxiety surge. More of his Catholic friends began coming to Laleham and the chanting did not abate. She finally snapped when, returning early from a trip to London, she found him entertaining two priests at dinner. Needing no reminder of what her life would be like if Tom were to embrace Catholicism again, she picked up several plates from the table and threw them to the floor. But neither broken crockery nor Julia's anger tempered Tom's behaviour and as the year wore on the signs grew increasingly ominous.

In September, while holidaying in France, he made a detour to Lourdes, a renowned site of Catholic pilgrimage, but still he said nothing. Even his Latin prayers appeared to become more muted, and Julia, ever hopeful that his disquiet might pass, began preparing for the first-ever performance of Dodgson's 'The Mad Tea-Party'. She and Tom were hosting it in their drawing room at Laleham. Judy, now thirteen, was playing the Hatter, and eleven-year-old Ethel, the March Hare.

As the New Year dawned, Tom's outbursts about their financial position grew louder, and his temper frayed more often. Julia's boarders were not yet stemming the financial bleeding caused by the decline in Tom's students, and renewed calls were made to the family for assistance. As, too, were renewed attempts to find Tom stable employment. Matthew was at the forefront of these attempts, keenly aware of the impact of Tom's declining fortunes on Julia and children. It was she who had to calculate how a diminishing income could meet all the demands of the family, and as Matthew commented, Tom had a placidity which deadened the sting of worry to him. When, early in 1875, a position as an assistant charity commissioner became vacant, various friends — among them the Archbishop of Canterbury, Charles Dodgson, and the Bishop of Exeter — lobbied for Tom and provided references. Matthew believed that if Tom got this position, he would be able to get rid of 'the barracks' — Matthew had always believed that Laleham was far too big and too expensive to maintain — and live in a small house on the pleasant side of London. Julia appreciated Matthew's attempts to find Tom a secure position, but she was less appreciative of his cavalier attitude to her home. It was, after all, their only source of income until Tom found a stable position.

When it appeared that Tom's application had been successful, jubilation broke out, but fate intervened before any final announcement was made. Sir James Hill, the chief charity commissioner, died in October 1875, and all appointments were put on hold. Julia was staying with her cousin Fanny and Fanny's husband, Sir Valentine Fleming, the former chief justice of the Supreme Court of Tasmania. When the news arrived, she rushed back to Oxford, knowing that this blow to Tom might trigger another crisis. She was right.

16

Into the Abyss

Tom was not there to greet her. Instead, Julia found a letter from him. Its address revealed that he was in London, but not staying with Jane and William Forster, as he usually did. It was not a good sign. Julia read on. His purpose in writing to her was there in the first paragraph. He was returning to Catholicism. Fearful that he might recoil at the last moment and fearful of her lack of moderation, he had fled Oxford rather than tell her directly. It was a long letter, in which Tom spoke of the inevitability of his act:

> For, my own darling Julia, it must come some day or
> other. I have fought and struggled with myself, God
> knows, if so I might be spared the necessity of inflicting
> so much pain on the wife whom I love unspeakably
> more than everything else in the world, hard and
> insensible as I may sometimes seem. But, as before God,
> my conscience seems to leave no other way open to me,
> and what other guide have we in this confused world

but our conscience? I would to God that you could think as I do; but as you say you cannot, you would not surely wish me to live on year after year, eternally self-condemned, and with no hope or idea to buoy me up. For though, on the whole, it has seemed best to me, everything being very perplexed, to go on as I have done, yet the time while that seemed allowable has pretty well come to an end. Do believe that my first earthly concern is now, and will be while we live, to make you happy, — as happy at least as being connected with such an unhappy erratic being as myself will let you be. For I do not deny that you may mostly justly condemn, and, from a certain point of view, despise me; and yet I feel that were I to renounce what I am firmly persuaded is the truth, I should deserve contempt much more ...

Julia did not hesitate. She left her daughters — Judy and Ethel were ill, and Polly was pregnant — and rushed immediately to London where she sought the support of the Forsters and Matthew in confronting Tom with all the likely consequences of his reconversion. The chair of Anglo-Saxon at Oxford was to be decided upon later that year, and Tom had applied for it. His years of scholarly work in Anglo-Saxon history and language had placed him in a very strong position and, if elected, it would give him both financial security and the chance to become the scholar he so fervently wished to be. If he reconverted, there would be no chair and any opportunity of work in Oxford, or elsewhere in England, would be closed forever. To be Catholic once might, they had found, be overlooked, but to return to it would brook no mercy. There were the four younger children to think of — Lucy was seventeen, Frank fourteen, Judy thirteen, and Ethel eleven —

and Theodore and Arthur still required assistance and probably would for some time to come. Their futures, precarious even now, were doomed if Tom failed to obtain a position that could support a family. And it wasn't only Tom's employment that would be threatened. Julia's boarding scheme would also be thrown into jeopardy if he became a Catholic again. Few families would send their daughters to lodge in a house where its head was known to be a Catholic.

Neither Julia's pleas nor those of his family had any impact on Tom. No one, least of all Julia, could convince him that he would still be able to lead a straightforward and honest life without reconverting. He argued that, as it was unlikely his reconversion would be reported in the press, nothing should hinder his chance of obtaining the Anglo-Saxon chair. Nor would it, he believed, destroy Julia's boarding scheme. Her *natural force and energy of character*, her experience of life, and her maturity, ensured its success — not his religion. As far as Tom was concerned, the only threat to the family came from her lack of moderation and discretion, not his reconversion. She should simply reconcile herself to his decision and not talk about it.

Julia had tried to keep in check her utter fury at what she thought were his ravings, but it was unleashed when he told her that he was absolutely sure that one day she would agree with him that he had had to reconvert, not just for himself but for her and for his children. Utterly distraught — she had never felt a greater sense of lovelessness or loneliness — and without thinking, she issued an ultimatum. If he reconverted, she would no longer live with him.

Julia's reactions had always been intense and spontaneous. She had never learned to contain her emotions, rehearse her responses, or construe strategies, and all Tom's nonsensical talk about loving her and acting in her best interests simply tormented her more. Only on her journey back to Oxford did she begin to regret her haste. A woman separated from her husband was outside the bounds of polite society, and Tom, if he wished to punish her, could ban her from having any contact with her own children. In the eyes of the law they were his property, not hers, and if she was not careful, her bitterness and intransigence would damage her children as much as herself. She pondered on the vow she had made twenty years earlier when Tom had first converted and she had threatened the same thing. She had decided then that her children would always come first. And they would again. She must offer him a compromise.

Unwilling to either meet him or write to him, Julia asked Polly to tell him that if he waited until the children were a little older and his prospects were more assured, and if he still wished to become a Roman Catholic, then she would consider it her duty not to oppose him. She would also, she promised, do her very best to abstain from saying bitter or wounding words to him in the future. It was as much as she could offer. Polly added her own pleas to those of her mother, asking Tom to reconsider his position and not take this step until his doing so would cause less misery to those around him. She was sure that if, out of affection and pity for those dependent upon him, he put off his open profession of Catholicism, then God would reward his great sacrifice, and they would all understand his *intention to make an open profession of Catholicism as soon as your doing so would not do grave injury to those nearest you.* Above all, Polly pleaded for peace between him and Julia, for their children's sake. Tom stepped back from the precipice.

Although Julia was profoundly grateful, she was also deeply mortified that once again he had acted, not as a result of what she herself had said, but because of what others had said. Nonetheless, she wrote to him immediately, eloquently, and thoughtfully. Alive to love, and pain, and shame, she expressed both her deep love for him and the anguish she had suffered as a result of her upbringing:

> What can I say to you that will make you believe that you are still dearer to me than life? You may doubt it, but God knows it is true. ... Never shall I forget the feeling of hopeless misery with which I left London where you were, to return to my, as it seemed to me desolate home. I do love you my darling in spite of all I have said and done, and a life apart from you would I am sure for me be a very short one. You must be blind indeed if you have not often felt sure of my love for you. Could a woman watch every change in a man's health and every change in his countenance as I have watched yours if she did not care for him. ... I do not know nor can I understand what has brought about your present determination but I concluded it is in consequence of what your brothers and sisters have said to you, & the utter ruin to your family which must have resulted if you had carried out the intentions mentioned in your letter to me written last Saturday. I can only feel that you have done, at their solicitation what you would never have done at mine, and I know that in many ways I have deserved that this should be so, but it is none the less bitter for this knowledge. I wish to say now that if at any future time you should have got permanent work which will enable us to live together, and will not have to be given up in consequence of your professing the R.C.

religion, & your heart and conscience still urge you to do so, that I will offer no opposition to your doing so. I do not mean to say that your doing so will ever cease to be a trial to me, but it is one that I shall feel bound for your sake to bear. If you can forgive me for all I have said and done do. You know well all the disadvantages of my early training, with such a training as yours I might have been different. Few families have been blessed with such a home training as yours, and certainly very few in our rank of life have been cursed with such as mine. I have often thought how much more it would have been for your happiness if when you learnt the facts connected with my childhood, you had banished all thought of me from your mind, of love from your mind. My heart is very full but I have great difficulty in expressing all I feel. ... Do write to me and tell me that you still love me, and believe me when I say that many many times when my tongue has been most bitter, I have loved you most.

Tom was likewise remorseful and passionate in his response:

My dearest Julia

God knows I love you most dearly; I feel indeed deeply humiliated and dejected, but it is at myself and my own insane conduct, not at anything on your part; for what you said & did considering your vehemence of nature, & the circumstances of the case, was far from unpardonable. I wonder now how I could ever have arrived at such a state of mind as to think myself free to make such a move at present. It is not the case that the solicitations of my brothers & sisters turned me; they did not solicit me at all; some things that they said perhaps made me realize what I was about more accurately; but before I saw them I had begun to doubt whether I was doing right, and on Monday night I lay awake the greater part of the night, and in that time the desolation that would ensue on my act painted itself to me in very vivid colours. I felt supremely miserable; however by the middle of the day on Tuesday I had resolved to draw back. But it is idle to go over it all again; what has past will have the effect of making me think more meanly of myself as long as I live; but, as the Bible says, 'it is good for us to be humbled.' What you say as to the future is kind & generous, and all that could be fairly expected of you …

Ever dearest dearest Julia,

Your loving husband.

His conscience soothed once more, Tom returned to Oxford. There, he continued to work furiously on his translation of *Beowulf* — if finished, it would certainly strengthen his chances for the Anglo-Saxon chair — and Julia began to hope for a more secure future. It was not to be. On the very eve of the election and without any warning, Tom withdrew as a candidate for the chair, telling the electors that he was returning to the Church of Rome. His promise to Julia, made only nine months earlier, that he would not reconvert until there could be no consequences for her or their children, was broken.

17

Separate Lives

The English novelist Rose Macaulay, a distant relative of Tom's, grew up listening to stories of his religious migration *from one church or no church to another and back again.* She used these stories as the inspiration for her satirical novel *Tale Told by an Idiot* which begins in 1879 with Mrs Garden coming briskly into the drawing room and telling her six children that poor papa has lost his faith again. The children are more irritated than concerned with their father's loss of faith. Mr Garden's daughter Victoria, who was named for her father's victory over unbelief in the year she was born, knew it was coming because his sermons have been so funny lately, and he's been reading Comte all day in his study. His son Maurice, who has fought and lost the battle of belief, asks cynically what religion he is joining this time, and Rome, who was named for the church of which her father was a member at the time of her birth, is annoyed that they might have to move, as their father always likes to live near a place of worship dedicated to his creed of the moment.

Sadly, this ironic, genteel scene, written by Macaulay some forty years later, bore little similarity to the way events unfolded at Laleham. Julia did not hear of Tom's decision from him, but from others. Having informed the electors of the chair first, and without informing Julia, Tom left Oxford immediately for Birmingham, where Newman received him back into the Roman Catholic Church. When Julia discovered Tom's whereabouts, she sent a blistering letter to Newman, cursing him from the bottom of her heart, blaming him for Tom's decision, and accusing him of having succumbed once more to the temptation of having Dr Arnold's son under his yoke, despite knowing that Tom was weak and unstable with a wife and eight children to support. Newman's attitude towards Julia was equally vituperative. It was, he wrote to his old friend Maria Giberne, also a Catholic convert,

> fitting, by way of contrast, that so sweet a fellow as Arnold should have such a yoke fellow — but except as an aesthetic contrast, it is marvellous that such a pair should be.

Julia was not alone in her grief and fury. Tom's whole family, his friends, his colleagues all reacted bitterly to the news. Polly, pregnant with her second child, ran to her friends the Greens and, with uncontrollable tears, poured out the story to them. Matthew, in an absolute rage, declared that Tom was beyond redemption. Jane Forster reserved her emotion for Julia, whom, she knew, would feel it *with peculiar poignancy*. Bonamy Price, the professor of political economy at Oxford, and friend to both Julia and Tom, believed Tom's decision was a *blow*, and he sought Jane Forster's help to persuade him otherwise. Charles Dodgson thought his behaviour extraordinary. Even those who did not know Tom were party to the shock that reverberated through the Oxford community.

In her reminiscences written years later, Margaret Fletcher, a friend of both Judy and Ethel at the Oxford High School for Girls, recalled the day vividly. The members of the family itself were absent from school, but the faces of the girls and mistresses who boarded at Laleham bore traces of tears causing Margaret and her classmates to wonder whether there had been a death, a suicide, or some tragedy. They were told that something very terrible and sad had happened in the family and Judy and Ethel must be pitied deeply and treated particularly kindly when they returned to school. This unspecified news rolled on vaguely, oppressively, all day with various explanations being suggested including murder, until the form mistress volunteered quietly, *'Mr Arnold has become a Catholic'*.

At Laleham it was indeed as if a death had occurred. Julia sent Lucy straight back to live with the Croppers, anxious that her prospects — she was on the verge of her 'coming out' — would be blighted by Tom's decision. Gussie took young Ethel to stay with her in London. Mary Hiley sent a food hamper from Woodhouse, and Tom's wider family immediately offered monetary support to Julia. Tom was so infuriated by this offer, he categorically refused the money until it was certain that he was unable to earn enough to support his own family. He could not, or would not, believe that Julia or his children would suffer as a result of his reconversion.

Polly, torn between looking after her mother and trying to understand her father's action, nearly miscarried, and Julia suddenly found herself nursing her eldest daughter. Only weeks after Tom's denouement, Polly gave birth to a boy, whom she named Arnold, but Julia could find no room in her heart for joy. She felt only despair as she realised that all her attempts to shield herself, her children, and even Tom himself had come to naught.

In the world that Julia and Tom inhabited, religion was never simply about belief. It was about position, about economic stability, about possible trajectories, not just for Tom and Julia, but also for their children. Tom's chances of getting secure, well-paid work in Oxford, indeed in the whole of England, were now extinct, unless his old mentor Newman could find him a position. His tutoring business — his livelihood, apart from writing — was finished, as no one would send their sons to live in the house of a professed Catholic. And if he remained living with Julia at Laleham, her boarding scheme would also be compromised for the same reason. Julia reacted decisively. She wrote to Tom, telling him quite bluntly that he had made his choice and he could not return to live with her in Oxford.

When Tom finally explained his actions, it was not to Julia, but to Polly and Humphry. His behaviour, he said, was quite simple. He had left Oxford without a word to Julia because it would *have led to no possible good, and might have led to much harm*. It was neither tolerable nor rational to him that he remain a Protestant until he retired and then choose to be anything he desired, because it was a forcible repression of his conscience and raised a partition between him and his God. Nor could he have honourably or honestly stood as an Anglican for the Anglo-Saxon chair and then, after a few months, or a year, or two years, declared himself to be a Catholic.

He knew Julia loved him, but whenever they collided, it was not his conscience that came between them, but her passion and her pride. Julia had simply married the wrong man and should have married someone more capable of satisfying the ambition and aspiration of her nature. He knew, too, that Polly loved him, but her love could not satisfy him for the loss of the love of God. As to his other children, he did not count for very much in their lives, nor did he deserve that he should. His wavering nature prevented friends from becoming attached to him and with no sources of comfort left, his sole joy was his God, who would, he believed, provide for those he loved.

Unable to return to Oxford, and with no prospect of work in Birmingham, Tom made his way to London, where, in lonely, squalid accommodation, he turned the blowtorch onto Julia. He blamed her for all that had happened to them. Her strong nature was set with the utmost rigidity against the things that he loved and would die for. Her wilful prejudice meant he could not discuss or explore ideas with her and he was forced *to look elsewhere for that intelligent cooperation and sympathy, which Nature so richly qualified* her to give. The only regret he had was that he had not persevered in being a Catholic. Had he done so, she would have been reconciled to what he was, and even if she could not have joined him, she would, at the very least, not have suffered the fearful shock of his latest action. From his point of view, only she could repair the schism between them, by reconciling herself to serving God in the way that *his* inmost convictions told him that God ought to be served.

Julia was willing to hold herself responsible in part for their divided lives, but she could never forgive his reconversion. She could never forgive him for breaking his promise to her. She could never forgive him for informing his Oxford colleagues of his decision before he had informed her. She could feel no pity for his delusional belief that his prayers would cause God to lighten her burden, or that he was trying to do all that he could for her. Nor could she bear the thought of him returning home. Lucy, she had already sent away, but Frank and the younger girls were still at school, Theodore was returning to Oxford to study, and Arthur was struggling — unable to find success in the colonies. Their lives were difficult enough, but if Tom returned to Oxford and her boarders left as a consequence, they would become unbearable. She banned him from returning to Laleham, declaring that they *must henceforth live as strangers.*

Julia's intransigence made Tom even more vengeful. Indifferent to the fact that her boarding scheme now formed the major part of the family's income, he told her that Laleham must be sold as soon as possible. It was unreasonable of Julia to take on the role of breadwinner — that was the husband's role — and therefore the family home should be where *he* could get work. Although their entire circle believed Tom's behaviour was reprehensible, Julia could do nothing to stop him, and Laleham was put on the market. Tom, isolated in London and shunned by his friends and colleagues, turned to his Catholic friends for support. Among them was Josephine Benison. Tom told her that he had given Julia abundant warning that he would reconvert at some time or other, but that her imperious will could not tolerate anything that injured her, or ran counter to her plans, or interfered with her own or her children's advancement in the world. Josephine did not disappoint him, greeting his reconversion as *good tidings of great joy.*

18

A Revolutionary Wife

Eight months later, in June 1877, Julia and Tom came together for Willy's wedding to Henrietta Wale. It was a rare moment of pleasure for Julia. She approved of Henrietta and she wanted this marriage for her son. Julia had been utterly wretched since her bitter separation from Tom. She was miserable without him, yet when he was with her, she made him miserable. *I love you my darling God knows how dearly, & yet I make your life miserable as well as my own!* She was full of yearning for him and wishing for reparation, but she had no sense of how they could live together, nor any illusions about its likelihood. She did not share Tom's faith that God would find a solution.

Julia was never a robust woman, and in her despair, she had become hauntingly thin, but it was the insomnia that eventually forced her to seek medical treatment — an occasion which gave her the opportunity to take another radical step. In the wake of her refusal to live with her husband or follow his religion, she now made an appointment with a female doctor, Emily Bovell, who immediately referred Julia to another female doctor, Elizabeth

Garrett Anderson. Both women were among the very first female medical practitioners in England. Julia had always turned to women for comfort and friendship, she had always believed in their competence and capacity, and she was now demonstrating her belief and her trust in these pioneers. She also felt, as did her sister-in-law Jane Forster, that it would be so much more pleasant to have a woman attend one, rather than a man. And on that first day of October in 1877, only months after her fifty-first birthday, Julia needed all the comfort and the competence that these woman could give.

Without any ambiguity, Dr Anderson diagnosed breast cancer and told Julia that if she were her mother, she would not rest until it was all removed. A mastectomy was required. Before Julia made any final decision, though, Dr Anderson wanted her to see Sir James Paget, surgeon to Queen Victoria, who had first described changes occurring on the nipple preceding breast cancer — a condition now known as Paget's disease of the nipple. Paget agreed with Anderson's diagnosis and her advice that the tumour be removed immediately, but Julia's distress and unhappiness was so intense, Dr Anderson advocated delaying the surgery.

Utterly bewildered by her diagnosis and full of fear for the future, Julia turned on herself. If only she had been a better wife this would not have happened. If only she could be with Tom then all would be well. Instead, here was a diagnosis that might be a further obstacle to resuming any life with him. And she was desperately anxious about the expense that both an operation and recuperation would incur. She knew Tom had no money and no capacity to either earn or manage it. Only months earlier he had sent her a bill for wine from three years earlier and asked her if she thought it could be right. She knew, too, that if she were unable to chaperone her boarders, then her income would also dry up completely. Again, it was her thoughts around her children that decided her. What would become of them if she was gone? It firmed her resolve. She decided to proceed.

The English novelist Fanny Burney had endured the same procedure just decades before Julia. Her screaming had continued from the moment the polished knife was plunged into her breast, cutting through the flesh and veins, arteries and nerves, until it was withdrawn. Unlike Fanny, Julia was anesthetised for her mastectomy, but she did endure extensive bleeding, infection, and pain and hovered between life and death for several days. It was a state she had inhabited before, and she showed the same determination to escape it. Weeks passed before she was well enough to be moved to Gussie's house, where her long recuperation began.

Julia's hope that her ordeal might bring her closer to Tom was in vain. He was certainly among those who visited her while she recuperated, but it would have been better had he not. Their exchanges became more heated than ever. She raged against what her life had become, letting flow her torrent of frustration and bewilderment, blaming him for her illness. He retaliated by declaring that he had been disappointed in everything other than her beauty, accused her of being incapable of having anything but the meanest and most contemptible feelings, and wished that she had remained in Tasmania when he had returned to England. After one such exchange, she wrote to him immediately, her strength of feeling and the misery they caused one another manifested in its smudged and frantic script:

> I thought my heart would break after you left me today.
> I am miserable when you are with me, & miserable when
> you are away. Why do I live? You never ought to have

married a woman with my turbulent passionate nature. You do not understand it and it repels you. And much that underlies it you do not see, and I am too proud to tell you, and if I did tell you a great deal of my inmost feelings, you would only sneer at me, and tell me that you do not believe me, and I am mean and selfish, and only care for the world & its judgements. If there is a future life you will see that this estimate of me is not altogether a true one. God knows I wish for your sake, that you had married a woman with a nature more like your own. Surely you must sometimes feel pity for me, you must see that I suffer but you have persuaded yourself that I am a fit person to be 'an inmate of St Luke's' wherever that may be & would fain dismiss me from your thoughts … God help me! I am miserably wretched.

Days later, she told him that she would still sooner be his wife, with all that she had suffered and still would suffer, than the wife of any other man whom she had ever seen. Surely he understood that the gulf between them was so bitter precisely because she was not indifferent to him? She began signing her letters as his *insufferably miserable … loving but broken hearted wife*. It was an apt description.

Julia remained with Gussie until the end of November when she was well enough to return home, and although she was delighted at being with her children again, of having Polly and the life force of her grandchildren nearby, she struggled to regain any strength. And she struggled to regain her spirits. Her vivacity and dauntlessness had sustained her through so much, and now these same traits had deserted her, leaving a grim frustration and a growing bitterness in their wake. She strained to share the excitement when Polly received the flattering request that she write for the *Dictionary of Christian Biography*. She became extremely agitated when Willy avowed no belief in Christianity, fearful that he and his young wife Henrietta would suffer the same sort of trauma that she and Tom had experienced. She felt utter despair that her fractured relationship with Tom had left her with *no strong arm to lean upon, no one to counsel, no one to comfort*. While he chanted and fasted, persuaded that he had found the truth, they remained *as wide asunder as the Poles*, Tom in London trying to scratch out a living and Julia in Oxford trying to maintain her boarding scheme. The breach between them was growing instead of diminishing.

Implacable and deepening financial woes only added to Julia's stress. As she had feared, her slow recovery was compromising her capacity to provide the level of chaperonage required, particularly for the older girls. Chaperones were sometimes required to stand all evening at a function, something Julia no longer had the strength to do. She also had no control over the money she herself was earning. The Married Women's Property Act that would allow married women to control their own money, was still more than ten years away, and all the fees Julia made from her boarding scheme had to be placed into Tom's bank account. She was then utterly dependent on him giving her the money she required when she required it. Inevitably, such a convoluted and humiliating arrangement caused further, and darker, disagreements and misunderstandings between them. Too often, Tom only paid the food bills and none of the other bills that she sent him. Needing more financial certainty, she asked him to pay her a fixed sum each month. He agreed in principle, but could not, he said, agree in practice until such time as he was earning money. Left with no alternative, Julia lived on credit and the hope that Tom would honour it. And with Laleham on the market, she needed to find alternative lodging for herself, her daughters, and her boarders. Life was utterly daunting.

Ironically, it was the wayward Arthur whose misdemeanours caused a breach in Julia's standoff with Tom, giving them a focus other than themselves. A slight thaw developed in their relationship, if Julia sending Tom some apricot jam could be taken as evidence of this. Arthur's sojourn in the colonies had entrenched his waywardness, rather than remedied it. When he returned to London in March 1877, he took up residence with his father and began borrowing more money, to add to the trail of debts he had left behind him in Tasmania.

Less than a month after Arthur's return, and after he failed to repay his father the money he had borrowed, Tom wrote to Julia *that wretched boy seems born to heap trouble on our heads and shame on his own. As I told him, he must have lied through thick & thin* … Desperate to be free of him, Tom used all his contacts and that of his wider family to find Arthur work. It was a thankless task. While Tom was directing his enquiries to the Post Office and the Civil Service Commission, Arthur had his eyes set on a theatrical career or something in the Irish Constabulary or the Sultan's irregular forces in Turkey. A dull life in the civil service was not for him, but, possibly to appease his father's growing irritation with him, he did return to Catholicism. He was the only one among Tom's sons to do so.

During the summer months of 1877, when Julia went to stay with friends, Tom returned to Oxford to the smaller house the family now lived in on Church Walk to be with his children. Arthur, however, continued to provoke him from near and afar with his crass behaviour, which included borrowing from Tom's friends and failing to return the money. Tom told Julia that he was *resolved that so worthless a person as he is, so incorrigible a liar, shall not stay here many days longer; he really is not fit to associate with his brothers & sisters.* Matthew was also wary of Arthur, at one time asking his sister Fan whether Arthur had applied to her for help and querying whether he could be trusted. So distraught was Tom by Arthur's life, he decided that if his son did not find work quickly then he would *offer him his passage to the Cape and £50 a year for two years.* Eventually, Arthur did find an occupation he thought might suit him. He joined the British army as a trooper in the cavalry and, at the beginning of 1878, he departed for South Africa with his unit, the Diamond Fields Horse.

Tom was thrilled at Arthur's departure — *what I have suffered this last month from that boy it is impossible to describe* — and hoped that his son might settle at something useful at last. He was, he told Julia, also encouraged by the fact that Arthur had spontaneously taken a third-class ticket to South Dock instead of any higher class and surmised from this that Arthur might at last be learning to live within his means. He hoped, too, that at last he, Tom, might have some peace. Julia wished for the same elusive thing. Yet it was Arthur who led to fresh disagreement between them when, after receiving a letter from South Africa, Julia expressed to Tom her utter horror at Arthur's sense of satisfaction and complacency when his troop executed *a mob of wretched half-armed Kaffirs.* Tom had no sympathy for her view, insisting instead that she be thankful that Arthur appeared to be gaining some character and had not yet been reported for misconduct. It was not the type of character Julia wished her son to have. In the event, her wish mattered little.

Only weeks later, Arthur was killed at Gomoperi. He was twenty-one years of age. In a letter to Julia and Tom, Arthur's commanding officer, Colonel Charles Warren, said that although Arthur had spoken very little in his last hours, he had asked for God's blessing on his parents and family. With nothing to guide them regarding Arthur's religion — some of the men thought he was Catholic — a Church of England service was read over his coffin when he was buried in the cemetery at Kuruman. The colonel reassured his parents that Arthur had behaved well in his regiment, although he had not been promoted because he was considered too careless with details for a man of his education. It was not an effusive obituary.

The wider family viewed Arthur's death as a tragic end to a stormy and restless career, but Julia felt her world had dissolved. She simply wanted to disappear and break her heart in silence. It was a moment when she and Tom, grieving over their son's untimely death, might have found a thread to unite them, but even this tragedy seemed to divide them further. Hopelessly miserable herself, Julia believed she made everyone around her miserable and began to feel that perhaps Tom was right when he said that she had inherited much that was evil. She decided to leave Oxford, where she had been happy, and take her younger daughters to the continent, where she might be at some remove from the debacle her life had become. Her desire was never realised. When Polly became pregnant at the beginning of 1879, Julia spoke no more of leaving. Instead, she slowly picked up the threads of her life and carried on. In the end, it was Tom who went to the continent — on holiday — an act that caused yet further talk among their family and friends about his behaviour towards Julia, Matthew even going so far as to rebuke him, something he rarely did, when he asked Tom how he could have gone off to Paris while his poor wife lay ill at home?

As the shock of Arthur's death receded, Julia's anxiety about Theodore increased. Just weeks after Theodore had graduated from Oxford, Arthur had died, and the event so shook him that he decided to leave England in search of a new life. Julia was greatly distressed — *I have already lost one son, and the parting from Theodore will be a terrible wrench* — but despite her fear that she would not live to see him again, she thought that it was best for his sake. She would not say a word to stop him. Instead, she concerned herself with his need for clothes, knowing that she could always picture him in one of the suits that she had packed, even if she could not always imagine the landscape he would find himself in.

Julia had lost Arthur, then Theodore, and before the end of 1879, Willy too had left Oxford. He had been content with his wife Henrietta, his teaching, and his apparent agnosticism, but this all changed when C.P. Scott, the editor of the *Manchester Guardian*, perhaps the most important provincial newspaper in England, came to Oxford searching for new staff. Impressed by Willy's wide range of interests, by his personality, possibly even by his physique — *he was nearly six feet high, sinewy and broad, a thirteen-stone athlete … [whose] face was, for an Englishman's, extraordinarily dark, with black hair* — Scott invited Willy to join the newspaper. He accepted. Julia's sadness at his going was countered by her pride in his appointment. Here was one son at least who was not only following his ambitions but who was also, importantly, able to care for his wife.

Throughout this period, the hopelessness of her relationship with Tom gnawed at Julia endlessly. She began to talk more openly of dying. It would, she said, be one solution to their estrangement, and, after the first shock of her death was over, Tom would be better and happier without her. There was a constant, often bitter, exploration on her part — and Tom's — as to what drew them together and what divided them so completely. When their relationship verged on the uncivil, they drew back immediately. Sorrowful, loving, almost poetic exchanges followed angry, bitter ones. It was an endless dance that neither could cease. Her hostility always focused on his adherence to conscience — it was his God and it had taken the place of wife and children — and on their widely different natures, hers passionate and uncontrolled, his equable, quiet, and beautifully trained. His hostility towards her always focused on her refusal to be his wife in what he saw as its truest sense — doing as he determined — and on her intense resentment towards him, his religious faith, and his conscience.

Tom's despair had also grown following Arthur's death. Unable to obtain any stable work, he was eking out an existence, taking commissioned writing where he could find it and relying on handouts from his relatives. In his desperation, he turned to Willy, suggesting that he assist in supporting Julia — a suggestion that astounded and mortified Julia. Rather than seek Willy's help, she would, she said, stop taking boarders and go into lodgings. Tom persisted in his plan, and weeks later, Willy and Humphry agreed to go as surety to raise £150 for Julia. Increasingly marginalised into the Catholic world, Tom missed Julia and was desperate to return to Oxford, to home. When he pleaded with her — *Are you not my own wife? Are you not a part of me, and I of you? Did not marriage make us one flesh?* — Julia lost all her fight. Bereft of physical strength, lonely to her core and feeling that she was neither wife nor widow, she wanted Tom back with her. She agreed to his return.

Tom was delighted and grateful — *I feel as if my heart was breaking. God bless you my darling* — but his gratitude did not deter him from setting out conditions for his return. She was *not* to worry herself about the places he thought fit to go to, or the meetings or religious services he might desire to attend. She was *not* to make things unpleasant for any Catholic acquaintance, priest or layman, who might call at the house wishing to see him. And she was *not* to destroy, under any circumstances whatever, any of his books or papers. Julia agreed. He did make one concession. If Julia did not feel equal to the prospect of living with him, then he would move into less expensive lodgings in Oxford and live in the most careful manner possible.

No one, other than Julia, was convinced that Tom's return to Oxford would be good for her. Polly, who had seen the effects of her father's presence and his anger on her mother, warned Julia that she ran a dangerous risk to her health if she and Tom were to see much of each other. Benjamin Jowett, who regarded Julia with great affection and was angered by Tom's behaviour towards her, was gravely concerned at the impact his return might have on her. Intent on discouraging Tom, he refused to help him find pupils to coach. Tom immediately blamed Julia for Jowett's action, sure she was setting people against him. Incensed that Tom should blame her for the judgement of their friends, and smarting from his censure, Julia retaliated by blaming him for her breast cancer. If he had not broken his promise to her, if he had remained as a candidate for the chair, if he had continued to live with her in Oxford, she would not have breast cancer. There was no homecoming.

Her body a barometer for her inner turmoil — she described her state as being *much worse than that of a widow* — Julia began suffering once more from insomnia and constant pain. She had been forced to let out all her dresses because of the swelling under her left arm and she could no longer lie on her left side. She again consulted Dr Anderson, who told her that further surgery was necessary, but concerned at her underlying fragility, Anderson decided to consult several prominent doctors before proceeding. Dr Lister, a pioneer of antiseptic surgery, thought the surgery should proceed, but Dr Paget was against it on the basis that Julia's heart was weak, and she lacked sufficient vitality to survive it. In the end, Julia decided to undergo the surgery. She had been buoyed by Lister's generosity regarding his fee, but strangely it was Tom's optimism — she could not, he said, be snuffed out *like a flickering candle* — that convinced her to go ahead. The operation took place at the end of March in 1880. It was another harsh ordeal — she was burned during the procedure — and although barely conscious for some time afterwards, she survived, and another long recuperation began.

During these difficult, exhausting weeks, Julia considered her position once again. She eventually decided that Tom's return to Oxford would threaten not only her capacity to earn an income through her boarding scheme, which was continuing in the smaller Church Walk house, but would also threaten her daughters' opportunities — Lucy was now twenty-one years old, Judy seventeen, and Ethel fifteen. It would also, importantly, undermine the independence that she had slowly and painstakingly gained in his absence.

After various attempts to convince Tom to allow her to keep the not-inconsiderable earnings from her boarding scheme, Julia had finally got him to agree — at that time, with eight pupils and a teacher, she was earning over £500 a year. She was now concerned that if Tom came back to Oxford, this arrangement would cease. Tom was furious when she expressed this worry, and his reaction to her anxiety was scathing. The picture that she drew of him — of his forcing her to work hard and screwing almost all that she earned from her — made him, he said, appear as a monster of rapacity. It was so grotesque and so unlike the truth that it would be laughable, were it not serious. He could only assume that people were again setting her against him. Nevertheless he did promise that if he came home to live, and she preferred to keep her earnings, then he would *accede to it without an instant's demur*. But Julia had lost faith in Tom's promises.

And she had every reason to. Once established in Oxford, he immediately broke his promise to pay her the full fees from her boarding scheme, and his aggressive behaviour towards her, particularly regarding her accounting, did not change. Despite Julia's further surgery, and despite her increasing fragility, Tom appeared unable to grasp the seriousness of her illness. Polly, who understood Julia to be dying, was appalled, and, although she adopted a restrained, thoughtful tone, she nonetheless lectured her father on his behaviour as a husband. She told him that Julia's accounting was quite plain and straightforward, and considering her health and loss of spirit and hope for the ordinary matters of life, it was hardly surprising that not every penny could be exactly accounted for. Polly then reprimanded her father for not keeping the financial agreement that he had made with Julia. It meant she did not know from one month to the next what she had to live on. It was an impossible way for her to live, it utterly exasperated her, and it made her deeply resentful. It was not the first time, nor would it be the last, that Polly intervened on behalf of her mother, but caught as she was between warring parents, she was always keen to mollify her father after she rebuked him.

Still, Tom did not dampen his demands on Julia. He continued to insist that she close her boarding scheme, move to a still smaller house, and undertake *the most careful scrutiny of every item & branch of the expenditure*. And if it was impossible for her, in her condition, to undertake this, then their daughter Judy should take over the management of the household. Tom was sure Judy would take an interest in it and do it well, but Julia refused to countenance the idea. She was determined that her daughter would not do housework, but instead continue her education. Judy had just been accepted into one of the first intakes of Somerville Hall, the institution that Polly had worked so hard to establish.

Tom did not give up. He turned to Polly, sure that she would agree with him, but Polly's response was as unequivocal as Julia's, although more carefully expressed. Explaining to him some of the finer points of housekeeping, she said that, as cooks were not machines, it was highly unlikely they *would take orders from a young and inexperienced girl of 17*, and it would take months of training before Judy could be any judge of quantities or prices, *especially as she had notoriously no aptitude for the kind of work*.

It should have been enough to stop Tom's campaign to close the house in Oxford, but it was not. As the summer light spread its charm over Oxford, his position became darker and more precarious — he likened it to facing an utter smash — and his anger grew with Julia's obstinate determination to remain in Oxford and her refusal to allow Judy to assume the role of housekeeper. So desperate was Tom that Julia close the house, he suggested to his sister Fan that she ask Julia and her younger daughters to live with her at Fox How. Julia was incensed. How dare Tom shunt her off to live with his sister. In response, Tom couldn't understand why she had *let so simple a matter* disturb her so much, when Fan, with little money, but a large house, had offered to help in the only way she could.

Nor could he understand Julia's anger when he suggested that she sell a portion of the furniture. The furniture. So prosaic, but to Julia, a powerful symbol of a diminishing life. As ill-health and poverty increasingly confined her to the house in Oxford, she was living more and more vicariously, torment of a special kind for someone of her vivacious and expansive nature. She refused to sell the furniture.

Julia's intransigence drove Tom to present her with what he called a simple choice — she could she be a revolutionary wife or a Christian one — and in his succinct summary of what each meant, it was abundantly clear which wife Tom would accept:

> A wife with revolutionary ideas is one who does not consider herself in duty bound to honour her husband, nor to lead her children to honour him, nor to submit to be guided by him, in all cases where conscience and the law of God do not oblige her to opposition. A wife with Christian ideas holds exactly the opposite view in all these matters ... There cannot be two rulers in one house. But this says nothing against its being alike the duty and the wisdom of the husband to consult with his wife on all important matters, and act in them so far as possible with her full consent & cooperation.

In a dramatic assertion of independence and a startling rejection of convention, Julia told Tom she would be a revolutionary wife. She would not go where Tom took her. She would not believe what he believed. She would not do as he asked.

Tom lashed out at her with a flurry of insult and condemnation. Putting her own comfort and convenience ahead of him did not accord with his understanding of marriage, where the first duty of a wife, after her duty to God, was *to be united in heart and will to her husband, and conform herself to his reasonable determination.* She was breaking the vow to obey her husband that she had made when they married. She was infected by the atmosphere of a debased civilisation and *the grovelling notions of a society which is fast losing all belief in God and duty.* She had unwittingly become a disciple of free thought, with *the corrupting breath of the modern world* upon her, and he condemned the *sham enlightenment which sees in the 'higher education of women' the culmination and the reward of human effort.*

When stridence did not work, Tom reverted to emotional pleading and charm — he had always used charm — wooing her in a manner reminiscent of a young man rather than a married man nearing sixty years of age and living in a state of estrangement from his wife. His landscape, he told her, was dominated by his great love for her, and although he may not have given her money or rank, he did love her most dearly and had never loved any woman but her. She had been beautiful enough in her prime *to justify a war of Troy, or the venture of an empire.* Had she been as pliable and as plastic as he had hoped, she would not have been what God and nature had made her. She would not have been the *sweet, wilful, passionate, original, ambitious Julia* whom he had married, but something much more tractable, which might have had charms of its own, but not her charms. She was always, in spite of jars and irritations, the delight of his soul, the glory of his life. Time crept when he was away from her and galloped when he was with her, and he pleaded that she not cast him aside, for although her children loved her as children ought, they could never love her as he did.

Julia steadfastly refused to enter into this discourse of love. Actions spoke to her, not words. She had a different definition of love — one that was enmeshed in parental responsibility and domestic routine. It was a love that bought his trousers, expressed concern for his health, encouraged him to eat fresh fish on Fridays, and sent him newspapers and cakes. It was a love that could no longer live alongside him.

19

Disintegration

While these shifts in Julia's marriage were unfolding, the fortunes of her sister and her daughter were coming into sharper focus. Disaster had struck Gussie when her husband, James Dunn, lost his fortune. There was considerable concern that if the Dunns remained in London, James would *either go out of his mind or kill himself — voluntarily or involuntarily ...* It was a great blow for Julia, who had come to rely on Gussie's presence in London, but ironically the Dunns' very lack of money prevented their return to Tasmania, and to Julia's great relief, Gussie and her family remained — although now in straitened circumstances.

In 1881 Humphry Ward accepted a position at *The Times* which meant that Polly and their three children would be moving permanently to London to be with him. Polly's future, too, was looking brighter. In November 1880, Macmillan accepted, for the princely sum of £60, the children's story that she had written the previous summer. It was a story that was dear to Julia, for, in framing the narrative of *Milly and Olly* — a play on Polly and Willy's names — Polly had intermingled parts of her own childhood in Tasmania with those of her children.

Just prior to her departure for London, Polly became enmeshed in her own Oxford battle when John Wordsworth, a contemporary of Humphry's, and afterwards Bishop of Salisbury, was announced as the 1881 Bampton Lecturer. It was a highly sought-after honour, and Polly was incensed that it had gone to someone whom she believed was on no higher a footing than Humphry, but she put aside her envy and attended Wordsworth's lecture on the present unsettlement in religion, with dramatic results. In an echo of Julia's behaviour twenty-five years earlier when she had gathered her basket of stones and marched to the church where Tom was being received into the Catholic religion, Polly, furious at Wordsworth declaring that holders of unorthodox views were definitely guilty of sin — among whom she counted thinkers like Benjamin Jowett and her own uncle Matthew Arnold — raced home and wrote a response.

She titled it *Unbelief and Sin: A Protest*, printed it as a pamphlet, and put it up in the window of the Slatter and Rose bookshop in High Street. When it was pointed out to the bookseller that the brochure bore no printer's inscription and was therefore illegal, he was forced to withdraw it and return the unsold bundle to its author. Polly laughed and submitted, and then sent her response privately to various friends. She had clearly inherited Julia's impetuousness and her need to be heard. But, unlike Julia, she did not have the heartache of a divided marriage nor an economically stressed household.

Julia and Tom continued to live apart, but a fragile peace prevailed between them until the end of 1881, when Tom finally obtained a position as professor of English literature at the Catholic University of Ireland in Dublin. Cardinal Newman — he had been made a cardinal in 1879 — had nominated him. It was sufficient incentive for Tom to reignite his campaign for Julia to join him.

Initially conciliatory, he declared his respect for her *tenacity of purpose, and devoted fidelity to her children's interests,* as she conceived them, and reminded her that if he was not always just to her in words, he would always be so in his heart. He then turned to the core of their division. They might love to a great extent the same things — *children, friends, animals, festivities, all that makes up the brilliancy and beauty of life* — but he loved *them all with a reference to something conceived to be higher than they,* a reference that she repudiated and rejected. Despite this, she could never call herself homeless while he was alive, for *wherever and whatever your husband was — worthless as he may be, and undeserving of any one's affection — there at any rate, while he lived,* would be a home for her, always open to her, hers by right and through his undying affection for her. On this basis, she should close her boarding scheme immediately, leave Oxford, and accompany him to Dublin. That, or allow their lives to become more separate. The choice was hers to make.

Julia made her choice. She refused his invitation. When, in April 1882, his position was confirmed, and he again insisted that she join him, she not only refused, but she also poured scorn on the idea. Her life, she told him, was in Oxford. It was her home. She had many friends there. She would not leave it. He had forgone the opportunity of a secure position that would have enabled him to live with her and his family, and had instead put them and any ambition he might have had aside for his conscience. He could now live with his conscience.

If Julia was repelled by Tom's permanent move to Dublin, other members of his family were relieved. Matthew was delighted, as it was Tom's first really solid post since he had left Hobart, and William and Jane Forster, too, were pleased, as it meant they would see more of him, although it was pleasure short-lived. Forster had been appointed chief secretary for Ireland in 1880, but before the end of April 1882, he would resign, and he and Jane would return to London.

When Forster had arrived in Ireland to take up his position, Charles Parnell was the accepted leader of the Irish nationalist movement, intent on galvanising support and funds for land reform in Ireland. The urge for reform erupted regularly into violence in the countryside and Forster was caught between a desire to remedy the grievances of the tenant farmers and a determination to quell the violence. When the 1881 Land Bill was passed and the violence did not cease, Parnell was arrested. Forster resigned his position as chief secretary following Parnell's release from prison at the end of March in 1882. In a violent finale to Forster's time in Ireland, Forster's replacement, Lord Frederick Cavendish, along with his under-secretary, Thomas Henry Burke, was murdered in Phoenix Park in Dublin on the day Cavendish took up his new position.

When the Forsters returned to London, Julia knew that Tom would be relentless in his pursuit of her, and she was right. His loneliness in Dublin only hardened his attitude towards her, a wife who, against her husband's wishes, lived in Oxford, while he lived in Dublin. He became even more vehement in his demand that she and Ethel join him, and Julia was forced to rebuff him in what she hoped would be a definitive declaration:

> Once for all I will not leave England & go to live in
> Ireland. I should loathe it, if things were not as they

are, but as things are I will not do it. You have pleased yourself & as you have made your bed so you must lie on it, but while I live I will never know one of your R. C. friends. Your whole life is outside mine & this is of yr own making. Ask Ethel if she would like to give up her life in England for what you could offer her in Dublin! No, whether we have to leave this house in September or not her home will be with me & I shall do what I think is best for her … If I were 10 years younger and in a good state of health it is questionable whether under all the circumstances I should consider myself in any way bound to follow you to Ireland, but as things are I belong to my children and they to me & I shall live amongst them.

If Julia recognised the intractability of their separate lives, Tom continued to assert that her place was by his side. She mocked the idea, telling him she was not the only woman she knew not living with her husband. Mary Bliss was not living with her husband William, who had converted from being an Anglican priest to being a Catholic in 1869. Surprisingly this had not precluded him from being appointed as keeper of periodicals at the Bodleian Library. In 1877, when asked by the Public Records Office to undertake research in the Vatican Archives, he had moved to Rome, where he spent nine months of the year. Mrs Bliss not only remained in Oxford, but she also remained an Anglican and it was she who brought up their eleven children.

Tom refused to accept this as a parallel case. Nor would he discuss the case of a man named Boyd, who, according to Julia, *tried to do as Mr Bliss has done but his two eldest children (girls I have been told) are now with their mother but a little girl of two he has taken away from her & she does not know where she is. He has also*

sent the one boy away from her to some Jesuit College & more than this
he has refused to live with her unless she goes over.

Ignoring all Julia's taunts, pleas, and arguments, Tom continued
to maintain that he was a married man whose wife lived in Oxford
while he lived in Dublin. He returned to Oxford several times
annually, determined to demonstrate the outward appearance of a
functional marriage. At one point it even appeared that he might
be able to return permanently when Matthew, who had been
visiting Oxford to discuss with Jowett the possibility of taking
the Merton Chair of English Language and Literature, told Tom
that if he decided against it he would raise the possibility of Tom
being offered the chair instead. Tom was immediately hopeful.
Julia was not, telling him that what he said *about a chair at Oxford*
is so visionary that it is not worth discussing. I do not think that
any one in your circumstances would have the slightest chance of being
elected here to any such post. The time had passed, she said, when
it might give her any gratification to see him in such a position:

> For your sake I should be glad, but once there the
> feelings would be mixed. My children are all now
> entered or entering the world, & what would have
> given me the greatest gratification which anything in
> this world could give when they were young now is a
> matter of absolute indifference to me. No one who has
> wasted the greatest part of his life as you have done has
> any right to expect such a blissful ending as you appear
> to contemplate.

She finished this harsh analysis of the situation by reminding
him that she hated Roman Catholics and telling him not to
hurry home as she infinitely preferred her rooms to herself

and that the prospect of sharing them was not a pleasant one. Her bitterness was turning rancid. As it was, Julia's grasp of the situation was realistic. Jowett decided against giving the position to Tom. His age was against him, he said, as was his religious conviction.

When Tom's assertions that Julia had failed as a wife had no effect, he began asserting that Julia had also failed as a mother. Impelled by the devil, she had kept their children, *by violence & other ways, from becoming Catholics, as they would otherwise have happily & surely been, sooner or later ... a sad & terrible responsibility to take.* Tom seemed oblivious to having spurned the religious views of his own parents and to the reality that his children, like Julia, had come to their own truth. Polly had told him on numerous occasions that her views were very different to his, that she believed *more in facts than doctrines*, and both Willy and Theodore had given up Catholicism as soon as they could and never returned to it. Julia refused to be provoked. She knew her children did not share Tom's view of her. And she was right.

Their children were, in fact, often appalled at Tom's behaviour. Polly felt its injustice particularly. She was closest to Tom, his favoured child — he admired her receptive and flexible mind — and his scholarship and gentleness were characteristics that she appreciated greatly. It was this affinity that made it all the harder for her to witness his cruelty to Julia, his intransigence, and his capacity to ignore pressing issues. And as Julia grew more frail, their mother and daughter roles began to reverse, Julia relying on Polly for advice, for help, for love, and Polly becoming the cajoler, the nurturer, the carer.

In order to reassure her boarders, and their parents, that she could continue chaperoning, Julia had become adept at hiding the full misery of her situation and the pain trapped inside her body.

She had always presented a cheerful face to the world — that was innate — but she could not hide her misery from Polly, and as her daughter witnessed and understood more of Julia's turmoil and struggle, she took up her cause more vehemently, intervening on her behalf when Tom became more dogmatic and negligent, and doing all she could to make her mother's life easier. When her novel, *Miss Bretherton*, was published in December 1884, one of the first things she did was buy her mother a fur-lined cloak. Julia's gratitude was palpable:

> How can I thank you and Humphry for all your goodness to me? I only hope my darling child that you have not pinched yourself in any way to send me the furlined cloak.

Julia's health had become more stable under a regime of homeopathic medicine — a situation that her local doctor thought was remarkable — and this hiatus allowed her to concentrate on her younger children, Lucy, Frank, Judy, and Ethel, whose futures weighed upon her, their prospects blighted by Tom's Catholicism. So sure had Julia been that Tom's reconversion would destroy Lucy's chances of marrying well, she had sent her daughter back to the Croppers, where she hoped she would be able to live without Tom's action blighting her life. She felt utterly vindicated when Lucy met and fell in love with the Reverend Edward Carus Selwyn, the principal of Liverpool College, a Cambridge graduate, and the son of an Anglican clergyman. Even Tom could find no fault with Lucy's choice. But that was not the case with Judy, who, in her first year studying English at Somerville Hall, had also fallen in love.

Leonard Huxley was a young undergraduate at Balliol College from a renowned intellectual family. His father, Thomas, was a biologist, anthropologist, and philosopher of history and science, who had come to public prominence as a supporter of Charles Darwin when publicly, eloquently, and often, he defended Darwin's theory of evolution. Leonard's parents, like Julia and Tom, had met in the Australian colonies — Thomas Huxley was serving as assistant surgeon on the H.M.S. *Rattlesnake* when he met Henrietta Heathorn in Sydney in 1847 — and they, too, found themselves on different sides of the religious spectrum. Thomas, the agnostic — he is said to have coined the phrase — and Nettie, the devout Christian. But unlike Julia and Tom, the Huxleys did not allow religion to divide them. Instead, they worked to bridge the worlds of science and theology.

Leonard's parents and Julia approved the match, and they agreed to a formal engagement, although not to a marriage until Leonard and Judy had finished their studies. But Tom refused to give his permission. He was unhappy that his daughter was marrying the son of an agnostic and he thought Leonard *a revolutionary, harebrained, unstable will of the wisp*. Judy deeply resented her father's attitude. She saw it as a condemnation of Leonard's religious beliefs and character and, importantly, as a condemnation of her own judgement. She was keen to defend herself and she did so with astonishing clarity for a nineteen-year-old.

However much she might be in love with a man, she said, she would certainly have enough common sense to know that there would be no chance of enduring happiness in a marriage with a man who had no high, ruling principles of life, who didn't trouble himself about religious matters, and looked down and scoffed at believers in Christianity. And in a telling, somewhat biting, finale to her plea for his permission, Judy told her father that she was certain that he would be able to reconcile it perfectly with his conscience, and that he would never have to reproach himself. Tom gave his consent.

The wedding of Lucy and Carus in July 1884 was a splendid affair, paid for and hosted by the Croppers, and Julia was determined that Judy's wedding in April 1885 should be as fine, an ambition that added further stress to the fragile relationship between Dublin and Oxford. Tom had promised cash for Judy's trousseau, but when he could not find the money, he demanded that Julia sell the furniture and move to a smaller house. He also renewed his threat to inform Oxford tradesmen that he would refuse to pay any credit granted to her. On this occasion, Tom's anger extended beyond Julia and embraced Ethel, who was helping her mother deal with the household bills. Knowing how much Julia and their daughters liked George Eliot and despite thinking her a sceptic and *a cold hard clever woman*, Tom quoted Eliot's thoughts on debt and begging as the two deepest dishonours short of crime.

Ethel responded by turning to Polly, asking her to put a stop to their father's attacks and to his sermonising. Polly did not hold back. She told her father that the household expenditure was not outrageous and Julia was not well enough to carry out his demands on her. She was *an invalid who ought indeed to have far more dainties than she ever allows herself*, and he was bound by every human and religious consideration to ensure that she was not thrown into a stressed state. He knew, as they all did, that a crisis of this kind was like poison to her, and he might as well *give her something deadly to drink as write letters to the tradesmen about her*. Every such action on his part shortened her chance of life, and, whatever the fault on her side, he was incurring a very heavy responsibility. That, said Polly, was the plain truth as his children saw it.

It was a stinging indictment. Tom drew back. Julia's credit was not cut off, but the damage was profound. She would never forget or forgive him for contemplating, for a second time, publicly humiliating her in Oxford:

> Your nature & mind are altogether mysteries to me. A man who cannot understand that a woman in the 36th year of her married life, even if she were of the most lethargic temperament instead of a very sensitive and proud temperament as mine is, would not resent her husband's contemplation of such a step as that contemplated ... You must understand that this is a step never to take except in cases of wanton personal extravagance on the part of the wife or in cases when the wife has dishonoured her husband's name & is still pledging his credit ... During the whole of my married life you have been so systematically unjust & unreasonable with me on the subject of money that I do not for the very short term of life left to me intend to have any dealings with you about money. What is done must be done through Ethel & if you cannot provide me with sufficient to live upon & remain in this house it will matter very little to me if I should be obliged to end my life in lodgings. But I cannot however bear expressions of sympathy and that sort of thing from a man who has shewn himself so absolutely devoid of feeling towards me as you have done & the only way therefore for me to live my life in peace and quietness is for us to go our

separate ways independently of each other ... However it is of no use writing or talking on the subject, the time for me here is very short and I do not intend to hasten my end by agitating myself, Let things be as they are.

Julia Arnold.

Amidst this considerable drama, Judy's wedding to Leonard Huxley went ahead. Julia's wound began bleeding again immediately after it. The disease had taken hold once more.

Twelve months later, in April 1886, Julia's brother-in-law William Forster died. Between his appointment as under-secretary for the Colonies in 1865 to his resignation as chief secretary for Ireland in 1882, Forster had worked assiduously inside the parliament as a Liberal Party politician, most notably steering through the various education Bills of 1867, 1868, and 1870, which effectively established a system of national education in England, and the Ballot Act of 1872, which introduced secret ballots for parliamentary and local government elections.

While William had been largely respected and loved by the wider world — the Queen herself had been given daily reports of his health — and deeply loved by the whole Arnold family, Julia mourned his death particularly. From the time of her arrival in England thirty years before, he had been a rock in her life, always in the background supporting and advising Tom, even if his advice was too often ignored. She felt even more bereft because she was too ill to attend his funeral. Her daughters, knowing how deep her mourning was, gathered in Oxford to be with her, causing Polly to reflect that except for their anxiety about Julia, *the 'gathering of the sisters' was very nice.* And her daughters had every reason to be very anxious. Julia's condition had deteriorated to the point where they believed she required a nurse, and they left Oxford determined that one would be provided with help from the whole family, Tom included.

By the end of April, a nurse was in place, and Julia's children were hopeful that she would prosper under this ministration. It appeared to work. She regained strength, but then as quickly as she rallied, a relapse would occur. Julia was using her warm interest in life and other people to distract her mind from the pain and weakness. Her capacity for friendship had sustained her throughout her life, and even Tom believed that there were very few women in the world whom the large circle of their friends thought could be spared less.

She was now dependant on something elemental in her nature, her capacity to absorb, to confront, and to persevere. These characteristics were often remarked upon by the wider family and friends and were, Polly believed, God's special gifts to her. Jane Forster spoke of her wonderful vital energy and her rallying power. Matthew often noted her pluck and how it made her suffering lighter. Fan wrote of her bravery, while Polly was in awe of her patience and her thought for others as her illness took hold.

None of this admiration could halt the disease. Nor did the summer spent by the sea have a recuperative effect. On her return home, with the Oxford damp descending, Julia developed bronchitis and went onto cocaine for pain relief. It may have been this or the fact that her old friends, the Müllers, had tragically lost another daughter — their eldest daughter, Ada, had died from meningitis in 1876 — that caused Julia to ponder on death more often and to clarify her understanding of what it meant. She came to think of death as an end, a tragedy, rather than the beginning of an eternal life, but she did not seek out any religious institutions for comfort. She had always thought the Christian church's teaching on punishment was odious, and she had far more respect for a man like Huxley, a scientist, than she had for ecclesiastics. She was sure that in the long term scientific, more secular views would prevail.

She shared these thoughts with Polly, not Tom, and despite her apparent non-religious views, Polly felt her mother's spiritual nature shone out and grew during those last years of illness. There was an extreme sincerity, she thought, in all that Julia said about religious matters, and while she took what others said with a gentle docility — the exception to this was Tom — she said nothing herself unless it meant something real to her. There was *no acquiescence in things, as it were, for safety's sake, & not the smallest terror of death. Truth & love — what can one want more?* When her young friend, Laura Lyttelton, died in childbirth, Polly described her as someone who met love with love. She and her sister Judy would use very similar words to describe Julia.

When Julia spoke to Tom about religion, it was generally to decry his choice. On one occasion, referring to one of their acquaintances who had been confined in a mental institution, Julia wrote that changing religion had clearly not answered in his case. In response, Tom told her he was reading the anti-feminist Eliza Linton's novel *Under Which Lord?*, and described as almost tragic one of the scenes in Linton's book when *the silly soft Hermione, after she has driven her husband away from her, goes one evening into the dismantled study, and instead of anatomical sections of diagrams, astronomical charts, microscope, scientific apparatus & so on, finds a dismal sense of vacancy & dullness, everything that could remind her of her husband having been swept away. She picks up in a corner a scrap of paper in his handwriting, & covers it with kisses & tears ...*

Did Tom hope or imagine that Julia, like Hermione, had gone into his study after his departure from Oxford and wept bitter tears of remorse at the part she may have played in driving him away? Julia gave him no hint. Instead she reiterated her opinion that the Christian church's teaching on punishment was odious and continued to send him any articles and snippets she found from the newspapers about the failings of the Roman Church.

As the end of 1886 approached and the pain intensified, Julia's handwriting bore pitiable witness to the spreading disease. Her script was increasingly frail and wobbly, no longer a flowing, decisive hand. It was now the tenth year of her separation from Tom, and although she was once more, on paper at least, his 'dearest Julia', she did not derive any comfort from his words. The wound had opened up further, and she was growing more dependent upon opiates — now a combination of cocaine and morphia — to allay the effects, yet he continued to deny the reality of her disease. He was alternately cruelly dismissive of her and her pain or full of overblown sympathy. But Julia was exhausted from the battle. She was only too familiar with the gap between Tom's prose and his practice and she no longer required, nor could she bear, expressions of sympathy from him.

Still, she continued to write regularly to him and he to her, domestic conversations about matters to be dealt with, misunderstandings to be cleared up, political events to be wondered at, gossip exchanged, anxieties about children and health and money, and constant dispute about religious history and its implications. These letters were ambiguous declarations of love, revealing what kept these two people tied to each other and underscoring what separated them. Julia ardently pressed her point, while Tom deflected, condescending, and occasionally took up what he considered were her more extravagant points and drew attention to her mistakes or her irrationality. Often these conversations were full of poignant reflections and pleas for comfort. At other times they were full of anger and bitterness. Between harsh 'facts', accusations, and regrets, there were occasional flashes of domestic humour, as when Julia advised him not to *eat fish when you are out of sorts*.

The 1887 festive season was not a happy one in Oxford. Julia's children and grandchildren had gathered around her, and Tom had joined them, but spending time with his family only made him more conscious of his own loneliness, and he lashed out at Julia. Polly reprimanded him swiftly, telling him that he would regret it very much someday if he went on treating Julia *as if she were in a state to bear argument and recrimination, and as if this illness of hers might last an indefinite time.* Smarting from Polly's rebuke, he paid his monthly allowance to Julia — Polly asked him to keep up the full payments — and quickly took himself back to Dublin. There, he sat down and wrote a fierce summation of Julia's singular failing. She had always been *too proud to render that respect, consideration and obedience to her husband*, which as a wife she was bound to render. It was *what every wife ought to render to every husband who is of sound mind, and requires nothing involving sin.*

Julia responded immediately:

> Your letter is just what I expected it to be & correspond-
> ence excepting upon the matters relating to our children
> is useless. I shewed your letter to Lucy who I thought
> as a young wife would appreciate it. I should like you
> to have heard her comments. I am thankful that I am
> proud, if I were not under the circumstances of my

married life things might have been different to what
they are.

These exchanges on marriage continued over the following
few weeks. In one such letter, Julia provided Tom with a bitter,
if succinct, summation of *his* singular failing, a tyrannical
understanding of marriage. She told him that the way he *spoke
of obedience on the part of a wife to her husband* was something out
of the Dark Ages and suited someone who was, as she described
it, *a pervert to Romanism*. She believed that Tom had inherited
this need for dominance from his father, after hearing from her
friend Mrs Bonamy Price, whose husband had taught at Rugby
under Dr Arnold, that he *must have [been] an extremely arbitrary
& tyrannical man & if your mother had not been of a very gentle &
yielding nature things might have been very different in your home to
what they were.* Julia's informant had also said that Mrs Arnold
*daren't interfere, although she was very fond of her husband she was
terribly afraid of him*, a situation that Julia felt was far from ideal
and one that she was thankful to say that none of her married
daughters were likely to experience. Fear. Such a small word, but
Julia had been determined that her daughters would not inhabit
it. Julia concluded the letter by hoping that when she died, Tom
would as soon as possible marry again, and then perhaps have his
ideal of married life realised.

In the midst of this never-ending attack and retreat came one
of those moments, so rarely referred to, yet fundamental to the
lives of women. As a postscript to a letter and marked Private,
Polly told Julia that her daughter's first menstrual cycle had begun.
*Poor Dot's troubles began yesterday. Rather early isn't it? Only twelve
and half. She was frightened out of her wits poor child.* So succinct
yet conveying so much, the news reminded Julia forcefully of her

own first period, when she, too, had been frightened, but unlike Dot, had not had a mother or a grandmother to turn to for reassurance.

The disease was progressing so quickly now that even those who saw Julia regularly were horrified by the change in her condition. As more and more people wrote to Tom of her decline, he finally began to take these reports seriously, and when he heard that Jowett himself had been to call on her, he expressed his sorrow at the pain she was in and thanked her for her kindness in writing to him, for sitting *up in your bed of pain and dazedness, after such a night and those two doses of morphia, in order to write to me; but it is like your unselfish and expansive nature.* Despite these sympathetic words, Tom also wrote to explain that he could not afford to maintain Julia's allowance and that other members of the family would have to help. That, or Julia and Ethel would need to move to a smaller house or into lodgings.

Polly and Lucy set about raising a fund for their mother, aware that moving house would probably be fatal to her. When various members of the family agreed to assist yet again, Polly told Tom that she was sure he would not find it difficult to manage his share and reminded him that Julia's comfort was the first consideration as it would in all probability be her last year. Frank, now working as a doctor in Oxford and taking an active role in assisting with his mother's dressings and her general medical care, also entered the fray. In a strongly worded letter to his father, he told Tom that Julia was a confirmed invalid, becoming more and more helpless, and would not live for several years as Tom appeared to believe:

The change in her condition since the beginning of the year has been very rapid & progressive. When cancer arrives at the condition in which hers is now it does not generally spare a patient many months. Of course her marvellous constitution & nervous energy must be taken into account, but this is likely to be of less effect in the future than it has been in the past in postponing that condition of a rapid growth of the tumour which is now unfortunately well established.

Moving house was an expensive business, and considering Julia's very precarious condition, any move taken on the assumption that she would live several years in the new house would be, he said, *a dismal farce*.

His son's words made an impact. Tom paid his share, Julia did not move, and Tom became more intent on pleasing her, rather than irritating or upsetting her. Knowing her love of gardens and flowers, he sent a fallen blossom from a camellia and some heliotrope. Julia, in turn, adopted a more gentle tone towards him and once more took to signing her letters as his affectionate wife. Writing was becoming more of an ordeal for her, particularly when her arm grew to the size of a child's body. On one occasion she described what this felt like and how temporary relief was obtained by inserting tubes into it to drain the excess fluid and blood:

> Yesterday was the day of the most appalling agony that I have yet had to bear & I write a few lines now in case I should not be able to write again or to anyone else. I had an unusually good night on Wednesday & up to about 10 o'clock I felt fairly well excepting that I felt weaker than usual. I then began to feel a good deal of pain in the bad arm & down that side of the back. This

went on increasing up 1.30 when Ethel got frightened & went to the hospital for Frank — he was amazed & alarmed at the state of things & after some deliberation he determined to put in two punctures. This he did, the first caused very little discharge but after the second the blood gushed out, & immediately coagulated into a jelly. The relief afforded was extraordinary & by 10 o'clock I was all but free from pain & very contrary to my expectations I had a very good night, & although terribly weak & in a good deal of pain which is only kept down by constant hypodermic injections of morphia.

By Easter the pain was excruciating and Julia's morphia dose was doubled.

Still she remained curious and concerned about others. It was the only way she knew to live. She comforted Polly, who was suffering from severe neuralgia and was anxious that she could not edit her novel. She encouraged Ethel to establish a life of her own — providing it was not, as Ethel had hoped, on the stage — to go to balls and dinners, to continue with her writing. She fretted about Frank, who, having completed medicine, still did not have a secure position and had fallen in love with the delightfully named, but somehow obscurely unacceptable, Miss Valentine. And she worried about Judy, who was pregnant and shortly to give birth a second time — her first baby had died at birth — and Julia, too ill to be with her daughter, could only wait for news. It came towards the end of June. Judy had given birth to a boy, and she and Leonard called him Julian Sorell Huxley. In an era when eldest sons were often named after their father or grandfathers, this was a singular honour to Julia.

Refusing to accept her declining strength, Julia continued to receive a steady stream of visitors through her door. Felicia Skene came to see her almost daily — she was one of the visitors Julia would never turn away — as did Mr Chavasse, the rector of St Peter-le-Bailey in Oxford. Julia had always liked his simple services. Her neighbours the Müllers and Charles Dodgson were also regular visitors. Benjamin Jowett called on her, too, and throughout the summer, people from beyond Oxford arrived, including her old friend from Ireland Edward Whately and her cousin Fanny. Even ravaged as she was, Julia's sense of humour did not desert her. When her neighbour Mrs de Brissay, the wife of the diocesan inspector of schools for the deanery of Oxford, burst into tears when she saw how ill she was, Julia was astonished. *I did not think that she cared that much whether I was alive or dead ...*

Her children came often, each in their own way giving comfort and providing her with a vital interest in living. Polly desperately wanted Julia to see her novel published, and Willy, who had read a draft of it, told Julia that she might look forward to finding herself the mother of a famous woman. Even Theodore, who, since the death of Arthur, had assumed the role of black sheep in the family, was there in spirit. A letter had arrived from him, telling Julia that her loving letters had been a great solace to him in his troubles. His life had become a shadow play of Tom's — he was in constant financial distress and now his short-lived marriage in New Zealand had broken down — and Julia felt his sense of hopelessness and the physical distance between them keenly. That, and the fact that she could provide no support for him.

Tom was one person who did not make his way to Oxford — instead, he visited his old Irish friend Josephine Benison. If Julia took offence, she did not reveal it. As summer morphed into autumn and then winter, she continued to send almost daily letters and parcels to him, and although these written conversations became increasingly punctuated by missing and scratched out words and blotches — the constant hypodermic injections of morphia she now required caused her to drop off to sleep with the pen in her hand — they were remarkably amiable. She offered sympathy when he became ill — wrap up properly and *take a glass of good stiff whisky & water when you go to bed* — and she even advised him on how he should negotiate his contracts and the fees he should seek.

Julia was no longer willing to vent any animosity. She wanted peace. She was preparing for her death. In fact, she wished for it, as she became more emaciated and weaker by the day. Her body was covered in eczema, and she needed oil to be applied several times a night to ease the pain. She felt *more & more incapable of doing anything either mental or bodily* and she was suffused with that *awful feeling, that of waking up to another day*, of the sun shining through a little, but not for her.

When, at the end of January 1888, Polly finally sent off the last corrections to her novel *Robert Elsmere*, Julia became extremely agitated. She was anxious about Tom's likely reaction to the book and the impact this would have on Polly. She had every reason to be concerned. In *Robert Elsmere* Polly had painted the world of religious division that had begun when Dr Arnold and Dr Newman became opponents in the 1830s, and one which was now, in the wake of Darwin's *On the Origin of Species*, engulfed in a confrontation between traditional orthodoxy and a new scepticism. In a classic tussle between love and conscience, Robert Elsmere, the young rector of Murewell, begins to doubt his own faith in the face of his work among the rural poor and the intellectual currents of his time. After much agonising he eventually turns his back on his traditional ministry and instead goes down the path of social activism, a path that leads to an estrangement from his wife, Catherine. It was a novelistic view of her own parents' struggle and the crisis in religion that had convulsed her family.

Tom did take umbrage at the novel, and Julia tried to blunt it by reminding him that Polly believed in God. It seemed to work, and he eventually conceded that *it was good that Polly should have her say, and make a clean breast, as she feels so strongly on what she writes about*, but he did hope that she might *return towards faith*.

If Tom did not recognise death was closing in on Julia — he talked of their having another pleasant summer together at Sea View — everyone else did. Her children now began taking turns to stay with her, and in a poignant note to his mother, Theodore told her that although he understood her death would be a release for her it would *be a terrible loss to us who are left behind*. One of his few champions would soon be gone, and he knew it. By the beginning of February in 1888, Charles Dodgson thought she was very near her end. They had a long talk covering more serious topics than they had ever discussed before. She told him her life had been lived and her faith was sufficient to have earned her God's mercy, and she summarised her understanding of the purpose of life by using the words from the prophet Micah, *to do justice, and love mercy, and walk humbly with thy God*. It was a text that resonated with her practical and intuitive nature.

On a very cold day towards the end of February 1888, as she lay on her bed watching the hundreds of blackbirds in her garden — poor birds, she thought, they *looked like little black demons on the snow* — Julia received the news that Lucy had given birth safely to another son, and that *Robert Elsmere* was finally published. On that same day, Frank wrote to his father in Dublin, telling him he should return as soon as he could. Fan Arnold travelled from Fox How, and although deeply shaken at the pain and suffering that made every movement agonising for Julia, she could only feel the deepest admiration for her spirit and courage and a great tenderness for her. Julia's favourite among Tom's sisters, Mary, also came, even though it meant leaving her own dying husband. And Matthew Arnold stayed overnight in Oxford in order to see her, writing to his daughter that Julia was *terribly wasted, one arm a yellow skeleton, the other monstrously swollen and discoloured; but her head and brow have still something fine and deer like about them. She liked my visit; I stayed more than an hour...* It caused him to write to Tom, saying that although Julia had wonderful vitality, the change in her since he had seen her last was very great, and that

> she seemed much distressed about the uncertainty of your coming; I can quite understand the difficulty of getting another man to take your lectures, unless the doctors absolutely summon you home, but I think, if you will allow me to say so, I would be careful not to hold out a prospect of your coming on this or that day, and then, changing your plans, to put off your return; as these changes worry an invalid and the mind goes on disturbing itself with them.

Tom finally arrived in Oxford, where he found Julia contemplating death with a steady calmness and acceptance. She had forgiven him. She wanted love and she wanted comfort. At night, when she had difficulty settling — she dreaded its length and darkness — she asked Tom to read psalms to her. It was a singular service he could and did perform for her. Polly found it extraordinary how Julia's feeling for Tom, which in spite of everything, had always been the most absorbingly fundamental thing in her, came out during this period.

At the beginning of April, she asked for her children. In the quiet of this house where death was hovering, she began her final farewells. After Dr Symonds visited her, she had five minutes alone with Tom. She gave him her wedding ring and, as he recalled afterwards, *she spoke in a lovely humble way of not having been as good a wife to me as she should have been.* She then farewelled her children and asked that Theodore, *poor darling*, be told that one of her last thoughts was for him. She said goodbye to Nurse Gooch, who had been with her for more than a year, and kissed her, and then asked to see the servants, Eliza and Lavinia, who, weeping, came up to her bed and kissed her. When Gussie arrived with her daughter Katie, Julia could no longer swallow and spoke rarely.

The following morning, the seventh of April, when Polly went in to sit with Julia, the nurse told her to call the others. They came at once:

> We asked her if she knew us, but she was past speech or recognition, and at 6.55 after a few gently labored breaths, with a meekness & piteousness of expression quite indescribable, she breathed her last. No one could see I think a more childlike rendering up of the soul.

Julia was sixty-one years old. Despite all the storms and friction, Polly said, Julia's nature had been sustained by love, and more particularly, her love for Tom. Her sister Judy agreed. Julia was, she said, *all love*, the basis of her character an *intense affectionateness*. She simply loved to love and be loved.

Julia's memorial service was held in Oxford a few days after her death, after which her family accompanied her body to Fox How where she was buried. Lucy's husband, the Reverend Carus Selwyn, gave the funeral address.

20

Aftermath

Despite her long, slow decline, Tom was completely unprepared for Julia's death. He was unprepared for the desolation her children and her friends felt, and he was unprepared for his own grief. He began to recast their relationship immediately, telling his sister Fan that the radiance had gone out of life and that living in Dublin without the hope of returning to Julia was far more dreadful than he had ever imagined. It was only now that she was gone that he knew just how much his spirit and being were linked and interwoven in hers. He told his old Tasmanian friend General Thomas Collinson, who had tried to dissuade him from marrying Julia, that he thanked God with all his heart for having given Julia to him, and he to Julia, and although Collinson had been right — he and Julia were unsuited to one another — Julia had so subjugated him by her beauty, he belonged much more to her than to himself, and it had been impossible for him to take Collinson's advice not to marry her.

In the verse he wrote about Julia for their children, Tom continued to recast his relationship with her. He had an intense desire, he said, that all the world should know how beautiful, how original, how valiant Julia was, and although she had been so little prepared by education to meet what she had to suffer, she had met it nobly and victoriously. Tom went so far as to claim that his life's single achievement was that his and Julia's *true love burn'd clear to the last*, this being despite the sorrow caused when *loving hearts cannot accord! When that which by one is deem'd holy, By the other is scorn'd and abhorred*. He wrote of Julia's fidelity, which he believed was stronger than reason, of her feeling, which was more potent than thought, and of the simplicity, courage, and kindness with which she bore her illness. She was, he said, a *true mother, true wife, and true friend*, ennobled by pain, exhaustion, and grief. Tom had always romanticised their life together, and when it was at its worst, he was at his most romantic. His children's reactions to his poetry are not recorded.

After burying Julia and writing his verse, Tom sold the furniture in Oxford and returned to Dublin with Ethel as soon as he could. When, some ten months later, he was re-elected a fellow at the Catholic University of Ireland, he no longer thought of returning to live in England. He would see his days out in Dublin, where he taught alongside poet and fellow Catholic convert Gerard Manley Hopkins — also received into the Catholic Church by John Henry Newman in Birmingham — and would number among his pupils the novelist James Joyce, who attended the University College from 1898 to 1902. Tom had another reason for staying in Ireland. Only a year after Julia's death, he had asked Josephine Benison to marry him, and she had accepted.

Months after his proposal, Tom reluctantly told Polly of his plans:

> I am afraid you will not like what I am going to tell you, but yet I think you will become reconciled to it after

a time. It is that I am going to marry again, not this year, but early in next. The person, as you would probably guess, is Josephine Benison.

He was anxious that she understood that despite his wish to marry Josephine, Julia *was, and remains, the wife of my youth, the wife of my manhood; and, as I have told Josephine, I shall be a mourner for her as long as I live.* And, almost to emphasise this point, he described Josephine as plain, *a queer honest Hibernian plainness*, but one that he had grown accustomed to. Josephine was, he argued, the perfect companion for his old age and one with whom he was in complete sympathy, something that he argued a man might rationally desire, *and without blame accomplish.*

To further demonstrate that his second marriage was practical rather than passionate, Tom emphasised that it would not have even been necessary had either Ethel or Polly been able to look after him as he grew old, but this had proved impossible. Polly was already married, and Ethel, who had gone to live with Tom after Julia's death, had quickly returned to Polly's in London, unhappy with being housewife to her father and unhappy living in Dublin. And as a final demonstration of his practicality, Tom told Polly that his remarriage would not involve any financial strain on him, as Josephine had £100 a year of her own. It is a remarkable letter, as much for what it expresses as what it does not. If there are none of the romantic flourishes of Tom the suitor, there is in plain sight his views about women and their place, views that Julia had found oppressive and had reared her daughters to reject.

Polly was gracious if cool in her response to Tom's news, and although she had expected his announcement and had nothing but sympathy and affection to give him with regard to it, she felt that to all grown-up children, *a father's second marriage must always carry with it something infinitely sad and moving.* She recognised that he had many needs that his children could not supply, however much they might wish to, and she rejoiced that he would find in Miss Benison the fundamental sympathy that he wanted. His children would be grateful to her if she made his life easier and happier, as would her *darling mother! — but neither you nor we can ever forget her — and if she knows, she no more than your children will begrudge you the help and tendance of one who understands and cares for you.*

Polly may have been expecting Tom's announcement, but she was startled when he married Josephine before the second anniversary of Julia's death had passed. It was a sentiment shared by all his children. The rift of indifference was widening between father and children, and it manifested itself further when, having refused to join his children for a Christmas hosted by Lucy at Uppingham, he made the trip from Dublin to Birmingham to attend Cardinal Newman's funeral in August 1890. No wonder, then, he felt like *Ulysses returning to Ithaca* when he arrived in Rugby for a commemorative service for Dr Arnold in June 1892. He believed that none of his children or grandchildren cared a rush for what he thought, and although he knew that it was in a great measure his own fault, it was, he acknowledged, a wretched situation. It struck him then how bewildered he was by the general ineffectiveness and unproductiveness of all that he had *been, said, and done.* But if Tom's own family had grown inattentive or even dismissive of him, Josephine's family liked him. They liked him for his kindness and for never allowing little things to worry him.

Tom had never been one to let big things worry him, either, although his refusal to have the last Christmas with his children before his remarriage did come to haunt him. It was the last time that all his daughters were together. Less than two years later, in 1894, Lucy Selwyn, his second daughter and mother to seven children, died suddenly from a blood clot in her brain at the age of thirty-six. She was buried beside Julia. Tom, unwell, did not attend his daughter's funeral, but Polly, Willy, Judy, Frank, and Ethel were there, with Lucy's husband, Carus, to bury her. Fan told Tom that his five children *looked such a remarkable band of brothers & sisters*. After they had buried their sister, Julia's children covered their mother's grave with white eucharises and chrysanthemums.

Julia had once said that if Tom remarried after her death he would perhaps realise his ideal of married life, and he did. His life with Josephine was content, if not passionate. She was noted for her charm, and he for his shyness. His days were spent researching and writing, and after dinner, he smoked his pipe while Josephine read his chosen book to him or darned his shirts and stockings. He was able to practise his religion unhindered. It was an ideal relationship for Tom — love with no loss of independence nor the burden of domestic responsibility. Josephine was a companion for his declining life — *a woman with whom on all sorts of subjects — religion first of all — I am in complete sympathy*. She was neither rebellious nor vehement. She did not throw stones or smash glass. She was keen to know and understand Tom's inner world, unlike Julia, who had always been uncomfortable at what she might find there. Josephine was, quite simply, in awe of him, and hoped that he would care for her and that she would *grow necessary* to him.

In November 1900, following the publication of his memoir *Passages in a Wandering Life* — a memoir which rarely reflected on his personal life — Tom became very ill with bronchitis. Polly was called to Dublin and when she reported back to her siblings that *our dear father is just fading away very peacefully and steadily,* Frank, Judy, and Ethel made their way to Dublin to farewell him. Willy was too ill to travel. Tom died on 12 November 1900 just short of his seventy-seventh birthday. He was buried in Ireland — his children did not wish to make his grave in England — and a tablet to his memory was placed in Newman's university church on St Stephen's Green with the words *Domine, Deus meus, in Te speravi.* O Lord, my God, in thee have I put my hope.

Following Tom's death, Josephine returned to charity work and to housekeeping for various members of her family. She died at Slieve Russell in 1919. She had always felt that living with Tom was a great privilege, and that *life beside him was so beautiful, only those who came into close contact could realize the tenderness and unselfishness of his character.*

Only weeks after Julia's death, Polly's novel *Robert Elsmere* was already on its way to making her a literary phenomenon in England. It would sell over one million copies and was published in many foreign languages, but Polly continued to regret bitterly that Julia had not lived long enough to share in the book's success. She regretted, too, the injustice of her mother's hard life, and although she had been unable to remedy that, she was able to bind Julia to her literary endeavours and to her success when she dedicated her next book, *The History of David Grieve,* published in 1892, to *the dear memory of my mother.* On seeing the dedication, Benjamin Jowett wrote to Polly immediately telling her how glad he was about it and saying that he hoped someone would tell Julia of it, adding that he *had a great respect for her. She told me when I last saw her that you had been the best of daughters to her.*

Polly continued to write popular books on significant social and religious issues and, in 1898, her most praised book, *Helbeck of Bannisdale*, was published. The novel, about the dilemma of passionate lovers who differ over religion, not only confronted again the deep division that had engulfed her parents' lives, but also explored the impact of women's lack of education and independence, and men's need to control them, two of the more destructive threads in Julia's life with Tom. Helbeck, a Catholic, and Laura, the daughter of a freethinking academic, fall in love, but when, despite her love for him, Laura cannot give up her own soul, cannot submit to Helbeck's need to convert her, their relationship becomes a battle to the death. With no education, no philosophical training to counter his religious conviction, Laura suicides. Keen that her father should approve the novel, but with Julia no longer there to protect her from his anger, Polly changed various aspects of her manuscript to make the Catholicism more appealing to him.

Between writing novels and raising children, Polly continued her involvement in women's education and expanded this interest to adult education for working men, to pre-school education, and to education for disabled children. She became the guiding spirit behind the establishment of the Passmore Edwards Settlement in Bloomsbury — which still exists today as the Mary Ward Centre — a place where working-class men and women were provided with adult education, and where planned day-care was available for their children. Her charitable work, like her novels, was born out of empathy for women's vulnerability, particularly as mothers. Strangely, in the context of her push for education, particularly women's education, Polly was one of the founding members of the Women's National Anti-Suffrage League in 1908. She believed that having the vote would not change women's lives. Only education could do that. Polly died in 1920.

Willy lived only four years beyond his father, dying in 1904. After he and Henrietta moved to Manchester in 1879 to take up his position with the *Manchester Guardian*, they constructed a content, childless life. Apart from his journalism, he dedicated himself to poetry (particularly Keats), art (he helped establish the Manchester School of Art), Roman history, and foreign contemporary literature. He published various essays and reviews, and his *Studies of Roman Imperialism* was published posthumously in 1906. His declining health — he had a painful, degenerative disease known as locomotor ataxia — forced his resignation from the *Manchester Guardian* in 1898, and in the following year, he and Henrietta moved to London, where they were cared for by Polly until his death in 1904. He was buried in Henrietta's family plot at Little Shelford, near Cambridge.

Theodore remained in New Zealand, and although Julia had been forever optimistic about his chances, he never fulfilled his mother's hopes for him. After divorcing his first wife, he remarried, and eventually bought some land at Hokianga, where he managed to survive with constant financial help from Polly.

Julia's youngest son, Frank, fared better. At her death, he had already been elected to a position at the Radcliffe Infirmary in Oxford and Julia was thankful that she had lived long enough to see this. After his marriage, in 1892, to Annie Reed Wilkinson — not Miss Valentine — he lost thousands of borrowed pounds in a calamitous business venture, before he and Annie moved to Manchester, where Willy and Henrietta lived. There, Frank practised as a doctor, and he and Annie raised their children.

Judy, like Polly, combined motherhood with a working career. She, too, was passionate about women's education, and in 1902 she established Prior's Field, a girls' school in Surrey. Only six years later, she was tragically struck down by cancer. Judy and

Leonard had four children, two of whom became widely known — Aldous Huxley as a novelist and philosopher, and Julian Huxley, Julia's namesake, as a renowned scientist and the first director-general of UNESCO.

When Julia's youngest daughter, Ethel, fled her role as housekeeper to Tom in Dublin, she returned to London where she joined the suffragette movement and forged a career as a literary critic and essayist, writing for the *Manchester Guardian* and *The Spectator* among others. She also carved out a career as a lecturer, her subjects ranging from the progress of women in Europe to the religious novel. Unlike her sisters, she neither married nor had children. She died in 1930.

Since her death, the life of Julia Sorell Arnold has been cast into a particular narrative form, shaped by the various obituaries, memoirs, and biographies written about her husband. In these, Tom has been portrayed as a cultivated scholar, a man of letters, whose gentle, principled nature, exquisite old-fashioned courtesy, high-minded devotion to what he thought right, and quixotic disinterest in getting on in the world, made him greatly loved. In this narrative, the one rash and foolhardy decision Tom Arnold made was to marry the beautiful, charming, passionate Julia Sorell. When Tom's attempt to change her wilful nature failed, he valiantly ignored her immoderation and prejudice, just as he ignored her nagging, her financial extravagance, and her deficiencies as a housekeeper — deficiencies that inevitably forced the family into poverty — and remained utterly devoted to her until her death.

In this account of the gentle, forbearing, scholarly Tom and his wild, profligate wife, there is no glimpse of the Julia who, in the face of her own mother's abandonment, forged close and loving relationships with her father, with her sisters and brothers, with her own children. There is no portrait of the Julia who was admired and befriended by so many, including accomplished, trailblazing women like Mary Louisa Whately and Felicia Skene, or intellectual and literary men such as Benjamin Jowett and Charles Dodgson. There is no sight of the Julia who refused to adhere to the Victorian ideal of a silent woman, of the Julia who grappled with the word 'independence' and who was resolute that her daughters should understand it. Nor is there any recognition of the Julia who stubbornly resisted the conventional understanding of marriage to retain control of her own soul.

Where is this Julia? Why has she remained hidden in the archive, and how many other unnamed women sit alongside her, women whose lives may have forged memorable fiction, but are deemed unworthy of biography, obscure women *who lived faithfully a hidden life, and rest in unvisited tombs*, and whose acts of resistance have paved the way for those who follow? If their voices remain opaque, their presence elusive, it is an essential part of their struggle. And ours.

Acknowledgements

I first met and was intrigued by Julia Sorell, a woman who refused to remain silent, while I was a student in the biography program at Monash University. Thank you, Julia, for an extraordinary journey in pursuit of your story. Monash also gave me three wonderful teachers in Professor Alistair Thomson, Bill Garner, and Ruth Morgan, and the generous administrative help of Melva Renshaw.

This biography would not have been possible without the support given by the Hazel Rowley Literary Fellowship, which was established by the great biographer's family and friends, to commemorate her life and writing. In particular I would like to thank Della Rowley, Lynn Buchanan, and Irene Tomaszewski, who have over the years provided me with much needed encouragement and advice and who led me to literary agent John Timlin, with whom every interaction has been informative and humorous.

John in turn, led me to Henry Rosenbloom's wonderful publishing house, Scribe, where he and his Associate Publisher Marika Webb-Pullman demonstrated great bravery in agreeing to publish the life of an ordinary, unknown woman, and where each person I have encountered — Chris Black, Jadan Carroll, Allison Colpoys, Sarina Gale, Caitlin Lawless, Kevin O'Brien, and Mick Pilkington — has been engaging, knowledgeable, and supportive. I must single out the best editor a writer could possibly have in Anna Thwaites, whose intelligence, care, and laughter have made me want to write many more books for the pure pleasure of being edited by her. Thank you, Anna.

I have sought help from many people on this journey, not least among them the staff at the various institutions where documents and images were to be found, including Bethany Hamblen, Amy Boylan, and Anna Sander, who helped me access the papers of Thomas (Tom) Arnold (1823–1900) held at the Balliol College Historic Collections, University of Oxford, and I am grateful to the Master and Fellows of Balliol College for their kind permission to reproduce excerpts from these letters. While all attempts were made to contact the donor of the papers, Mrs Janet Davies, sadly we did not succeed. I am grateful also to Tanya Kato and Sara Chetney from the Special Collections at The Claremont Colleges Library in California; to Tony Marshall and Annaliese Claydon from Tasmanian Archives and Heritage; to Jane Stewart, Jacqui Ward, and Sue Backhouse from the Tasmanian Museum and Art Gallery in Hobart; to Ashleigh Whatling and Bridget Arkless at the Queen Victoria Museum and Art Gallery in Launceston; to my friends Peter and Ruth McMullin for sending me to Joanna Gilmore, who curated the wonderful 'Elegance in Exile' exhibition at the National Portrait Gallery in Canberra, thereby bringing me face to face with many of the characters wandering in and out of Julia's story; to Susie Shears, Norm Turnross, and my sister Anne Hoban, at the Baillieu Library at Melbourne University, who helped find and scan some of the more esoteric documents required; and to Sharon Sutton and Gillian Whelan from the Digital Collections at The Library of Trinity College Dublin, Lucinda Walker from Historic England, Haley Drolet at Wycliffe Hall in Oxford, and Deborah Walsh and Sue Osman at the Armitt Museum and Library at Ambleside, all of whom helped locate specific images for the book.

Other people who have provided invaluable assistance on this journey include the writers and academics Alison Alexander and Lucy Frost, whose work has been an inspiration to me, and whose words led me to Toni Sherwood, who was remarkably generous in giving me a full transcription of all Annie Baxter's writing in Van Diemen's Land, which she had produced as part of her PhD research. Others in Tasmania, wonderfully generous in giving their time and energy, were Jon Flach, Ian Broinowski, who first alerted me to Julia's friendship with Charles Dodgson, and Reg Watson, who was indefatigable in his pursuit of sources and images for me. From further afield, Edward Wakeling, Jon Lindseth, and Mark Richards were all wonderfully generous in providing images and information about Charles Dodgson's photographs of Julia and her daughters, as was writer Janie Hampton from the Oxford-based blog *The History Girls*, who provided me with background on Julia's friend Felicia Skene.

On a more personal level, many people have been directly or indirectly involved in the making of this book: my father, Kevin Hoban, who instilled in me a great love of history and story; Christine Bayly, who introduced me to Tasmania and shared her Tasmanian connections and stories with me; Meg Mitchell and Brian Parkinson, who not only introduced me to knowledgeable Tasmanians, but who also hosted me on numerous trips to Hobart and showed me many of the sites in Julia's story; Martin Clark and Sophie Rigney, who spent several days researching documents in London; Marg McCaffrey and Jan Cossar, who prompted me to apply for the Hazel Rowley Fellowship; artist Julie Irving, who shared with me some wonderful insights into portraiture in painting, which helped me in ways I could not have foreseen; James McCaughey, William Henderson, and Jonah Jones, who encouraged me to write, just write; Hilary Maddocks, Hilary Ericksen, Rosie Clark, Andrew Funston, Pru Black, David Wilks, Elizabeth Keyishian, Chris Brewer, Sarah Riordan, Helen Nevin, Michael Heyward, Penny Hueston, Linda Michael, Tiziana Mantynen, and Rosemary Barker, who have either encouraged, advised or assisted me on this wild ride; the women in my book groups who have listened with such compassion and interest to the travails (mostly) and triumphs (rarely) of writing and publishing; the wonderful bibliophiles who work at Avenue Bookstore in Albert Park, who continue to share the pleasures of reading with me, and more particularly, Kristin Otto, who has provided me with excellent advice and friendship; Giulia Giannini McGauran for her photographic skill and her laughter; Bernadette Maher, who closely read and critiqued my writing with care and enthusiasm and a clarity that I will forever respect and admire; and Ellen Koshland, with whom I began my writing career and whose intelligence and poetic sensibility helped me so much in shaping and writing this book.

To Robert Tuck, Nikolas Pefanis, and Emma Barnett — thank you. I will treasure your words of love and encouragement and your pleasure (and relief) in seeing this journey reach its destination.

List of Photographs and Illustrations

Julia Sorell. Watercolour portrait by Thomas Griffiths Wainewright, c. 1846. Collection: Tasmanian Museum and Art Gallery, Hobart.

Tom Arnold. Reproduced with the permission of the Tasmanian Archive and Heritage Office.

Tom and Julia's house in New Town. Henry Gritten, *The main road New Town with the coach Perseverance 1857*, oil on canvas. Collection of the Queen Victoria Museum & Art Gallery, Launceston. QVM: 1949:FP:0440

Aurora Raby. Artwork by W.P. Frith, A.R.A, in *Heath's Book of Beauty, 1847*, edited by the Countess of Blessington.

Amy Robsart. Engraved by W.H. Mote, drawn by J. Hayter. Antiqua Print Gallery/Alamy Stock Photo

William Sorell. A family photograph from Jane Sorell's Governor, William & Julia Sorell, reproduced with the permission of the Flach family.

Mrs Arnold at Fox How. Photographed by M. Bowness, from the Arnold family correspondence and miscellanea IE TCD MS 5102, Trinity College Dublin, reproduced with kind permission of The Board of Trinity College Dublin.

Dr Thomas Arnold of Rugby. H. Cousins/Public Domain

John Henry Newman. Adolphe Beau/Public Domain

Fox How, by Herbert Bell c. 1890. Courtesy of the Armitt Trust, Ambleside

Laleham, now part of Wycliffe Hall and Lollard Theological College, Banbury Road, Oxford. Reproduced by permission of Historic England Archive.

Charles Dodgson (Lewis Carroll). Oscar Gustave Rejlander/Public Domain

Benjamin Jowett. Elliott & Fry/Public Domain

Judy & Ethel Arnold. Photograph by Charles Dodgson, from the Jon A. Lindseth Collection of C.L. Dodgson and Lewis Carroll, by permission.

Polly (Mrs Humphry Ward). Photograph by Charles Dodgson, from the Edward Wakeling Collection, by permission.

Willy Arnold. Image sourced from Mrs Humphry Ward & C.E. Montague, *William Arnold: journalist and historian*, 1907.

Theodore Arnold from the Balliol College Historic Collections, Papers of Thomas (Tom) Arnold (1823–1900), reproduced by kind permission of the Master and Fellows of Balliol College.

Julia (Judy) Huxley with her son Aldous, 1898. This photograph is part of the Prior's Field School archive, and is reproduced with kind permission.

Ethel Arnold. This photograph is taken from an advertising brochure announcing Ethel Arnold's 1910 lecture tour of the United States.

Julia Sorell Arnold. Photograph by Charles Dodgson, Christ Church Studio, Oxford, 26 June 1875, from the Edward Wakeling Collection, by permission.

Bibliography

Archives

Papers of Thomas (Tom) Arnold (1823–1900), Balliol College Archive and Manuscripts, Oxford

Correspondence, literary MSS and papers of Mary Augusta Ward (1851–1920), Special Collections of The Claremont Colleges Library, Claremont

Books and Articles

Alexander, Alison, *The Ambitions of Jane Franklin: Victorian lady adventurer*, Allen & Unwin, Sydney, 2013.

Alexander, Alison, 'Gender', *Tasmanian Essays*, Centre for Tasmanian Historical Studies, Hobart, 2006.

Alexander, Alison, *Governors' Ladies: the wives and mistresses of Van Diemen's Land governors*, Tasmanian Historical Research Association, Sandy Bay, 1987.

Alexander, Alison, *Obliged to Submit: wives and mistresses of colonial governors*, Montpelier Press, Sandy Bay, 1999.

Altholz, Josef L., 'A Note on the English Catholic Reaction to the Mortara Case', *Jewish Social Studies*, vol. 23, no. 2, April 1961, Indiana University Press.

Anderson, Tony, 'Thomas Wainewright', *Dictionary of Australian Artists Online*, <www.daao.org.au/main/read/6382>.

Arnold, Ethel M., 'Reminiscences of Lewis Carroll', *The Windsor Magazine: an illustrated monthly for men and women*, vol. 71, December 1929–May 1930, Ward, Lock & Co Limited, London & Melbourne, 1930.

Arnold, Ethel M., 'Social Life in Oxford', *Harpers New Monthly*, July 1890.

Arnold, Mary, 'The Poem of the Cid', *Macmillan's Magazine*, 24 October 1871.

Arnold, Matthew, *The Letters of Matthew Arnold*, ed. Cecil Y. Lang, University Press of Virginia, Charlottesville, 1996–2000.

Arnold, Matthew, 'Rugby Chapel', November 1867 in *The Poetical Works of Matthew Arnold*, Thomas Y. Crowell & Company, New York, 1897.

Arnold, Thomas, 'Account of Julia Sorell Arnold's Last Illness', May 1887–7 April 1888, Balliol College Archives and Manuscripts.

Arnold, Thomas, 'The Oxford Malignants and Dr Hampden', *Edinburgh Review*, vol. 63, April–July 1836.

Arnold, Thomas, *Passages in a Wandering Life*, E. Arnold, London, 1900.

Arnold, Thomas, 'A Memoir Written by Thomas Arnold After Julia Arnold's Death and Intended for His Children', dated Dublin, 17 Feb 1889, Balliol College Archives and Manuscripts.

Arnold, William, *Oakfield or Fellowship in the East*, Leicester University Press, New York, 1973, (1853).

Arnold, William Thomas, *Studies of Roman Imperialism*, with an introduction by Mary Humphry Ward & Charles Montague, Manchester University Press, 1907.

Arnold, William Thomas, 'Thomas Arnold the Younger', *The Century Magazine*, vol. 66, The Century Co., New York, Macmillan & Co. Ltd, London, May–Oct 1903.

Baker, A.D., *The Life and Times of Sir Richard Dry*, Oldham, Beddome & Meredith Pty Ltd, Hobart, 1951.

Barrett, W.R., 'Francis Russell Nixon', in *Australian Dictionary of Biography Online Edition* at <adbonline.anu.edu.au/biogs/A020252b.htm>.

Barry, William, 'The Oxford Movement (1833–1845)', *The Catholic Encyclopaedia*, vol. 11, Robert Appleton Company, New York, 1911, accessed at <www.newadvent.org/cathen/11370a.htm>.

Battiscombe, Georgina, *Reluctant Pioneer: the life of Elizabeth Wordsworth*, Constable, London, 1978.

Bebbington, D.W., review of *Anatomy of a Controversy: the debate over essays and reviews, 1860–1864* by Josef L. Altholz, *Victorian Periodicals Review*, vol. 28, no. 2, Summer, 1995.

Bedford, Sybille, in Shusha Guppy, 'An Interview', *The Paris Review*, no. 126, Spring, 1993.

Bergonzi, Bernard, *A Victorian Wanderer: the life of Thomas Arnold the Younger*, Oxford University Press, Oxford, 2003.

Bertram, James, ed., *Letters of Thomas Arnold the Younger 1850–1900*, Oxford University Press, London & Wellington, 1979.

James Bertram, ed., *New Zealand Letters of Thomas Arnold the Younger with Further Letters from Van Diemen's Land and Letters of Arthur Hugh Clough 1847–1851*, Oxford University Press, London & Wellington, 1966.

Bock, Carol A., 'Charlotte Brontë: 1816–1855', Poetry Foundation at <www.poetryfoundation.org/bio/charlotte-bronte>.

Bolger, Peter, *Hobart Town*, Australian National University Press, Canberra, 1973.

Boughton, Gillian Elisabeth, *The Juvenilia of Mrs Humphry Ward (1851–1920): a diplomatic edition of six previously unpublished narratives derived from original manuscript sources*, Durham theses, Durham University, 1995.

Boyce, James, *Van Diemen's Land*, Black Inc., Melbourne, 2008.

Boyce, Peter, 'Britishness', *The Companion to Tasmanian History*, Centre for Tasmanian Historical Studies, 2006.

Boyes, G.T.W.B., *Extracts from the Journal of G.T.W.B. Boyes, Colonial Auditor, December 10th 1829–July 31st 1853*, ed. J.W. Beattie, unpublished typescript, Allport Library, State Library of Tasmania.

Briggs, Asa, *Victorian Cities*, Pelican Books, 1968.

Brittain, Vera, *The Women at Oxford: a fragment of history*, Macmillan, New York, 1960.

Brontë, Charlotte, *Villette*, Harper Press, London, 2011 (1853).

Brown, Rosemary, *Madge's People: in the island of Tasmania and beyond*, Berriedale Trading, Hobart, 2004.

Burney, Frances, *Journals and Letters*, selected with an introduction by Peter Sabor and Lars E. Troide, Penguin, New York, 2001.

Burritt, Elihu, *Walks in the Black Country*, S. Low, Son, and Marsden, London, 1868.

Button, Henry, *Flotsam and Jetsam: floating fragments of life in England and Tasmania: an autobiographical sketch with an outline of the introduction of responsible government*, A.W. Birchall & Sons, Launceston; J. Walch & Sons, Hobart; Simpkin, Marshall, & Co., Ltd., London, 1909.

Chadwick, Owen, *The Victorian Church*, SCM Press, London, 1966.

Chapman, Peter, ed., *The Diaries and Letters of G.T.W.B. Boyes*, vol. 1, 1820–1832, Oxford University Press, Melbourne, 1985.

Chapman, Peter, 'G.T.W.B. Boyes and Australia: the pursuit of a vision?' *Papers & Proceedings: Tasmania Historical Research Association*, vol. 33, no. 3, 1976.

Clark, Christopher & Wolfram Kaiser, eds, *Culture Wars: secular-Catholic conflict in nineteenth-century Europe*, Cambridge University Press, Cambridge, 2003.

Clark, Ronald W., *The Huxleys*, Heinemann, London, 1968.

Cohen, Morton N., ed., *The Letters of Lewis Carroll*, in 2 vols, vol. 1, Oxford University Press, New York, 1979.

Conway, Jill Ker, *The Road from Coorain*, William Heinemann, Australia, 1993.

Courtney, Janet E., *Recollected in Tranquillity*, William Heinemann, London, 1926.

Courtney, Janet E., *The Women of My Time*, Lovat Dickson Limited, London, 1934.

Creighton, Louise, *Life and Letters of Mandell Creighton, Sometime Bishop of London*, vol. 1, Longmans, Green and Co., London, 1904.

Crossland, R., 'Wainewright: the Tasmanian portraits', *Tasmanian Historical Research Association Papers and Proceedings*, vol. 2, no. 5, August 1953.

Daly, Mary E., *Dublin: the deposed capital; a social and economic history 1860–1914*, Cork University Press, Cork, 1984.

Daly, Mary E., 'Dublin Life', in Tom Kennedy, ed., *Victorian Dublin*, Albertine Kennedy Publishing with Dublin Arts Festival, 1980.

Dessain, Charles Stephen, et al., eds, *The Letters and Diaries of John Henry Newman*, 32 vols, Oxford & London, 1961–2008.

Dodgson, E.O., 'Notes on Nos. 56, 58, 60, 62 and 64 Banbury Road' in *Oxoniensia*, vol. 32, 1967, accessed at <http://oxoniensia.org/volumes/1967/dodgson.pdf>.

Dwyer, Philip, 'Boney and his Balcombe girl', Spectrum, *The Age*, Saturday 14 November 2015, p. 26

Edwards, Paul Bathurst, 'Anthony Fenn Kemp: a new appraisal', *Tasmanian Ancestry*, vol. 23, no. 4, March 2003, pp. 215–37.

Edwards, Paul Bathurst, *Of Yesteryear and Nowadays: my children's family history*, Hawley Beach, Tasmania, 1995.

Eliot, George, *Middlemarch*, Penguin, New York and Harmondsworth, 1965.

Elkin, Susan, 'Travels and Travails of a Troubled Literary Man: a review of *A Victorian Wanderer: the life of Thomas Arnold the Younger*, Bernard Bergonzi', *The Independent*, Wednesday 20 August 2003.

Fenton, James, *A History of Tasmania from Its Discovery in 1642 to the Present Time*, J. Walch & Sons, Hobart, 1884.

Fitzpatrick, K., 'Mr Gladstone and the Governor: the recall of Sir John Eardley-Wilmot from Van Diemen's Land', *Historical Studies, Australia and New Zealand*, vol. 1, no. 1, April 1940–Oct 1941.

Flanders, Judith, *A Circle of Sisters: Alice Kipling, Georgiana Burne-Jones, Agnes Poynter and Louisa Baldwin*, Penguin Books, 2002.

Fletcher, Margaret, *O, Call Back Yesterday*, The Old Hall Press, Leeds, 2000 (1939).

Flood, Alison, 'Plinth Commemorates Huxley-Wilberforce Evolution Debate', *The Guardian*, 10 September 2010.

Frost, Lucy, *A Face in the Glass: the journal and life of Annie Baxter Dawbin*, William Heinemann Australia, Port Melbourne, 1992.

Gaskell, Elizabeth, *The Life of Charlotte Brontë*, with an introduction and notes by C.K. Shorter, Harper & Brothers, New York & London, 1900.

Gilchrist, Cate, '"The Victim of his own Temerity"?: silence, scandal and the recall of Sir John Eardley-Wilmot', at <http://www.api-network.com/main/pdf/scholars/jas84_gilchrist.pdf>.

Gilmour, Joanna, *Elegance in Exile: portrait drawings from colonial Australia*, Canberra National Portrait Gallery, 2012.

'A Grandmother's Tales', *Macmillan's Magazine*, 1898, accessed at <archive.org/stream/macmillansmagaz47grovgoog#page/n446/mode/2up/search/a+grandmother's+tales>.

Grant of Rothiemurchus, Elizabeth, *The Highland Lady in Dublin 1851–1856*, edited by Patricia Pelly & Andrew Tod, New Island Books, Dublin, 2005.

Graves, Kathleen E., *Exile: a tale of old Tasmania*, William Earl & Company, Ltd, Bournemouth & London, 1947.

Green, Roger Lancelyn, ed., *The Diaries of Lewis Carroll*, vol. 2, Cassell & Company Ltd, London, 1953.

Green, Vivian, *Love in a Cool Climate: the letters of Mark Pattison and Meta Bradley, 1879–1884*, Clarendon Press, Oxford, 1985.

A Hand-book for Travellers on the Continent: being a guide through Holland, Belgium, Prussia, and Northern Germany, and along the Rhine, from Holland to Switzerland, 2nd edn, John Murray and Son, London, 1838, accessed at <archive.org/stream/ahandbookfortra20firgoo#page/n3/mode/2up>.

Heath's Book of Beauty, 1847, Longman, Rees, Orme, Brown, Green & Longman, 1847.

Heilbrun, Carolyn G., *Writing a Woman's Life*, The Women's Press, London, 1989.

Hinchcliffe, Tanis, *North Oxford*, Yale University Press, New Haven & London, 1992.

Hoe, Susanna, *Tasmania: women, history, books and places*, HOLO Books, The Arbitration Press, Oxford, 2010.

Howell, P.A., 'Thomas Arnold the Younger in Van Diemen's Land', *Tasmanian Historical Research Association*, 1964.

Hughes, Kathryn, *The Short Life & Long Times of Mrs Beeton*, Harper Perennial, New York, 2006.

Hulse, Michael, 'Introduction' in Johann Wolfgang von Goethe, *The Sorrows of Young Werther*, Penguin Classics, 1989.

Huxley, Julian, *Memories I*, Allen & Unwin, Sydney, 1970.

Huxley, Julian, *Aldous Huxley 1894–1963: a memorial volume*, Chatto & Windus, London, 1965.

Jones, Enid Huws, *Mrs Humphry Ward*, Heinemann, London, 1973.

Jones, Tod E., *The Broad Church: a biography of a movement*, Lexington Books, Lanham, 2003.

Kemp, M.C. & T.B. Kemp, 'Captain Anthony Fenn Kemp', *Journal of the Royal Australian Historical Society*, vol. 51, 1965.

Lancaster, G.B. [Edith Joan Lyttleton], *Pageant*, Endeavour Press, Sydney, 1933.

Lepore, Jill, *Book of Ages*, Alfred A. Knopf, New York, 2013.

Lispector, Clarice, 'Jimmy and I', *The Complete Short Stories of Clarice Lispector*, trans. Katrina Dodson, New Directions Press, New York, 2015.

Loring, Chris, *Compelled to Tiers: the gripping account of an escaped convict's survival amidst the wilderness of 19th-century Tasmania*, Regal Press, Launceston, 1996.

Macaulay, Rose, *Told by an Idiot*, Virago Press, London, 1983.

MacCarthy, Fiona, *The Last Pre-Raphaelite: Edward Burne-Jones and the Victorian imagination*, Faber and Faber, London, 2011.

Mackaness, George, ed., *Recollections of Life in Van Diemen's Land*, Review Publications, Dubbo, 1977 (1850).

Mackaness, George, ed., *Some Private Correspondence of Sir John and Lady Jane Franklin (Tasmania, 1837–1845)*, pts 1 & 2, D.S. Ford, Sydney, 1947.

Markus, Julia, *J. Anthony Froude: the last undiscovered great Victorian*, Scribners, New York, 2005.

Mary Ward House website, accessed at <www.marywardhouse.com>.

Meredith, Louisa, *My Home in Tasmania*, Griffen Press Ltd, Adelaide for Sullivan's Cove, 1978 (1852).

Mickleborough, Leonie C., *Colonel William Sorell, Lt-Gov of VDL 1817–1824*, MA thesis, University of Tasmania, March 2002, accessed at <eprints.utas.edu.au/11816/1/Sorell_Thesis.pdf>.

Mickleborough, Leonie C., 'Lieutenant-Governor William Sorell: appearances of respectability', accessed at <www.femalefactory.com.au/FFRG/pdfs>.

Mickleborough, Leonie, *William Sorell in Van Diemen's Land: Lieutenant-Governor, 1817–24: a golden age?*, Blubber Head Press, Hobart, 2004.

Müller, Max, *The Life and Letters of The Right Honourable Friedrich Max Müller*, ed. Georgina Müller, vol. 2, Longmans, Green, And Co., London, 1902.

Newman, John Henry, *The Letters and Diaries of John Henry Newman*, eds Charles Stephen Dessain, Vincent Ferrer Blehl, Edward E. Kelly, Francis J. McGrath, Thomas Gornall, Ian Ker, Gerard Tracey, 32 vols, Oxford University Press, Oxford, 1961–2008.

Nixon, Norah, ed., *The Pioneer Bishop in Van Diemen's Land 1843–1863: letters and memories of Francis Russell Nixon, D.D., first bishop of Tasmania*, J. Walch & Sons, Hobart, 1953.

Norris, Rev. Canon, Rev. R.E. Bartlett, John Flint, & Thomas Wyles, 'Is an Unsectarian Scheme of Education Inconsistent with Religious Teaching?', a paper to the National Association for the Promotion of Social Science (Great Britain), Bristol Meeting, 1869, reproduced in *Transactions of the National Association for the Promotion of Social Science*

(Great Britain), Bristol Meeting, 1869, ed. Edward Pears L.L.B., General Secretary of the Association, Longmans, Greed, Reader, and Dyer, London, 1870.

Peterson, William S., *Victorian Heretic: Mrs Humphry Ward's Robert Elsmere*, Leicester University Press, 1976.

The Popular Science Monthly, conducted by E. L. Youmans, vol. 9, May–October 1876, D. Appleton and Company, New York.

Rae-Ellis, Vivienne, *Louisa Anne Meredith: a tigress in exile*, Blubber Head Press, Sandy Bay, 1979.

Richardson, Joanna, *An Annotated Edition of the Journals of Mary Morton Allport*, vol. 1, 7 Feb 1853, PhD thesis, University of Tasmania, 2006.

Rickards, E.C., *Felicia Skene of Oxford: a memoir*, John Murray, London, 1902.

Roberts, Shirley, *Sophia Jex-Blake: a woman pioneer in nineteenth century medical reform*, Routledge, London & New York, 1993.

Roe, Michael, 'Eardley-Wilmot, Sir John Eardley (1783–1847)', *Australian Dictionary of Biography*, accessed at <adbonline.anu.edu.au/biogs/A010329b.htm>

Rowley, Hazel, 'The Ups, the Downs: my life as a biographer', Friends of the University of Adelaide Library, Radio Adelaide, University of Adelaide, 7 June 2007, accessed at <http://hdl.handle.net/2440/39350>.

Russell, Penny, 'Ornaments of Empire?: Government House and the idea of English aristocracy in colonial Australia', *History Australia*, vol. 1, no. 2, July 2004.

Russell, Penny, 'Unsettling Settler Society', *Australia's History: themes and debates*, UNSW Press, Sydney, 2005.

Schama, Chloë, *Wild Romance: a Victorian story of a marriage, a trial, and a self-made woman*, Walker Publishing Company Inc, New York, 2010.

Scott, C.P., *The Making of the Manchester Guardian*, Frederick Muller Ltd, London, 1946.

Seigel, Jerrold, *Marx's Fate: the shape of a life*, Penn State University Press, Pennsylvania, 1993.

Shakespeare, Nicholas, *In Tasmania*, Random House, Milsons Point, 2004.

Sherwood, Toni Anne, *Complete Transcription of All Sections of Annie Baxter's Journal Written in Van Diemen's Land, 1834–51, March 1845*, PhD thesis, University of Tasmania, 2006. The original diaries are held at the Mitchell Library, State Library of New South Wales.

Showalter, Elaine, *A Literature of Their Own: from Charlotte Brontë to Doris Lessing*, Virago, London, 1999.

Shrimpton, Paul, *A Catholic Eton? Newman's Oratory School*, Gracewing, Herefordshire, 2005.

Smith, Elizabeth Grant, *Memoirs of a Highland Lady: the autobiography of Elizabeth Grant of Rothiemurchus afterwards Mrs Smith of Baltiboys 1797–1830*, ed. Lady Strachey, John Murray, London, 1911.

Sorell, Jane, *Governor, William & Julia Sorell: 3 generations in Van Diemen's Land*, Citizens Advice Bureau: Eastlands, Tasmania, 1986.

Southey, Robert, *Letters from England*, David Longworth, New York, 1808.

Stegner, Wallace, in James R. Hepworth, 'Wallace Stegner, The Art of Fiction No. 118', *The Paris Review*, no. 115, Summer, 1990, accessed at <www.theparisreview.org/interviews/2314/the-art-of-fiction-no-118-wallace-stegner>.

Steinbach, Susie L., *Understanding the Victorians: politics, culture and society in nineteenth-century Britain*, Routledge, New York, 2012.

Stokes, Eric, 'Misguided Tom', review of TA Letters, *London Review of Books*, vol. 3, no. 4, 5 March 1981.

Stoney, Captain H. Butler, *A Residence in Tasmania: with a descriptive tour through the island, from Macquarie Harbour to Circular Head*, Smith, Elder & Co., London, 1856.

Strachey, Dorothy, *Olivia*, Vintage Press, London, 2008, (1949).

Strachey, Lytton, *Eminent Victorians*, Penguin Books, Middlesex, England, 1986 (1918).

Sutherland, John, *Mrs Humphry Ward*, Clarendon Press, Oxford; Oxford University Press, New York, 1990.

Tasma [Jessie Couvreur], *Piper of Piper's Hill*, Harper & Brothers, New York, 1989.

Thackeray, William Makepeace, *Vanity Fair: a novel without a hero*, Könemann, 1998 (1847).

Tilsley, Clive, 'Bookselling', *The Companion to Tasmanian History*, Centre for Tasmanian Historical Studies, 2006, accessed at <www.utas.edu.au/library/companion_to_tasmanian_history/B/Bookselling.htm>.

Trevelyan, Janet Penrose, *Evening Play Centres for Children: the story of their origin and growth*, Methuen, London, 1920.

Trevelyan, Janet Penrose, *The Life of Mrs. Humphry Ward*, Constable, London, 1923.

Trevor, Meriol, *The Arnolds: Thomas Arnold and his family*, Bodley Head, London, 1973.

Tuckwell, William, *Reminiscences of Oxford*, E.P. Dutton & Co, New York, 1908.

Turnbull, C., 'R. Crossland, Wainewright in Tasmania, Melbourne 1954. A Review', *Papers and Proceedings: Tasmanian Historical Research Association*, vol. 4, no. 2, July 1955.

Uglow, Jenny, *Elizabeth Gaskell: a habit of stories*, Faber and Faber, London, 1993.

Vertigan, Graham, 'Some Tasmanian Events and Their Ephemera', paper presented to a meeting of the Tasmanian Historical Research Association on 10 December 2002, *Papers and Proceedings: Tasmanian Historical Research Association*, vol. 51, no. 2, June 2004.

von Stieglitz, K.R., *Six Pioneer Women of Tasmania*, CWA Tasmania, Hobart, 1956.

Walker, James Backhouse, *Reminiscences of Life in Hobart 1840s–1860s*, (unpublished, 1890), University of Tasmania Library Special and Rare Materials Collection.

Ward, Mrs Humphry, *Milly and Olly*, Macmillan & Co., London, 1881, accessed at <archive.org/stream/millyandollyora00wardgoog#page/n28/mode/1up>.

Ward, Mrs Humphry, *Robert Elsmere*, Macmillan & Co., London, 1888, accessed at <www.gutenberg.org/files/24898/24898-h/24898-h.htm#BOOK_IV>.

Ward, Mrs Humphry, *Marcella*, Macmillan & Co., New York, 1894, accessed at <www.gutenberg.org/cache/epub/13728/pg13728-images.html>.

Ward, Mrs Humphry, *Helbeck of Bannisdale*, Penguin Classics, 1983 (1898).

Ward, Mrs Humphry, *Delia Blanchflower*, Hearst, New York, 1914, accessed at <www.gutenberg.org/cache/epub/9665/pg9665-images.html>.

Ward, Mrs Humphry, *A Writer's Recollections*, W. Collins Sons & Co., London, 1918, accessed at <www.gutenberg.org/files/9820/9820-h/9820-h.htm>.

Ward, Mrs Humphry & C.E. Montague, *William Thomas Arnold: journalist and historian*, University Press, Manchester, 1907.

Whately, Mary Louisa, *Ragged Life in Egypt*, Seeley, Jackson, and Halliday, London, 1863.

Whately, Mary Louisa, *More About Ragged Life in Egypt*, Seeley, Jackson, and Halliday, London, 1864.

Woolf, Jenny, *The Mystery of Lewis Carroll: discovering the whimsical, thoughtful, and sometimes lonely man who created 'Alice in Wonderland'*, Haus Publishing Ltd, London, 2010.

Woolf, Virginia, *A Room of One's Own*, Triad/Panther Books, St Albans, 1977 (1929).

Newspapers

Hobart Town Gazette (Tas: 1825–27)

The Colonial Times (Hobart, Tas: 1828–57)

The Cornwall Chronical (Launceston: 1835–80)

The Courier (Hobart, Tas: 1840–59)

The Hobarton Mercury (Tas: 1854–57)

Hobart Town Courier (Hobart, Tas: 1827–39)

The Observer (Hobart, Tas: 1845–46)

Chapter Notes

Abbreviations used in Chapter Notes

ABJ   Toni Anne Sherwood, *Complete Transcription of All Sections of Annie Buxter's Journal Written in Van Diemen's Land, 1834–51, March 1845*, PhD thesis, University of Tasmania, 2006. The original diaries are held at the Mitchell Library, State Library of New South Wales.

AVW   Bernard Bergonzi, *A Victorian Wanderer: the life of Thomas Arnold the Younger*, Oxford University Press, Oxford, 2003.

AWR   Mrs Humphry Ward, *A Writer's Recollections*, W. Collins Sons & Co., London, 1918.

BCAM   Balliol College Archives and Manuscripts

GTWB   G.T.W.B. Boyes, *Extracts from the Journal of G.T.W.B. Boyes, Colonial Auditor, December 10th 1829–July 31st 1853*, ed. J.W. Beattie, unpublished typescript, Allport Library, State Library of Tasmania.

GWJS   Jane Sorell, *Governor, William & Julia Sorell: 3 generations in Van Diemen's Land*, Citizens Advice Bureau: Eastlands, Tasmania, 1986.

JA   Julia Sorell Arnold

LJHN   John Henry Newman, *The Letters and Diaries of John Henry Newman*, eds Charles Stephen Dessain, Vincent Ferrer Blehl, Edward E. Kelly, Francis J. McGrath, Thomas Gornall, Ian Ker, Gerard Tracey, 32 vols, Oxford University Press, Oxford, 1961–2008.

LMA   Matthew Arnold, *The Letters of Matthew Arnold*, ed. Cecil Y. Lang, University Press of Virginia, Charlottesville, 1996–2000.

LMADE   *The Letters of Matthew Arnold, A Digital Edition*, ed. Cecil Y. Lang, The University of Virginia Press, ©2006 by the Rector and Visitors of the University of Virginia.

LOMHW Janet Penrose Trevelyan, *The Life of Mrs. Humphry Ward*, Constable, London, 1923.

LTAY   James Bertram, ed., *Letters of Thomas Arnold the Younger 1850–1900*, Auckland University Press, London & Wellington, 1980.

MA   Matthew Arnold

MHW   Mary Humphry Ward (Polly)

NZL   James Bertram, ed., *New Zealand Letters of Thomas Arnold the Younger with Further Letters from Van Diemen's Land and Letters of Arthur Hugh Clough 1847–1851*, Oxford University Press, London & Wellington, 1966.

PWL   Thomas Arnold, *Passages in a Wandering Life*, E. Arnold, London, 1900.

TA   Thomas Arnold

TAAM   Tom Arnold, 'A Memoir Written by Thomas Arnold After Julia Arnold's Death and Intended for His Children', dated Dublin, 17 Feb 1889, Balliol College Archives and Manuscripts.

TAHF   Meriol Trevor, *The Arnolds: Thomas Arnold and his family*, Bodley Head, London, 1973

TCCL   The Claremont Colleges Library

VDL   Van Diemen's Land

WTA   Mrs Humphry Ward & C.E. Montague, *William Thomas Arnold: journalist and historian*, University Press, Manchester, 1907.

Where letters have been published in books, the book references are provided for easier access for readers.

Introduction

'Smashed the windows' from Huxley, *Memories I*, pp. 12–13. Renowned Australian biographer Hazel Rowley claimed she chose her subjects according to the way in which particular words struck a chord in her, see Rowley, 'The ups, the downs'. **On women being seen but not heard** see Heilbrun, *Writing a Woman's Life*, p. 15; Woolf, *A Room of One's Own*, p. 86; and Dwyer, 'Boney and his Balcombe girl'.

1 – A Tumultuous Inheritance

On morbid Catholicism see Strachey, *Olivia*, p. 13. **On hanging bodies** see Button, *Flotsam and Jetsam*, p. 43. **On Hobart Town:** Although Hobart was known as Hobart Town until 1875 when it was renamed Hobart, the shortening to Hobart is used frequently in the manuscript for ease of reading. **On the Sorell family background, Sorell's reign as Lieutenant-Governor, and on Anthony Fenn Kemp** see Brown, *Mudge's People*; GWJS; Edwards, *Of Yesteryear and Nowadays*, & 'Anthony Fenn Kemp: a new appraisal'; M.C. & T.B. Kemp, 'Captain Anthony Fenn Kemp'; Shakespeare, *In Tasmania*; Alexander, *Governors' Ladies*, pp. 75–77; Mickleborough, 'Lieutenant-Governor William Sorell: Appearances of Respectability'; '… the most seditious, mischievous' from Mickleborough's thesis for MA; Chapman, *The Diaries and Letters of G.T.W.B. Boyes*, vol.1, p. 360. **On Ellinthorp Hall** see *Hobart Town Gazette*, Saturday 15 Sep 1827, p. 4; Hoe, *Tasmania*, p. 336. **On departure ball** see *Hobart Town Courier*, 7 Dec 1838, p. 2. **On life on board sailing ships** see Button, *Flotsam and Jetsam*, pp. 25, 34–35. **'One of the loveliest days that it was possible to conceive'** JA to TA, 4 May 1887, BCAM. **'Second-rate dandies and roués'**, Thackeray's *Vanity Fair*, vol. 2, p. 819. **On life and schools in Brussels** see Bock, *A Hand-book for Travellers on the Continent*;

Brontë, *Villette*, ch. 9; Strachey, *Olivia*, p. 13; and Frost, *A Face in the Glass*, p. 5. **On Julia's Huguenot forebears** see AWR, p. 6; GWJS, p. 19. **On Captain Chalmers** see Chapman, 'G.T.W.B. Boyes and Australia', p. 69; NZL, p. 191.

2 – Entering Society

Descriptions of colonial society in VDL in the 1840s found in Bolger, *Hobart Town*, pp. 63, 55–56; Button, *Flotsam and Jetsam*; Loring, *Compelled to Tiers*, p. v; Fenton, *A History of Tasmania*; Graves, *Exile*; Stoney, *A Residence in Tasmania*; GTWB; and Walker, *Reminiscences of Life in Hobart 1840s–1860s*. **On the silence around the decimation of the Indigenous population** see Russell, 'Unsettling Settler Society' and Mackaness, *Recollections of Life in Van Diemen's Land*, p. 33. **On the lives and difficulties of women & the impact of gossip and scrutiny in the small community of Hobart** see Meredith, *My Home in Tasmania*; Rae-Ellis, *Louisa Anne Meredith*; Russell, *This Errant Lady*; Nixon, *The Pioneer Bishop in Van Diemen's Land 1843–1863*; Clarke, *A Colonial Woman*; Alexander, *The Ambitions of Jane Franklin*, particularly chs 12–13 and her article 'Gender'. **On JA's reference to her upbringing** see GWJS, p. 133; JA to TA, 18 Feb 1876, BCAM; and LTAY, p. 179. **On the problems of servants** see Richardson, *An Annotated Edition of the Journals of Mary Morton Allport*, p. 121; GTWB; Tilsley, 'Bookselling'; and for a fictional version see Graves, *Exile*. **On the cultural life of early Hobart, including the cultural role of the Franklins** see Mackaness, *Some Private Correspondence of Sir John and Lady Jane Franklin*, and *Recollections of Life in Van Diemen's Land*; Russell, *This Errant Lady*; Nixon, *The Pioneer Bishop in Van Diemen's Land 1843–1863*; Stoney, *A Residence in Tasmania*; Clarke, *A Colonial Woman*. **On JA's riding skill** see *The Observer*, 23 Sep 1845, p. 2. **On turfy conversation and preference for dancing** see Meredith, *My Home in Tasmania*, pp. 12, 173. **On JA's participation in Government House tableaus** see Lady Caroline Denison to JA, Sat 1849(?), BCAM and in AWR, p. 5. **On the art scene in Hobart** see Meredith, *My Home in Tasmania*; Gilmour, *Elegance in*

Exile; GWJS; Boyce, 'Britishness'; Barrett, 'Francis Russell Nixon'. **On JA's physical appearance** see NZL, p. 198 and *Aurora Raby* by W.P. Frith, A.R.A. in *Heath's Book of Beauty, 1847*. **On Thomas Bock** see GWJS, p. 132 and Gilmour, *Elegance in Exile*.

3 – A Colonial Belle

On Boyes's view see GTWB, p. 103. **'Plebeian blood'** see Annie Baxter in ABJ, p. 67. **On Annie's responses to JA** see ABJ, pp. 70–71. **On Waverley's Amy Robsart** see NZL, p. 198. **On Richard Dry** see Baker, *The Life and Times of Sir Richard Dry*, pp. 42–43. **On rumours** see ABJ, p. 80. **On JA's father** see AWR, p. 6 and TA to JA, 11 Mar 1887, BCAM, in which TA refers to JA's father as 'a thorough gentleman if ever there was one'. **On New Norfolk cottage scene** see ABJ, p. 85 and GTWB, p. 84. **On trust** see Chester Eardley-Wilmot to JA, 1844, BCAM. **On Eardley-Wilmot's governorship and dismissal** see Russell, 'Ornaments of Empire'; GTWB, p. 84; Gilchrist, 'The Victim of his own Temerity'; Stieglitz, *Six Pioneer Women of Tasmania*, p. 32; Fitzpatrick, 'Mr Gladstone and the Governor', pp. 31–45; Alexander, *Obliged to Submit*, pp. 168–77; Roe, 'Eardley-Wilmot, Sir John Eardley'. **On Boyes's view on engagement** see GTWB, p. 105. **On JA seeking reassurances from Richard Dry** see ABJ, p. 108. **On Annie's response to the engagement being broken off and Chester's marriage** see ABJ, pp. 99, 265. **On Wainewright and JA's portrait** see Crossland, 'Wainewright: the Tasmanian portraits', pp. 99–103; Turnbull, 'R. Crossland, Wainewright in Tasmania, Melbourne 1954. A Review', pp. 32–33; Anderson, *Dictionary of Australian Artists Online*. **On JA's further alleged flirtations and engagements** see ABJ, pp. 134–41, 155–57; NZL, pp. 178–79. **On Percy's expulsion** see Edwards, *Of Yesteryear and Nowadays*, p. 95 and *Colonial Times*, 26 Sep 1848, p. 4. **On fixation on marriage:** Elizabeth Grant Smith, in her memoirs, said everybody was always busying marrying her off, except her mother who 'had no wish for any marriage, it would only throw so much more trouble on her … she did not understand this craze for marrying'. See

Smith, *Memoirs of a Highland Lady*, pp. 395–99. The same fixation is picked up in Lancaster's novel *Pageant*, set in nineteenth-century Tasmania, and the historian James Anthony Froude recalled his grandmother saying that she had been a fool to marry. She had, she said, 'everything a young woman could desire; a kind father, an ample property. Her picture had been painted by Sir Joshua. What could have possessed her?' in Markus, *J. Anthony Froude*, p. 6. **On William Sorell's view of marriage and his closeness to his children** see William Sorell to JA, 10 Feb 1860, BCAM; ABJ, p. 384.

4 – An Unusual Man

On Dr Arnold biography: *Life of Arnold* was written by Arnold's former pupil Arthur Penrhyn Stanley and first published in 1844. **On Dr Arnold** see TAHF, ch. 1; AWR, vol. 1, ch. 1; AVW, pp. 12–13. **On young TA's looks and character** see TAHF; AVW, pp. 25, 31; W. Arnold, 'Thomas Arnold the Younger', p. 128; GWJS, p. 133; AWR, vol. 1, p. 40; MA, *The Scholar-Gipsy*; *NZL*, p. 72. **On TA's appointment as inspector of schools and the usefulness of Dr Arnold's name** see NZL, pp. 116, 130; AVW, pp. 54–63. **On TA and JA's meeting** see TA, TAAM, BCAM; Graves, *Exile*, p. 75; NZL, p. 183. **On JA's character** see TA, TAAM; MHW, *Helbeck of Bannisdale*, pp. 47–59; and AWR, ch. 1. **On Arnold, Rugby School, and Queen Adelaide's visit** see Strachey, *Eminent Victorians*; AVW, pp. 12–13; <www.rugbyschool.net/ history>; MA, 'Rugby Chapel'; <www.rugbyrelics.com/museum/exhibitions/ nr125/02.htm>. **On Tractarian wars and religious conflict in Oxford:** one description of the religious conflict at Oxford while TA was there held that 'espionage, delation, quarrels between heads and tutors, rejection of Puseyites standing for fellowships, and a heated suspicion as though a second Popish Plot were in the air, made this time at Oxford a drama which Dean Church likens to the Greek faction-fights described by Thucydides. The situation could not last.' See Barry, *The Oxford Movement (1833–1845)*; *Catholic Encyclopaedia*; Chadwick, *The Victorian Church*, p. 210; Arnold, 'The Oxford Malignants and Dr Hampden', pp. 225–39; <www.oriel.ox.ac.uk/content/

newman-window>; Markus, *J. Anthony Froude*, ch. 1; Uglow, *Elizabeth Gaskell*, p. 228; Clark & Kaiser, *Culture Wars*; Thomas Hughes, *Tom Brown at Oxford*, John W. Lovell Company, New York, 1888–92, p. 8; TAHF, pp. 31–46; AVW, p. 15; PWL, p. 18. **On Dr Arnold as a father** see W. Arnold, 'Thomas Arnold the Younger'; MA, 'Rugby Chapel', dedicated to Dr Arnold's memory. **On life at Fox How** see AVW, p. 18; Arnold, *Oakfield*, vol. 11, p. 169. **On TA and Henrietta** see NZL, pp. 54, 212, 217. **On TA's attraction to Goethe's young Werther** see Hulse's 'Introduction' to Von Goethe, *The Sorrows of Young Werther*, p. 19; NZL, pp. 212, 217. **On TA's inefficiency** see TA to Frances Arnold, 14 Mar 1896, BCAM; LTAY, p. 236; **On moving to NZ and life there** see W. Arnold, 'Thomas Arnold the Younger'; NZL, pp. 4, 54–56, 83, 108, 162, 210; AVW, pp. 49–50; for Collinson's description see LTAY, p. xix. **On TA's view of marriage** see NZL, p. 108.

5 – Finding Love

On TA's fascination for and pursuit of JA and their engagement see TA, TAAM; NZL, pp. 108, 178–84; ABJ, pp. 294, 324. **On JA causing jealousy** see TA, TAAM; NZL, pp. 183–84. **On reaction to JA's engagement** see ABJ, p. 294; LTAY, p. 219. **On Thomas Collinson falling in love with JA** see LTAY, p. 219; **For TA's letters to JA while travelling** see NZL, pp. 180–83. **On TA's desire for Julia and his desire to change JA completely** see TA, TAAM; NZL, p. 184; LTAY, p. 4. **For description of the ball held at the Custom-house** see *The Courier*, Wednesday 24 Apr 1850, pp. 2–3. **On JA's reasons for marrying** see ABJ, p. 320; MHW to Willy Arnold, 7 Apr 1888, TCCL; and TA, TAAM, BCAM. **On Julia's search for a deeper connection with life** see TA, TAAM, BCAM and also MSS of a novel he began writing in c. 1853, with his character Lucy based on Julia. He writes in his novel of Lucy (Julia) going frequently to church

> and meditation on the verities of religion threatened to make war
> on that addiction to the world which had hitherto characterized

her soul. In this new temper of mind, I have reason to believe that
one reason why she received with pleasure the addresses of Nebulo,
was that she knew him to be the son of a truly religious and
excellent parents, supposed him to have inherited the opinions and
principles of his noble father, and which conscious to herself of the
frail and dubious hold which her new found religious impressions
had as yet conquered in her heart, she welcomed with a secret and
honest pleasure the thought of being confirmed and guided in
them by the like-minded son of a religious father. If these were her
calculations, sadly were they falsified.

On the wedding and reception see ABJ, p. 329; NZL, p. 184. **On marriage
determining the shape of a woman's life:** in her biography of Jane Franklin,
Lepore writes that 'marrying the man she did when she did, determined the
whole course of Jane Franklin's life. Marriage determined the whole course of
every woman's life.' See Lepore, *Book of Ages*, p. 52.

6 – A Woman's Destiny

On JA's early married life see NZL, pp. 187, 190; LTAY, p. 12; ABJ,
pp. 332, 336, 353, 357. **On encounter with bushranger** see NZL, p. 194;
Lancaster, *Pageant*, p. 51. **On JA's travels and network of friends** see AWR,
vol. 1, p. 14; TAAM; LTAY, p. 192. **On JA and Gussie, TA's attitude to
her, and his expectations of JA** see LTAY, pp. 5, 12, 14, 24; ABJ, p. 305;
TAAM; JA to TA, 7 Feb 1887, BCAM. **On financial pressures** see TA to
his brother William, Mar 1858; JA to TA, 7 Feb 1887, BCAM; LTAY, pp. 7,
12. **On maternal mortality rate** see Irvine Loudon, 'Deaths in Childbed
from the Eighteenth Century to 1935', *Medical History*, 30 Jan 1986, no. 1,
pp. 1–41. **On pregnancy and impact of motherhood** see LTAY, pp. 5,
40; TAAM. **On battle over christening, JA's views of religion, and TA's
instability** see AWR, vol.1, p. 13; LTAY, pp. 10, 31, 55. **On opposition to
transportation and desire to leave VDL** see NZL, pp. 193, 196, 205; LTAY,

pp. 27, 35. **On moving to the former Normal School** see AVW, p. 76; LTAY, p. 40. Mrs Humphry Ward, *Milly and Olly*, ch. 2. **On death of Arthur and grieving** see LTAY, p. 47; Uglow, *Elizabeth Gaskell*, p. 92; Lepore, *Book of Ages*, p. 57; Flanders, *A Circle of Sisters*, p. 16. **On impact of death on JA and TA** see LTAY, pp. 51–55; AWR, vol. 1, p. 13; AVW, p. 31. **'I love you dearest Tom'** see LTAY, p. 63.

7 – An Impossible Choice

On JA's abhorrence of Catholicism and her reaction to TA's conversion see LTAY, pp. 55, 63; TA, 'Fragment of a novel', p. 9; MHW, *Helbeck of Bannisdale*, pp. 20, 74, in which her daughter Polly used aspects of JA's attitude to Catholicism in her heroine, Laura, who is horrified by what she sees as the overriding sense of sin in Catholicism and its attendant attitude to women as inferior and works of the devil. 'What a gross, what an intolerable superstition! — how was she to live with it, beside it?' **On TA's anti-Catholicism** see NZL, pp. 56, 142–43, 167; and LTAY, pp. xxi–xxiii. **On TA's conscience and his martyr's compulsion** see NZL, pp. 4, 215. **On TA's lack of friends to talk to in VDL** see LTAY, p. 12. **On TA's reasons for becoming a Catholic** see PWL, pp. 153–57; TAAM; AWR, vol.1. **On the similarity between Dr Arnold and Newman** see Jones, *The Broad Church*, p. 229. **On Newman's approval** see Tuckwell, *Reminiscences of Oxford*, p. 180. **On the help of friends and reactions** see LTAY, pp. 61–63; Bishop of Tasmania (Francis Russell Nixon) to JA, 11 Jul 1856, BCAM. **On 'fearful gulf' and 'morbid caprice'** see JA to TA, Jun 1855 and TA to JA, 25 Jun 1855, BCAM; LTAY, pp. 62–64. **'A force, not an organism'**, MHW, *Helbeck of Bannisdale*, p. 59. **'I know you don't want to force me'**, MHW, *Helbeck of Bannisdale*, p. 285; **'The home consecrated by love'**, MHW, *Robert Elsmere*, p. 343. **'Unjust and half-frantic language'**, see LTAY, pp. 66–67. **On this view of Newman** see Tuckwell, *Reminiscences of Oxford*, p. 180. **On leaving children:** if there was no Tom, there could be no children. It was still several years away from the passing of the

Matrimonial Causes Act of 1857, which gave men the right to divorce their wives on the grounds of adultery. However, married women were not able to obtain a divorce if they discovered that their husbands had been unfaithful. Once divorced, the children became the man's property and the mother could be prevented from seeing her children. **On TA breaking his promise, JA talking too much and Willson's advice** see TA to Mrs Arnold, 21 Feb 1856, BCAM and LTAY, p. 68. **On sectarianism in Australia** see Conway, *The Road from Coorain*, p. 176. **On JA throwing stones** see Huxley, *Memories I*, pp. 12–13.

8 – Between Two Worlds

On education in VDL & reaction to TA's conversion both for and against see 'The Inspector of Schools', *The Courier*, 18 Jan 1856, p. 2; *The Cornwall Chronicle*, 23 Jan 1856, p. 4; Howell, 'Education in Van Diemen's Land', p. 23; LTAY, pp. 36, 68–69; Letter from Sir Henry Young to TA, BCAM. **On TA's pay rise** see Howell, 'Education in Van Diemen's Land', p. 30. **On negotiations regarding his position** see LTAY, pp. 61, 67–72; Howell, 'Education in Van Diemen's Land', p. 48; LJHN, vol. 32, Supplement, p. 145. **On ignoring advice** see MA to TA in LMA, vol. 1, p. 211; Mary Arnold to TA, 1 Jan 1856, BCAM. **On JA's deep feeling for TA** see MHW, *Helbeck of Bannisdale*, p. 256. **On departure and life at sea:** the high regard in which TA was held was revealed by a deputation of public schoolmasters who presented him with an Address, signed by seventy-two teachers, which spoke of his kind assistance, courteous manner, conscientious rigour, and the simplicity and modesty of his demeanour towards them. It also reflected that 'the admirable system of education at present in force in this colony, which promises fair to place Tasmania in the front rank of educated nations, was initiated during your period of office, and has been fostered by your care', *Colonial Times*, 12 Jul 1856, p. 3; TAAM; Bishop of Tasmania to JA, 11 Jul 1856, BCAM; *The Hobarton Mercury*, 14 Jul 1856, p. 2; LTAY, pp. 58, 69–76; AWR, vol. 1, p. 4.

9 – Facing Reality

On arrival in England & impressions of Fox How and its mistress see AWR, pp. 4, 15, 22; Gaskell, *Life of Charlotte Brontë*, p. 493; NZL, p. 38; MHW to Willy Arnold, 14 Jun 1886, TCCL; William Arnold, *Oakfield*, p. 157. **On TA's sister Mary Hiley** see WTA, pp. 7–8; LOMHW, pp. 8, 13. Mary had been tragically widowed in 1848, only a year after her first marriage, when her young husband, a physician at St Bartholomew's Hospital, had developed paralysis of the brain. After his death, she remained in London, took up social work and became a follower of F.D. Maurice, who was at the forefront of higher education for working men, and later, women. Only months before Julia's arrival at Fox How, Mary had married again, this time to the Reverend James Hiley, a clergyman who owned a small estate, Woodhouse, in Leicestershire. John Frederick Denison Maurice, known as F.D. Maurice, was another fascinating player in the religious culture wars of the nineteenth century. A major theologian of the nineteenth-century Anglican Church, who, like Dr Arnold, had initially been unable to graduate because he could not subscribe to the Thirty-nine Articles, he was also one of the founders of Christian Socialism, which tried to combine the principles of Christianity with the principles of socialism emerging as a result of the new industrial age. In 1854 he founded the first Working Men's College and became its first head. **On the family's reaction to TA's conversion** see LTAY, pp. 80, 85–86; Jane Forster to TA, 19 Sep 1855, BCAM; TAHF, p. 125. **On negotiations with Newman** see LJHN, vol. 17, p. 532. In the same volume in a letter written on 25 Mar 1857 to Joseph Dixon, Archbishop of Armagh, Newman wrote, 'Mr Arnold is the son, and (I believe) the cleverest son, of the late famous Dr Arnold of Rugby. His Father sent him to Australia and there he became a Catholic, and had to give up his place. It is one of the most wonderful instances of conversion I know, considering how energetic Dr Arnold was in his opposition to the church and the Oxford movement.' See also AVW, p. 92. **On JA at Fox How** see AWR, pp. 21–22. In her novel *Delia Blanchflower*, Polly drew on the feeling of disapproval that

Julia believed she triggered on her arrival at Fox How, particularly in Tom's mother and his sister Fan. See *Delia Blanchflower*, ch. 8. **On news from Tasmania** see Gussie to JA, 18 Sep 1856, BCAM. **On discussions with Newman re JA's conversion** see LTAY, p. 85. **On letters between JA & TA** see LTAY, pp. 81–85. **On leaving Polly & Willy & departing for Dublin** see Susanna Cropper to JA, 30 Jan 1857 & 8 May 1857; Catherine Reibey to JA Apr 1857; Mary Arnold to JA, 26 May 1857, BCAM. In her novel *Marcella*, Polly drew on her mother's stratagem when Evelyn Merritt Boyce sends her daughter away to various schools to keep her as free as possible from the social consequences of her husband's actions. See MHW, *Marcella*.

10 – A New Beginning

On Dublin see Daly, *Dublin: the deposed capital*, pp. 1, 16, 74. **On Julia's reaction to Dublin** see Gussie to JA, Sep 1857 & Jane Forster to TA, 3 Mar 1857, BCAM. **On servants:** Elizabeth Grant of Rothiemurchus was born in Edinburgh towards the end of the eighteenth century. After her marriage to Colonel Henry Smith in 1829, they moved to his estate, Baltiboys, in County Wicklow in Ireland. Elizabeth wrote her memoirs — based on the journals she had kept throughout her life — and they were published after her death under the title of *Memoirs of a Highland Lady: the autobiography of Elizabeth Grant of Rothiemurchus*. See Pelly & Tod, *The Highland Lady*, p. xv. **On Rathmines** see Daly, 'Dublin Life', pp. 83, 156, 159. **On Mrs Arnold's advice** see Mary Arnold to JA, 19 Jun 1857, BCAM. **On JA's reaction to living in a Catholic world** see MHW, *Helbeck of Bannisdale*, pp. 273, 279. **On Newman's view of JA** see LJHN, vol. 24, p. 34. **On Newman's resignation & TA's reaction** see AVW, pp. 109–10. **On Polly's remaining at Fox How** see Susanna Cropper to JA, 8 May 1857; Mary Arnold to JA, 26 May 1857; JA to James Dunn, 1861; & Fan Arnold to JA, 26 Apr 1860, BCAM. **On raising children as Catholics** see Catherine Reibey to JA, Apr 1857, BCAM. **JA's energy** was noted by Lord Carlisle, see TAHF, p. 127. **On the Whately family & JA's relationship** see AWR, p. 14;

Fan Arnold to TA, Jun 1857; Mary Louisa Whately to JA 1857, BCAM; Whately, *Ragged Life in Egypt* & *More About Ragged Life in Egypt*. **On the relationship with the Benisons** see AVW, pp. 103–05. **On Dr Arnold's views on converts** see Peterson, *Victorian Heretic*, p. 23. **On JA's refuge with Mary Hiley** see TA, Diary, BCAM; WTA, pp. 7–8; Fan Arnold to JA, 26 Apr 1860; JA to TA, 12 Jan 1859, BCAM. **On differences between JA & TA** see TA to JA, 26 Dec 1858; JA to TA, 28 Dec 1858; JA to TA, 15 Jan 1859, BCAM. **On move to Kingstown** see Jane Forster to TA, 3 Mar 1859, BCAM; Daly, *Dublin: the deposed capital*, p. 195; WTA, p. v. **On financial woes, family assistance, and advice** see AVW, pp. 113–20; TA's siblings William, Director of Public Instruction in the Punjab in India, and Jane were particularly helpful — see TA to William, 24 Mar 1858, BCAM; at the same time Julia's father was expressing his regret that it was not in his power to match the £100 given to them by Tom's sister, but was hoping that Tom could procure some permanent appointment within the government, as, given his experience in the Colonial Service, he had both the ability and the interest for such a position. See William Sorell to JA, 1 Apr 1858; T Penrose to Mary Arnold, 6 Jun 1859; TA to JA, 27 Feb 1861; Mary Arnold to TA, 8 Apr 1858 & 23 Sep 1862; MA to TA 26 Aug 1858; JA to James Dunn, 1861, BCAM; TAHF, p. 130. That TA was not adept financially was demonstrated in the negotiations regarding his replacement tutor for his private students in Dublin. TA had offered Mr Stuart £18 for the term he would be in Birmingham, and JA had to point out to him that it was senseless to pay Mr Stuart £18 for tutoring when TA himself only received £13 for it. See JA to TA, 3 Mar 1862, BCAM. **On the constant demand for money** see JA to TA, 28 Jan 1862; William Forster to TA, 24 Jun 1862 & 28 Jun 1862, BCAM. **On Marx's financial situation** see Seigel, *Marx's Fate*, p. 255. **On William Sorell's death** see Percy Sorell to JA, 23 Nov 1860; Gussie to JA 18 Sep, 1856 & 23 Jan 1861; Mary Hiley to JA, 17 Jan 1861; JA to James Dunn 1861; JA to TA, 14 Feb 1861; JA to TA, 4 Aug 1861; MA to TA, 13 Mar 1861, BCAM; AVW, p. 124; £170 in 1860 would be the

equivalent of approximately AUD$36,000 today. **On the Yelverton case &
JA's religious experiences in London** see TA to JA, 27 Feb & 1 Mar 1861;
JA to TA, 5 Mar 1861, BCAM. See also Schama, *Wild Romance.* **On mutual
desire** see JA to TA, 15 Jan 1859 & TA to JA, 27 Feb 1861, BCAM. **On JA's
encounter with her step-grandmother** see JA to TA, 14 Feb & 28 Feb 1861,
BCAM.

11 – Adrift

On plea to James Dunn see JA to James Dunn, 1861, BCAM. **On TA's job
applications and JA's increasing dread** see AVW, p. 124; JA to TA, 4 Aug
1861, BCAM. **On offer from Oratory** see LJHN, vol. 32, pp. 218–19; AVW,
p. 125. **On moving to Birmingham** see LTAY, p. 118 & JA to TA, 28 Jan
& 17 Feb 1862, BCAM. **On JA's unhappiness & anxiety about being a
mother, TA as a father, & religious division in the nursery** see JA to TA, 20
Feb, 2 Mar, & 6 Mar 1862; MA to TA, 21 Dec 1861; MA to Mary Arnold,
9 Jan 1862, BCAM. **On TA as teacher** see Shrimpton, *A Catholic Eton?*,
p. 196 for Newman's analysis of Tom as being a superior man, but unable to
teach younger students because he could not control them. **On Lucy being
removed** see MA to TA, 21 Dec 1861; MA to Mrs Arnold, 9 Jan 1862; TA
to JA, 9 Mar 1862; Susanna Cropper to JA, 31 Oct 1862; TA, Diaries, 8 Nov
1862, BCAM. **On Mortara case** see PWL, p. 185 & Altholz, 'A Note on
the English Catholic Reaction to the Mortara Case', pp. 111–18. **On JA's
photograph** see JA to TA, 14 Feb & TA to JA, 15 Feb 1862, BCAM.

12 – A Dark World

On TA's desire for JA see TA to JA, 28 Feb & 9 Mar 1862; JA to TA, 6 Mar
1862, BCAM. **On Birmingham** see TAHF, p. 111; MacCarthy, *The Last Pre-
Raphaelite*, p. 24; Briggs' *Victorian Cities*, pp. 186, 196, 202; Southey, *Letters
from England*, pp. 191–92. **On relations with Newman** see JA to TA, 17 Feb
& 3 Mar 1862, BCAM; AWR, chs. 6 & 7. **On social life & friendships in
Birmingham** see PWL, p. 172; JA to TA, 2 Mar 1862, BCAM; MA to TA

in LMA, vol. 2, p. 312. The Arnold name had cachet in Victorian England and people were always anxious to meet the family of the famous Dr Arnold of Rugby. On one occasion while visiting London, TA's mother and sister had been accompanied by the Lord Chamberlain to Whitehall Chapel to hear Arthur Stanley preach. It was noted in *The Guardian* newspaper that 'after the Service at Whitehall at which the P & Princess of Wales were present, the Very Rev The Dean of Westminster was observed to conduct out of the Chapel with the greatest care & attention an elderly lady, who, on enquiry, proved to be Mrs Arnold, the widow of the great Head Master of Rugby ...' from Fan to TA, 9 Jun 1864, BCAM. **On Birmingham's climate & family illnesses** see TA to JA, 28 Feb, 9 Mar & 15 Apr 1862; TA, Diaries, Nov & Dec 1863, BCAM; Briggs, *Victorian Cities*, p. 199; Burritt, *Walks in the Black Country*, ch. 1; Steinbach, *Understanding the Victorians*, p. 22. **On TA's issues with the Oratory** see LTAY, pp. 137–40; LJHN, vol. 20, p. 563, vol. 21, pp. 4–5, vol. 32, p. 250. **On troubles with the boys & consequences** see Courtney, *Recollected in Tranquillity*, p. 64; TA's Diaries, Jan, Mar–Apr & 18 Aug 1864; TA to JA, 15 Jun 1865; MA to Mrs Arnold, 9 Jan 1862, BCAM; LTAY, pp. 155–56, 166; MA to TA in LMA, vol. 2, p. 112; MA to Mrs Arnold in LMA, vol. 3, p. 54; W. Arnold, 'Introduction', *History of Rome*; *The Popular Science Monthly*, p. 497; Rev. Canon Norris, et al., 'Is an Unsectarian Scheme of Education Inconsistent with Religious Teaching?', p. 273. **On Polly's change of school** see TA, Diaries, 24 Jan, 30 Sep & 7 Oct 1864, BCAM; LOMHW, p. 17. **On TA's growing dissatisfaction** see TA to JA, 16 Feb 1864, BCAM; MA to Mrs Arnold in LMA, vol. 2, p. 286; LOMHW, p. 18.

13 – Returning to the Fold

On TA's fall away from Catholicism see PWL, pp. 171, 185; TAHF, p. 152; TA to General Collinson, 24 Apr 1888 in LTAY, pp. 219–20 in which TA writes, 'Towards the end of 1864 a sort of cloud settled down over my mind; perhaps a long continuation of ill health had something to do with it. I gradually lost faith in things unseen altogether; nothing but science and its methods commended itself to me.' **On the controversy re Temporal Power of the Pope in the 1860s** see TAHF, pp. 132–33, 147–154; LJHN, vol. 24, p. 34; AWR, ch. 6. **TA's conversion:** in a letter to Josephine Benison, TA explains his defection: 'I had come reluctantly to the conviction that the claim of the Catholic Church to the exclusive possession of religious truth was unfounded, and to the further conviction — closely connected with the former, that the supposition of an infallible authority, permanently residing in the church, was a dream.' See AVW, p. 160. **On reaction to Newman & his *Apologia*** see MA to TA in LMA, vol. 2, p. 312; McCarthy, *The Last Pre-Raphaelite*, p. 22. **On Josephine Benison's response** see TA, Diaries, 7 Jun & 24 Aug, 1864, BCAM and AVW, p. 161. **On JA's knowledge** see Penelope Fitzgerald, *The Blue Flower*, Flamingo, London, 1996, p. 27. **On application for pay rise** see LTAY, pp. 143–45; Shrimpton, *A Catholic Eton?*, p. 196. **On Mrs Arnold's reaction** see Mary Arnold to TA, Nov 1864, BCAM. **On new-found harmony between JA & TA** see TA to JA, 4 Dec 1864 & TA to JA, 16 May 1865, BCAM; AVW, p. 136. **On proposal for TA to be head of Catholic College in Oxford** see AVW, p. 133. In a letter dated 6 Jul 1863, Newman refers to TA having just returned from Oxford and saying that there was bitter feeling against Catholics there just now and that the Liberals are strong against any separate Catholic body. See LJHN, vol. 20, pp. 480, 485. **On reactions to TA's tutoring scheme** see PWL, p. 91; MA to TA in LMA, vol. 2, pp. 373, 382; William Forster to TA, 21 Jan 1865, BCAM; TA to Dean Arthur Stanley, 5 Apr 1865 in LTAY, p. 146. **On Matthew's reaction to TA's move away from Catholicism, advice re children, frustration & employment prospects** see MA to TA in LMA, vol. 2, pp. 376, 385, 388. **On JA in Birmingham following TA's move to Oxford & Willy's move to Rugby** see TA to JA, 24 Apr & 2 May 1865, BCAM; LTAY, p. 147. **On Willy's view of religion** see W. Arnold, 'Introduction', *History of Rome*. **On JA's Oxford visit & TA's attempts to get pupils** see TA to JA, 16 May & 13 Jun 1865, BCAM. **On public outing of**

TA as non-Catholic see TA to JA, 16 May; 1 Jun 1865 & 26 Jul 1865; Mary Arnold to JA, 27 May 1865, BCAM. TA's wavering religious fervour was by no means unusual in the milieu in which he and JA mixed. His old Oxford contemporary Gifford Palgrave, who had converted to Catholicism and had become a Jesuit priest, told him at the same time that he too was about to do a volte-face and, like TA, renounce his Catholicism. (See TA to JA, 1 Jun 1865, BCAM) It was also a time 'when Bishop Colenso had to go because he couldn't swallow the Pentateuch whole, when Kensitites pelted Ritualists, when priests renounced their Orders and took to lecturing at the universities ...' see Courtney, *The Women of My Time*, p. 225. **On Newman's reaction** see LJHM, vol. XXIV, p. 34. **On Polly's reaction** see LOMHW, p. 18.

14 – A Landscape of Desire

On reactions to Oxford see Mary Arnold to JA, 27 May 1865, BCAM; McCarthy, *The Last Pre-Raphaelite*, p. 27; Uglow, *Elizabeth Gaskell*, p. 441; AWR, vol. 1, ch. 6. **'The meadows were strewn...'** see Fletcher, *O Call Back Yesterday*, p. 4. **On religious turmoil in Oxford** see Green, *Love in a Cool Climate*, p. 17; Bebbington, *Review*, pp. 158–60; Flood, 'Plinth commemorates Huxley-Wilberforce evolution debate'; 'A Grandmother's Tales', p. 433. **On JA's relationship with Benjamin Jowett** see Arnold, 'Social life in Oxford'; AWR, vol. 1, ch. 6. **On a united family at Oxford** see LOMHW, p. 15. Polly used her return to her family's home in Oxford to inform the opening chapter of her novel *Marcella* (published in 1894), when her heroine, after years of poverty and parental neglect, returns to her family home eager '... to put the past — the greater part of it at any rate — behind her altogether. Its shabby worries were surely done with, poor as she and her parents still were, relatively to their present position. At least she was no longer the self-conscious school-girl, paid for a lower rate than her companions, stinted in dress, pocket-money, and education, and fiercely resentful at every turn of some real or fancied slur ... She was something altogether different ...' See MHW, *Marcella*, book 1, ch. 1; Peterson,

Victorian Heretic, p. 18. **On building of Laleham** see TA to JA, 30 Apr &
24 Dec 1865; TA, Diary, 30 Aug 1867, BCAM. Laleham was no ordinary
house. It was built on Banbury Road, just north of where they were living
in St Giles', on land that had recently been released by St John's College.
Several properties had already been built there, one of which belonged to the
chemist Mr William Walsh, whose architect was John Gibbs, the designer
of the Banbury Cross. Possibly because he liked Walsh's house, but more
probably because of Gibbs' reputation for economy, Tom chose Gibbs to
design his house. See AVW, p. 163. For further information on Laleham
and North Oxford see <britishlistedbuildings.co.uk/101392912-wycliffe-
hall-oxford#.W2jjSvZuIeE>; Hinchcliffe, *North Oxford*, p. 152; Christy
Anderson, Review [of *North Oxford by Tanis Hinchcliffe*, New Haven and
London: Yale University Press, 1992], *Journal of the Society of Architectural
Historians*, vol. 54, no. 4, Dec 1995, pp. 502–04; Dodgson, *Notes on*. **On
Lansdale Manor** see Boughton, *The Juvenilia of Mrs Humphry Ward*, ch. 3.
Many writers have spoken about experience driving narrative. See for
example Macaulay, *Told by an Idiot*, p. xi; Stegner in Hepworth, 'The Art of
Fiction No. 118'; Bedford in Guppy, 'An Interview'. **On crisis between JA
& TA in Devon** see TA to JA, 31 Aug 1866 & 1 Sep 1866, BCAM. **On
views of marriage** see *Life and Letters of Mandell Creighton*, pp. 64, 122, 132.
On the death of JA's baby see TA to JA, 13 Nov 1867, BCAM; Hughes'
The Short Life & Long Times of Mrs Beeton, pp. 319–20. Isabella Beeton had
died, six days after giving birth in 1865, from peritonitis and puerperal fever,
despite the fact that three quarters of women who caught puerperal fever
in the 1860s survived. **On Theo's return home & Laleham as one of TA's
ill-fated schemes** see Mary Arnold to TA, 29 Apr 1868; Mary Arnold to
MHW, 30 Sep 1868, BCAM; MA to Mrs Arnold in LMA, vol. 3, p. 283;
William Forster to TA, 21 Oct 1868 & 17 Jan 1869, BCAM. **On young
Tom's death and MA's response** see MA to Tom Arnold, 24 Nov 1868,
BCAM. **On JA's bequest** see TA to JA, 4 Jan 1869, BCAM. **On JA hearing
ominous sounds from TA's study** see LOMHW, p. 16. **Views on JA's**

personality and friendships in Oxford see TA's account of JA's last illness, BCAM; MA to Mrs Arnold in LMA, vol. 3, p. 417; Rickards's *Felicia Skene of Oxford*, p. 135; Arnold, 'Social life in Oxford'; *The Life and Letters of the Right Honourable Friedrich Max Müllers.* **On meeting Charles Dodgson and his impact on the Arnold household** see Arnold, 'Reminiscences of Lewis Carroll', p. 43; Arnold, 'Social life in Oxford'. Carroll's charm was beguiling. When Judy and Ethel failed to return a book he had lent them, he wrote one of his delightful letters, telling them that he didn't think he 'would find in all history, even if you go back to the times of Nero and Heliogabalus, any instance of children so heartless and so entirely reckless about returning story-books. Now I think of it, neither Nero nor Heliogabalus ever failed to return any story-book they borrowed. That is certain, because they never borrowed any, and that again is certain because there were none printed in those days.' See Green, *The Diaries of Lewis Carroll*, vol. 2, pp. 309, 310, 321; Cohen, *The Letters of Lewis Carroll*, vol. 1, pp. 174, 209. **On the absent boys** see TA to JA, 4 Jan & 7 Jan 1869, BCAM. **On Polly's life in Oxford** see LOMHW, ch. 2, in which Trevelyan writes, 'Like Julia, Polly was dark-haired and dark-eyed; striking rather than pretty; and elegant, as was noted by the French literary critic, Monsieur Hippolyte Taine, when he visited Oxford in May 1871 and was introduced to her by Professor Jowett at one of his dinner parties.' See also Boughton, *The Juvenilia of Mrs Humphry Ward*, vol. 2, pp. 459–500; MHW, *Helbeck of Bannisdale*, vol. 1; Nearly forty years later Virginia Woolf needed just such a connection as Mark Pattison to ease her entry into the library at Cambridge University. Instead, she was barred by 'a deprecating, silvery, kindly gentleman, who regretted in a low voice as he waved me back that ladies are only admitted to the library if accompanied by a Fellow of the College or furnished with a letter of introduction', see Woolf, *A Room of One's Own*, p. 9; Courtney, *The Women of My Time*, p. 145; JA to James Dunn, 1861; TA to JA, 23 May 1869, BCAM; Polly to TA, 13 Jan 1874 in LTAY, p. 174; Sutherland, *Mrs Humphry Ward*, pp. 50–53. Humphry had won a fellowship at Brasenose in 1869 and, unlike most fellows, was not ordained. He favoured a more secular life and was more interested ultimately in a journalistic career than an academic one. See also Rickards' *Felicia Skene of Oxford*, p. 134; Huxley, *Memories I*, p. 13; TA to Mary Arnold, 16 Jun 1871, BCAM; MHW, 'The Poem of the Cid'. **On Gussie's arrival & Budge's death** see Gussie to JA, 10 Sep 1857 & MA to TA, undated, BCAM.

15 – Coming Adrift

On cost of trousseau see Flanders, *A Circle of Sisters*, pp. 223–24. **On Polly's wedding:** Dean Stanley officiated and as he 'had recently buried the theologian Frederick Denison Maurice, his speech at the wedding breakfast was quite as much concerned with graves and worms and epitaphs as with things hymeneal'. See TAHF, p. 172. **On impending financial ruin** see TA to JA, 27 Apr 1872; MA to JA, 22 Jan 1876; William Forster to TA, 17 Jan 1869, BCAM; AVW, pp. 172–74. In her biography of Polly, her daughter Janet Penrose said that in order to live comfortably in that period, a family needed between £800 and £900 a year. This was the amount that together Humphry and Polly were earning. It was an amount that Tom would never earn, despite his perception 'of having a tolerably large income'. See LOMHW, p. 29; see also Clark, *The Huxleys*, p. 73; Battiscombe, *Reluctant Pioneer*, p. 53. **On Mrs Arnold's death and TA's reaction** see TA to Fan Arnold, 30 Nov 1873, BCAM. **On education of women and girls in Oxford:** Charlotte's husband, the philosopher Thomas Hill Green, also supported the women, as did other men in Oxford. See Sutherland, *Mrs Humphry Ward*, p. 56; LOMHW, p. 30: 'The idea of the founding of Women's Colleges was already in the air, for Girton and Newnham had led the way at Cambridge, and all through 1878 plans were being discussed to this end. In the next year a special committee was formed for the raising of funds towards the foundation of a "Hall of Residence".' See also Brittain, *The Women at Oxford*. **On JA's role** see entry for 15 May 1875 in Green, *The Diaries of Lewis Carroll*, vol. 2, p. 321, in reference to Maud and Ethel

Conybeare (about sixteen and twelve) who lived with the Arnolds; Violet
A. Sydney Smith to TA, 5 & 7 Jun 1895, BCAM. TA always resented JA
earning income despite its usefulness. In one letter he wrote, 'That you
should attempt to take the part of the "breadwinner" is not reasonable, till
my incompetence for it has been proved. Also I doubt much whether you
do not over estimate your strength, when you speak of carrying on so large
an establishment as you talk about. Then the furnishing of so large a house
would have to be considered and twenty other things. Nor do I see that the
mistress of the house need ever want plenty of "occupation" even though she
should not take boarders ...' See TA to JA, 31 Mar 1877, BCAM. **On JA's
intense pride in her children** see Violet A. Sydney Smith to TA, 5 & 7 Jun
1895, BCAM; WTA, pp. 10–11. **On JA & TA becoming grandparents** see
Fan Arnold to TA, 23 Jul 1874, BCAM. The whole family were delighted
with Dorothy's birth, especially Judy and Ethel who were rapturous when
they heard the news; LOMHW, p. 29 & Trevelyan's *Evening Play Centres for
Children*; the Mary Ward Centre website; Sutherland, *Mrs Humphry Ward*.
On JA's two wild boys, Theodore and Arthur see TA to JA, 31 Aug 1866
& TA to Mr Price at the Bank of England, 27 Dec 1871, BCAM; MA to
TA, 30 Nov 1875, LMADE. Unlike Willy, neither Theodore nor Arthur had
ever fitted in or shone or settled into the discipline and routine that came
with school. After being moved from the Oratory School at Birmingham,
Theodore had been sent first to the grammar school at Loughborough, then
to another at Burton upon Trent, and finally to Cheltenham College, each
move being triggered by his disruptive behaviour. When he turned seventeen,
Tom had tried to find him a position — beginning with the Bank of
England — clearly hoping that the Arnold name would open doors for him.
In his letter to the bank, Tom stated that his son had 'plenty of intelligence,
and if he gets into the Bank of England, will soon, I am convinced, make
himself useful'. **On TA's allegiance to the Anglican Church** see LOMHW,
pp. 26–27; Huxley, *Memories I*, p. 13; TA to Fan Arnold, 27 Oct 1874,
BCAM. **On first-ever performance of Dodgson's 'The Mad Tea-Party'**

see Green, *The Diaries of Lewis Carroll*, vol. 2, 7 Dec 1874, p. 335. Carroll thought the performance 'very creditably done'. **On TA's increasing vulnerability** see TA to JA, 25 Feb 1875, BCAM. **On financial worries and trying to find TA a job:** Tom didn't have enough money to send to Julia, who was staying in London, and advised her to 'borrow it from Jane, or else from Fanny'. Jane offered to send some money to TA, see Jane Forster to TA, 18 Mar 1875. William Forster sent 'out of brotherly sympathy' a cheque for £50, see William Forster to TA, 9 Apr 1875. TA, in Wales, tells JA to pay, if she can, a part of the bill for Polly's wedding cake (the wedding had been held over a year previously) but *not* to pay any interest! in TA to JA, 13 May 1875; MA to JA, 22 Jan 1876, BCAM; MA to TA, 28 Jan & 1 Feb 1875, LMADE; Lewis Carroll to Lord Salisbury, 31 Jan 1875, in Cohen, *The Letters of Lewis Carroll*, vol. 1, pp. 219–20.

16 – Into the Abyss

On exchanges between JA & TA in London see TA to JA, 12 & 13 Feb 1876; JA to TA, 18 Feb 1876, BCAM. **On JA's ultimatum** see Polly to TA, 16 Feb 1876; JA to TA, 18 Feb 1876; TA to JA, 18 Feb 1876, BCAM.

17 – Separate Lives

On TA's religious migration see Macaulay, *Tale Told by an Idiot*, pp. xi, 3. **On reactions to TA's reconversion** see LJHN, vol. 18, pp. 124–26 & vol. 28, p. 157; AVW, p. 189; LOMHW, p. 27; Jane Forster to JA, 18 Oct 1876; TA to JA, 22 Oct 1876; MA to TA, Oct 1876, BCAM, in which he said to TA '… As to the Catholicism, that is a long story. Catholicism is most interesting, & were I born in a Roman Catholic country I should most certainly never leave the Catholic Church for a Protestant; but neither then or now could I imagine that the Catholic Church possessed "the truth", or anything like it, or that it could possess it'; see also Green, *The Diaries of Lewis Carroll*, vol. 2, p. 356. Margaret Fletcher, who later converted to Catholicism herself, remembered Oxford being enveloped by Protestantism, a place where only Catholics were 'excluded as dangerous'. She also went straight to the dilemma that Tom's nature and his actions posed for Julia, his family, and his friends when she remembered 'the indignant reaction most of us felt that the soul-journey of the chivalrous and courteous man who was a familiar figure to many of us was being held up to public bewailing'. See Fletcher, *O, Call Back Yesterday*, pp. 16, 29, 39; GWJS, p. 167; TAHF, pp. 178–79. **On TA's explanation** see TA to Humphry Ward, 14 Oct 1876, BCAM & TAHF, pp. 177–79. **On TA blaming JA for all that had happened & her response** see TA to JA, 22 Oct 1876; 4 Apr 1877; 9 Jun 1877, BCAM. See also MHW to TA, 23 Oct 1876, TCCL; TAHF, pp. 178–79. **On TA's view of his role as breadwinner** see TA to JA, 31 Mar 1877, BCAM. **On Josephine Benison's response** see AVW, pp. 187, 190.

18 – A Revolutionary Wife

On Willy's marriage: after his graduation, Willy had remained in Oxford in lodgings and had set himself up as a coach and as a lecturer for the women's courses Polly and her friends were developing. It was enough to enable him to support a wife. See WTA, pp. 14–15, 30. **On JA's misery** see JA to TA, 29 Aug 1877; 21 Sep 1877, BCAM. **On JA's illness & surgery** see TA to JA, 22 Oct 1876; 16 Jan 1877; JA to TA, 21 Sep, 1 Oct & 2 Oct 1877; Jane Forster to JA, 30 Oct 1877, BCAM; Roberts's *Sophia Jex-Blake*, p. 28. In 1870 Elizabeth Garrett Anderson had become the first woman to earn a medical degree from the Sorbonne; in 1872 she had opened the New Hospital for Women in London, staffed entirely by women; and in 1877, not long before Julia was sent to her, Anderson and another woman, Dr Sophie Jex-Blake, had established the London School of Medicine for Women. Bovell had also been among the first group of women to gain admission to the Medical School at Edinburgh University in 1871. When protesting male students and faculty members forced the women out of the course without being granted degrees, Bovell went to Paris in 1873 to complete her course. Bovell was appointed physician to the New Hospital for Women in Marylebone Road in 1877 and in 1880 she was nominated by the French Government as an *Officier d'Academie*, a distinction conferred for scientific and literary merit. **On JA's deliberations** see JA to TA, 1 & 2 Oct, 1877; TA to JA, 20 Feb 1877, BCAM; **On Burney's operation** see Burney, *Journals and Letters*, pp. 431–43; **On JA's relationship with Tom & her poor recovery** see JA to TA, 6 & 12 Nov & 3 Dec 1877, BCAM; LOMHW, pp. 26–27; MA to Victor Marshall, 18 Oct 1877, in LMADE. **On increasing financial stress** see TA to JA, 27 Feb 1878, BCAM; TA's letter of 23 Jan 1878 written to Mrs Clough in LTAY, p. 195, in which Tom writes to accept her offer of staying the repayment of the loan that her husband Arthur had extended to him years before, saying, 'I do not know how to thank you enough for the great kindness of your letter. It would not be right for me to accept it, were I not in truth a very poor man, that is, relatively to the demands which those whom I have to support make upon me ...' **On JA sending TA jam** see TA to JA, 26 Mar 1877, BCAM. **On Arthur's wayward character and TA's attempts to get him a position** see Ada Belstead to JA, 2 Sep 1876, in which she says of Arthur while he was staying with her in Tasmania,

> I think dearest Julia that if Tom is in a position to do so he had far better have him home so that for the next few years he may be under his control. The appointment he has got here is not enough to (occupy) him and the longer he stays the deeper he will be (in debt) ... I should strongly advise you to get him away from their influence if you possibly can. I do all I can in the way of advice but he is rather inclined to 'hough his own (row)' I'm afraid and I think his whole ... life depends upon the influences he is under for the next two or three years. I think he has the making of a good man with judicious treatment and a kind but firm hand to control him such as his Father's.

See also TA to JA, 27 & 28 Mar 1877 & 8 Jan 1878, BCAM; MA to Frances Arnold 9 Jul 1876, LMADE. **On disagreement about Arthur's military**

exploits see TA to JA, 16 Jun, 1878, BCAM. **On Arthur's death and reactions to it** see Col. Charles Warren to TA, 1 Oct 1878; Fan to TA, 17 Aug 1878; JA to TA, 23 Oct 1878, BCAM; Sutherland, *Mrs Humphry Ward*, pp. 160–61; 'South Africa', *South Australian Register*, 16 September 1878, p. 5; MA to TA, 19 Nov 1878, LMADE. Not even an invitation from Max Müller to a private viewing of Graham Bell's new invention, the telephone, could lift JA's spirits. It was the first time it was ever heard in England:

> A large company gathered together, and intense interest and surprise
> were felt by everyone, even the scientific men present ... Mr. Bell also
> brought down a microphone, only just invented, and a phonograph.
> The wire of the telephone was stretched from one end of the garden
> to the other, and even a whisper was distinctly heard. The wire of
> the microphone was brought from a room on the second story, and
> the sound made by a fly crawling along a board in the room upstairs
> sounded in the garden like the tramp of an elephant.

From Mrs Müller, *The Life and Letters of The Right Honourable Friedrich Max Müller*. **On Theodore's departure** see Jane Forster to TA [undated]; JA to TA, 21 Sep 1879; JA to TA, 23 Sep 1879, BCAM. In this letter JA spoke of the suits that Willy and Humphry Ward had given Theodore before he left. **On Willy's departure from Oxford** see WTA, p. 82. **On JA's increasing despair & TA's increasing hostility** see JA to TA, 29 Jun 1879; JA to TA, 29 June 1879; TA to JA, 5 March 1880, BCAM. **On family financial assistance:** even TA's younger, single sister Fan was providing assistance when she could. In April 1879 she had enclosed a cheque for £5 to TA, saying she had been given a gift and that it would give her pleasure to make even a week or fortnight of his life a little easier. See Fan to TA, 27 Apr 1879; JA to TA, 6 Nov 1879, BCAM. **On TA's isolation:** partly to counter his isolation and to earn some money TA joined forces with William Addis to write a Catholic dictionary. Like TA, Addis was also a religious vacillator, although he would make TA's vacillation look minor — an Anglican, he became a Catholic priest, returned to Anglicanism, then became a Unitarian minister, before rejoining the Church of England to become a vicar. **On TA's mooted return to Oxford & reactions** see TA to JA, 10 & 12 Mar, 22 Apr 1880; JA to TA, 27 Feb 1880, BCAM; Polly thought that whatever mental worry JA experienced when TA was away, she had double that when he was at home. His mere presence made her think about topics that, if he were not there, she 'might forget, or at any rate not take to heart in such a wearing and painful way'. See Polly to JA, 23 Jan 1880, BCAM; TAHF, p. 180 & LTAY, pp. 201, 239 for Jowett's reaction; TA refers to the rector of Lincoln, Mark Pattison, setting JA against him again and thinks he is a little like Mephistopheles. See letter from TA to JA, 10 Feb, 1878; TA to Frances Arnold, 10 Oct 1897, BCAM; Stokes's 'Misguided Tom'. **On JA's surgery** see JA to TA, 25 Feb 1880; TA to JA, 20 Mar 1880; Fan to TA, 25 Mar 1880, BCAM. **On JA's financial position and TA's behaviour towards her** see JA to TA, 30 Mar 1880; TA to JA, 23 Apr 1880, 30 May 1880, 1 Jun 1880, BCAM; MHW to TA 21 May & 7 Jun 1880, TCCL; TAHF, p. 181; LTAY, p. 201. **On Polly's relationship with TA:** in this instance, knowing how much it would please him, she told TA that she and Humphry were going to meet Newman at Trinity College, where a reception was being held for him. When Polly's turn came to meet him, she recalled her father to him and their days in Edgbaston. Newman's face, she recorded, 'lit up — almost mischievously. "Are you the little girl I remember seeing sometimes — in the distance?"' Neither Polly nor Newman spoke of the woman who had placed that distance between them. See MHW to TA, 21 May 1880, TCCL & TAHF, p. 182. **On selling furniture** see TA to JA, 1 Jun & 2 Jun 1880, BCAM. **On which wife** see TA to JA, 26 Apr, 14 & 16 Jun, 11 Sep, 9 Nov 1880, BCAM. TA was always fluent in his love letters to JA. Even when telling her she, too, had faults like everyone else, he told her that to mitigate against her faults he had, at least, had her to look at, had her as the presiding spirit in the house, had her bright decisiveness and charm, all of which 'was always "an overpayment of delight", as Wordsworth says, which far exceeded any grievance there might be. Do not hate me altogether, my dear one, and do not drive me from you. Though it be rather a pain than a pleasure to you to see me, yet support me.' Examples like this can be found in TA to JA, 27 Oct & 23 Dec 1879, 5 Mar & 16 Jun 1880, 3 Sep 1882, 16 Mar 1884, 21 Oct 1886, BCAM.

19 – Disintegration

On family members see LOMHW, pp. 26–33; TA to JA, 14 Jun & 18 Oct 1880; JA to TA, 5 Jul 1880; Ada to JA, 12 May 1880; Sutherland, *Mrs Humphry Ward*, pp. 73–76, p. 78; AWR, p. 224. **On Polly's marriage as a stark contrast to that of her parents** see Sutherland, *Mrs Humphry Ward*, p. 81. Approaching her tenth wedding anniversary, Humphry had, according to Polly, given her 'ten years of real and great happiness and constant tenderness and care and cherishing', and she was expecting that the next ten years of her life with him would be even happier. **On TA's appointment as professor of English literature at the Catholic University of Ireland in Dublin, reactions to it, & his reignited campaign for JA to join him** see TAHF, p. 181; TA to JA, 13 Dec 1881, 1 Jun 1882, 30 Nov 1883; JA to TA, 22 Mar 1884; MA to TA 19 Apr 1882, BCAM; MHW to JA 3 Mar 1882, TCCL; Sutherland, *Mrs Humphry Ward*, p. 86. **On JA's definitive declaration & on other women living apart from their husbands** see JA to TA, 15 Feb & 22 Mar 1884, BCAM. **On TA's attacks on JA as a mother & her children's responses** see TA to JA, 1 Jun 1882; 18 & 30 Nov 1883; TA to MHW, 6 Feb 1884; TA to Frances Arnold, 26 Oct 1883; JA to TA, 22 Oct 1884, 12 Feb 1888; JA to MHW, 14 Dec 1884, BCAM; MHW to TA, 25 Nov 1882, 4 Aug 1883, 5 Feb & 5 Mar 1884, TCCL. **On possibility of TA getting chair in Oxford** see JA to TA, 8 Mar 1884, BCAM; MA to TA, 5 Apr 1885, LMADE; AVW, p. 216. **On financial wrangling between JA & TA** see TA to JA, 22 Nov 1884; TA to Ethel Arnold, 7 Mar 1885; JA to TA, 2 Feb 1887; JA to TA, 12 Feb 1888, BCAM; MHW to TA, 18 Feb 1885, 11 Mar 1885, TCCL. **On TA quoting George Eliot:** JA and Polly had met George Eliot at an evening with the Pattisons in Oxford in 1871. When the ladies had retired after dinner, Eliot, knowing that Polly was studying Spanish history, thought she might like to hear about her own journey through that country. Her kindness was always remembered. See AWR, vol. 1, pp. 144–46. **On Judy's marriage to Leonard Huxley** see MHW to JA, 27 Dec 1881, TCCL; Cohen, *The Letters of Lewis Carroll*, vol. 1, pp. 467, 533; Judy Arnold to TA, 15 Feb 1882; TA to JA, 22 Nov 1884, BCAM; see also LTAY, p. 233. **On JA's deterioration and TA's responses** see Frances Arnold to TA, 17 Sep 1885; Frances Arnold to JA, 6 Jul 1886; TA to JA, 15 & 18 Apr 1883, 9 Mar 1884, 24 Mar, 18 Oct, & 6 Dec 1886, 19 Feb 1887; JA to TA, 28 Apr 1884, 2 Feb 1887; Jane Forster to TA, May 1886, BCAM; MA to TA, 30 Nov 1886, LMADE; MHW to TA, 13 Sep 1885, 29 Mar & 1 Apr 1886; MHW to JA, 3, 13, & 27 Apr, 29 Jun, 17 Oct, & 6 Dec 1886, TCCL. **On JA's spiritual beliefs** see MHW to JA, 27 April & 9 Sep 1886; MHW to Willy Arnold, 7 Apr 1888, TCCL; JA to TA, 13 Oct & 14 Dec 1886; TA to JA, 3 & 6 Nov 1886, BCAM; LTAY, p. 218. **On Polly's rebuke of TA** see MHW to TA, 23 Jan 1887, TCCL. **On TA's summary of JA's failings and her responses** see TA to JA, 19 Feb 1887; JA to TA, 4 & 7 Feb 1887, BCAM. **On Dot's menstruation** see MHW to JA 1 Feb 1887, TCCL. **On responses to progress of disease** see JA to TA, 14 Dec 1886; Frances Arnold to TA, 19 Feb 1887; TA to JA, 8 Dec 1886, Mar 1887; TA to Ethel Arnold, 14 Feb 1887; Frank Arnold to TA, 11 Mar & 6 May 1887; Ethel Arnold to TA, 8 May 1887; TA's Account of Julia Sorell Arnold's last illness, May 1887–7 April 1888, BCAM; MHW to JA, 6 Dec 1886 & 28 Feb 1887; MHW to TA, 9 Mar 1887; MHW to Willy Arnold, 14 Mar 1887; MHW to JA, 7 May 1887, TCCL; MA to Jane Forster, 9 Apr 1887, LMADE. **On 'appalling agony'** see JA to TA, 17 Feb 1887, BCAM. The tubes used to relieve JA, known as Southey's Tubes, were invented by Reginald Southey, a friend of Charles Dodgson. **On Ethel's theatrical ambitions:** Ethel, unlike Judy, had failed to win a scholarship to Somerville, and had instead expressed an ambition to become an actress, causing concern to her mother and family. This was a time when the editor of *Punch*, Frank Burnand, who was also a prolific playwright, declared categorically that no parent would wish their daughter to go on the stage. 'A well-brought-up girl would react to the stage in one of two ways, either recoiling in disgust at "life behind the scenes" and fleeing, or else succumbing to its corruption "until the fixed lines of the moral boundary have become blurred and faint"'. Curiously, Burnand's two wives were both actresses. With no likelihood of ever winning her parent's approval for such a life, Ethel began writing. Before long she had had several short stories published and was offered the opportunity of writing a serial for the *Temple Bar* magazine, one of the leading literary magazines of the time. See TA to JA, 13 Dec 1881; JA to TA, 14 June 1884, BCAM; MHW to JA, 27 Dec 1881, TCCL; Michael Sanderson, *From Irving to Olivier: a social history of the acting profession in England 1880–1983*, The Athlone Press, London, 1985 (1984), pp. 10–11; Claire Tomalin, *The Invisible Woman*, Penguin Books, 1991, p. 21. **On Julian Huxley:** towards the end of July, Judy brought the newborn Julian Huxley to stay in Oxford, and JA's delight was intense when, for all the pain it caused, she held the child in her arms. See Frances Arnold to TA, 2 Jun 1887, BCAM; MHW to JA, 7 & 11 May 1887, TCCL. **On visitors to JA** see JA to TA, 10 & 17 Feb 1888, BCAM. Chavasse's pastoral skills were widely appreciated and it was to him that JA had turned for spiritual advice and solace. Chavasse was, she told Tom, 'esteemed & respected by men of all shades of opinion', including Mr Talbot, the Warden of Keble, and Benjamin Jowett, the Master of Balliol. LTAY p. 241; Frances Arnold to TA, 11 Aug 1887; Theodore Arnold to JA, 22 Aug 1887; JA to TA, 31 Jan & 6 Mar 1888, BCAM; MHW to JA, 8 Sep 1887, TCCL; Rickards's *Felicia Skene*, p. 135. **On Theodore's marriage:** the problem with Theodore's wife was never articulated fully, except in one rather bitter sketch left by TA in which he described her as 'such an impracticable dreadful creature as his wife is it is seldom a man's lot to meet with; she is an octopus'. When word reached JA of the failed marriage, she felt it should not have come as such a surprise to everyone, and referred to him as the 'poor old boy', an expression oddly reminiscent of how TA's family had always referred to him.

See TA to JA, 15 Jul, year undated (written from Dublin); JA to TA, 11 Nov 1885, BCAM; MHW to JA, 4 & 13 Apr 1886, TCCL. **On Willy Arnold's prediction** see LOMHW, p. 53. **On TA visiting Josephine Benison** see TA to JA, 15 Jul 1887, BCAM. **On better relations between JA & TA** see JA to TA, 31 Jan 1888, 10 & 19 Feb 1888, & Ethel Arnold to TA, 15 Feb 1888; TA's account of JA's last illness, BCAM. **On *Robert Elsmere* & TA's reaction to it** see JA to TA, 12 Feb 1888; TA to JA, 12 Feb 1888, BCAM. **On TA's failing to recognise the seriousness of JA's illness** JA wrote,

> I could not help being both astonished and amused to a certain extent at what you say in yr letter of this morning about my 'wonderful vitality' & the probability of our all having a pleasant summer together at Sea View. Horatio Symonds happened to come just as I had finished reading it, & I read what you said on the subject of my health to him. The remark he made was, 'Well he certainly is a most extraordinary man, does he not see that you are simply living on morphia? This will last for a certain time but it cannot go on for an indefinite time.'

See JA to TA, 1 Feb 1888, BCAM. **On discussion between JA and Charles Dodgson** see Cohen, *The Letters of Lewis Carroll*, p. 697. Dodgson disagreed with JA believing that another text — 'Believe on the Lord Jesus Christ, and thou shalt be saved.' — stated the necessary truth. **'On a very cold day towards the end of February'** see JA to TA, 25 & 26 Feb 1888, BCAM; MA to Lucy Whitridge, 16 Mar 1888; MA to TA, 11 Mar 1888, LMADE. **On JA's death** see TA, 'Account of Julia Sorell Arnold's Last Illness, May 1887–7 April 1888'; Ethel Arnold to TA, 19 Feb & 3 April 1888; Frank Arnold to TA, 25 Feb 1888; JA to TA, 5 Mar 1888; Frances Arnold to TA, 3 & 4 Apr 1888; Mary Hayes to TA, 12 Apr 1888, BCAM; Sutherland, *Mrs Humphry Ward*, p. 123; MHW to JA, 30 Mar 1887; MHW to Dorothy Ward, 3 Apr 1888; MHW to Willy Arnold, 7 Apr 1888; MHW to TA, 19 Apr 1888, TCCL; TAHF, p. 195.

20 – Aftermath

On TA's reaction to JA's death see TA to Frances Arnold, 29 Apr 1888 &
25 Sep 1890; TA, 'Account of Julia Sorell Arnold's Last Illness, May 1887–7
April 1888', BCAM; LTAY, p. 219. **On TA's remarriage to Josephine
Benison & Polly's reaction** see AVW, pp. 227–30; TA to MHW, 19 Oct
1889; MHW to TA, 4 & 15 Apr, 29 Jun, 23 Oct, 22 Nov, 20 Dec 1889,
TCCL; TA to Frances Arnold, 25 Sep 1890, 12 Jun 1892; JA to TA,
7 Feb 1887, BCAM. **On Ulysses returning to Ithaca** see TA to Frances
Arnold, 12 Jun 1892, BCAM; LTAY, p. 229. **On Lucy Selwyn's death** see
Sutherland, *Mrs Humphry Ward*, pp. 165–66; Frances Arnold to TA, 4 Oct
1894, BCAM. Of all JA's daughters, Lucy's life followed the most traditional
path. When, in 1887, Carus was appointed headmaster of Uppingham,
Lucy assumed the role of headmaster's wife whilst giving birth to seven
children in ten years. On her death her devastated husband turned to Maud
Dunn, JA's niece and Gussie's daughter, for support, eventually marrying
her. **On TA's death and Josephine's death** see LTAY, pp. 245–46, 248;
TAHF, pp. 197–98. **On reception of *Robert Elsmere*:** by October of 1888,
the book was into its fifteenth edition, and sales had reached 1200 a week.
Weeks later, the novel was selling in America to great acclaim and was into
it eighteenth edition. It was to go on and sell over one million copies and
be published in most foreign languages. See MHW to TA, 13 Oct, 16, &
23 Nov 1888, 10 Feb 1889, 7 Apr 1898, TCCL; Peterson, *Victorian Heretic*,
p. 159; Sutherland, *Mrs Humphry Ward*, p. 108; Jones, *Mrs Humphry Ward*,
pp. 85–87. **On Jowett's response to dedication** see letter from Frank Arnold
to TA, 27 Jan 1892, BCAM. **On JA as inspiration for *Helbeck*** see MHW,
A Writer's Recollections, vol. 1, ch. 1, where she writes, 'There was in her an
instinctive dread of Catholicism, of which I have suggested some of the
origins — ancestral and historical. It never abated. Many years afterward,
in writing *Helbeck of Bannisdale*, I drew upon what I remembered of it in
describing some traits in Laura Fountain's inbred, and finally indomitable,
resistance to the Catholic claim upon the will and intellect of men.' See also

Peterson, *Victorian Heretic*, pp. 106, 114, 137. **On Polly's desire for TA's approval of *Helbeck*:** Polly wrote in her autobiography that she consulted her 'Catholic father, without whose assent I should never have written the book at all; and he raised no difficulty'. And later she wrote that her first anxiety was her father, and she was seized with misgivings lest certain passages should wound or distress him. 'I, therefore, no sooner reached Italy than I sent for the proofs again, and worked at them as much as fatigue would let me, softening them, and, I think, improving them, too.' AWR, vol. 2, ch. 6; see also LTAY, p. 242; Jones, *Mrs Humphry Ward*, p. 132. **On Polly's involvement in education, including pre-school & for disabled children & her anti-suffrage activities** see the various biographies of Polly, including these: Sutherland, *Mrs Humphry Ward*; Jones, *Mrs Humphry Ward*; LOMHW & Showalter, *A Literature of Their Own*, pp. 230–31. **On Willy** see Sutherland, *Mrs Humphry Ward*, p. 164; WTA; *The Times*, 30 May 1904; WTA, *Manchester Guardian*, 30 May 1904; WTA, *Quarterly Review*, Oct 1905; Rugby School Register, 1842–1874, p. 266; TAHF, pp. 190–92; LTAY, p. 242; Scott, *The Making of the Manchester Guardian*, ch. 3. **On Theodore:** In the year following JA's death, Polly spent more than £500 helping Theodore, the Dunns, Ethel, Frank, and Humphry's family. See letter from MHW to TA 30 Nov 1888, TCCL. JA had always felt very protective towards him, believing that he had experienced a difficult life and was forever optimistic about his chances. JA to TA, 6 Mar 1888, BCAM; LTAY, p. 242. **On Frank** see JA to TA, 23 Jan 1888, BCAM; LTAY, p. 242; TAHF, p. 192. **On Judy** see Huxley, *Memories I*, pp. 14–15, 64–65, 206; TAHF, p. 190. In addition to *Brave New World*, Aldous Huxley's other major works include *Antic Hay*, *Point Counter Point*, and *The Doors of Perception*. Julian Huxley, besides becoming the director-general of UNESCO in 1946, was also a founding member of the World Wildlife Fund, was awarded the Kalinga Prize for the popularisation of science in 1953, the Darwin Medal in 1956, and knighted in 1958. **On Ethel:** in 1884 Ethel suffered a nasty horse accident, and in so doing had dashed JA's expectations of an imminent engagement. Whether

Ethel's hopes were likewise dashed is unclear, but she never married, and given her parents' marital estrangement, she may have had no desire to follow suit. She suffered constant and various illnesses, a traditional evasive weapon in women's armoury against an uncertain or undesirable future. See JA to TA, 22 Mar 1884, BCAM; LTAY, p. 242; *Cambridge Chronicle*, 16 Jan 1909. **On how JA & TA have been portrayed:** TA has generally been portrayed as a charming, gentle, often impractical saint, for whom real life only took place in thought, and JA as not an easy woman, whose deficiencies as a housekeeper meant that the family was always short of money, and whose histrionics caused TA untold problems. For example, in the short biography accompanying her portrait in *Elegance in Exile* (p. 74), Julia 'was considered a disreputable woman of "undisciplined and tempestuous nature" ... By her mid twenties [she] had broken off two engagements, indulged in flirtations and allegedly seduced her first fiancé's father ... Her personal history, however, did not deter ... Thomas Arnold ...' In his biography of TA, Bergonzi says, 'One gets the sense, that while Tom, in his way, tried to be a dutiful father, Julia preferred her daughter at a distance' (p. 123), and 'Mary remembered and gave a jaundiced picture of Julia's housekeeping in her description of Mrs Hooper in *Lady Connie* (1916) "[She] was the most wasteful of managers; servants came and went interminably; and while money oozed away, there was neither comfort nor luxury to show for it. As the girl grew up, they learned to dread the sound of the front doorbell, which so often meant an angry tradesman"' (p. 133). Sutherland reflects on JA's poor management in his biography of MHW, (p. 30) while Shakespeare suggests she was an 'undisciplined', vain, vituperative, and air-headed young woman (p. 122) who used her marriage as an escape from the military and settler society, (p. 123) whose husband quickly discovered that she was not simply beautiful, but financially extravagant, prone to passionate outbursts of temper, and liked to 'nag, nag, nag him til he almost lost his sense' (p. 124). **On obscure women 'who lived faithfully a hidden life, and rest in unvisited tombs'** see George Eliot, *Middlemarch*, Penguin, New York & Harmondsworth, 1965, p. 896.

Index